OP 75c

Our Time Has Come

Lucius J. Barker

Our Time Has Come

A Delegate's Diary of Jesse Jackson's
1984 Presidential Campaign

University of Illinois Press
Urbana and Chicago

© 1988 by the Board of Trustees of the University of Illinois
Manufactured in the United States of America
C 5 4 3 2

This book is printed on acid-free paper.

Library of Congress Cataloging-in-Publication Data

Barker, Lucius Jefferson, 1928–
   Our time has come.

   Bibliography: p.
   1. Jackson, Jesse, 1941–   2. Presidents—United
States—Election—1984.   3. Primaries—United States.
4. Afro-Americans—Suffrage.   I. Title.
JK526 1988   324.973′0927   87-24357
ISBN 0-252-01426-X (alk. paper)

To the Jesse Jacksons
who challenge America's potential

Contents

A Note of Appreciation

Friday the thirteenth was anything but a bad omen, for it was Friday, July 13, 1984, the day I left for the San Francisco Democratic National Convention. As I expectantly waited to board my flight at St. Louis's Lambert International Airport, I heard this voice call out, "Lucius, Lucius." To my great but pleasant surprise it was a long-time friend and fellow political scientist whom I had not seen in some time. He had just deplaned for a stopover and, as it turned out, was about to board the same flight as I was for San Francisco. He was also going to the convention, not as a delegate, but as an observer.

And when my friend found out that I too was going to the convention, not as an observer, but as a duly elected Jackson delegate, he became ecstatic, bubbling over with enthusiasm and advice. He immediately and repeatedly encouraged me to keep a diary. "Don't try to write it as a political scientist," he implored. "Enough of that will come through anyway. Try to write it," he emphatically suggested, "from an *actual delegate's perspective and experience!*" I then recounted how I had already been taking notes, clipping papers, keeping files for something I wanted to write about my observations and experience in the Jackson campaign, although I had not really thought of it in diary-like terms. But the more my friend and I talked, the more the diary idea took hold. And by the time I landed in San Francisco some three or four hours later, I had already started my diary. Obviously, I appreciated my friend's off-the-cuff remarks. They were timely, and as I trust this book reflects, they were altogether helpful.

I found the diary format a great way to record my views and impressions of a tightly organized, fast-paced event such as the convention. But more than this, my diary-keeping at the convention proved so fulfilling that it led me to think about using a diary-like format to recount my views and impressions of the whole Jackson campaign. This would permit me to tell the story of that campaign as I saw it—to recount the excitement and challenges, successes and achievements, and the problems, disappointments, and frustrations of the Jackson campaign as I saw and experienced them; to describe what I believed to be the campaign's deeper sense and meaning; and to record my views of its great historical significance. Thus, though the participant-observer approach had occurred to me much earlier, during the airport conversation with my friend the "diary" idea really began to blossom. As a result, I owe my friend a great measure of appreciation, greater than his modesty would ever permit him to fathom.

But I owe an even greater debt to my family, friends, and colleagues at Washington University (and elsewhere) who made it very easy for me to keep up with the Jackson campaign. They gave me encouragement, tips, and a lot of advice, mostly their own views, which were quite often *unsolicited*. But this was exactly what I needed; these interactions were challenging, provocative, stimulating. My family and friends were great informers, flooding me with news clippings, articles, Op-Ed pieces, apparently determined not to let me miss *one* thing, whether I wished to or not. Regardless of what I was doing at home, if a newscast came on the television or radio, my wife or two daughters or any one or combination thereof shouted, "Jesse's on" or "They're talking about Jesse, turn to channel so and so." Their constant vigilance reminded me anew that television remains a remarkably potent medium of information and influence, giving as good a first-hand feel as one possibly could without actually being there in person.

I also profited greatly from the print media. Even if I missed something in my own avid reading, certainly nothing appeared in the two papers we read daily (the *New York Times* and the *St. Louis Post Dispatch*) or other papers that we read occasionally (e.g., the *Christian Science Monitor, Wall Street Journal, Washington Post*) that my family or friends did not call to my attention. The black press (e.g., *Ebony, Jet*, local black newspapers) kept me in touch with what the "brothers and sisters" were thinking and doing. In addition, family and friends from literally around the country (New Jersey, California, Maryland, Florida, Louisiana, Illinois) sent or saved clippings from all types of journals and even called long distance for long conversations about "what Jesse's up to now."

Certainly all these sources proved helpful—some more than others—to my information and education on the Jackson campaign. I am less certain, however, about how much influence they had on how I saw things and what I accepted as fact or believed to be fiction. But such influences as I was able to recognize and profit from are duly acknowledged in the footnotes which an academic like myself simply cannot forego.

But my *active* participation and involvement in the Jackson campaign provided influences and information which footnotes can never record. To have been a part of Jackson's effort at so many levels was really an honor, and for that I shall always be grateful. I felt humbled and honored by my fellow Missouri supporters who accorded me the privilege of serving as a fully accredited Jackson delegate to the 1984 Democratic National Convention. But I am even more indebted to the Reverend Jackson, whose undaunted courage and determination gave us all a rare opportunity to grow and be of service. His contributions will not soon be forgotten. Neither will those of professional colleagues and outside referees who read all or parts of the manuscript and offered numerous helpful suggestions and comments. I profited particularly from rather detailed comments of an anonymous reader for the University of Illinois Press, who, though suggesting that it is not the easiest task to comment on the "impressions and experiences" of someone else, nonetheless did an excellent, almost exquisite, job of doing just that. Several others also read the entire manuscript and invariably offered provocative and useful comments. These included Linda Williams of Howard University and the Joint Center for Political Studies; Richard L. Fenno, Jr., of the University of Rochester; William Crotty of Northwestern University; Michael Combs of the University of Nebraska; and my brother, Twiley W. Barker of the University of Illinois–Chicago. Others who read certain sections of the manuscript or otherwise offered suggestions that helped greatly include Robert Salisbury and Charles Franklin of Washington University, George Shulman of Yale University, and H. W. Perry of Harvard University.

This volume would have been impossible without secretarial and research assistance received from the department of political science at Washington University. Sally Outten somehow translated and skillfully fashioned my writing and tapes into a quite readable first draft. Marilyn Schad exhibited enviable patience and endurance in negotiating revisions necessary to put the manuscript in final form. And along the way, other members of the office staff—Jean D'Wolf and Natalie Sekuler—were always ready to lend a helping hand. I must also acknowledge valuable research assistance on this and related projects rendered by several graduate students: Christopher Hillcoat, Diane Schmidt, LeeAnn Banaszak, and Kevin Lyles. Lyles's contributions were especially helpful: a doctoral student in American politics with a special interest in Jackson's campaign and black politics generally, he was an uncommonly strong "sounding board" and an informal collaborator in reviewing the entire manuscript for final revisions.

Clearly, I appreciate the assistance of those at the University of Illinois Press (and its referees) who saw the value in publishing this kind of volume. The keen detective eye and publisher's instincts of Larry Malley, editor in chief, led to my original submission of the manuscript, and his unfailing encouragement and support have been with me throughout. The copyediting expertise of Cynthia Mitchell, an assistant editor, led to comments, queries, and suggestions that forced me to unearth, develop, and state more clearly and directly ideas, impressions, and observations that were otherwise vague and implicit. I also want to thank others at the press who helped in the production and promotion of this volume.

My final acknowledgements, of course, go to my family: Maude, my wife, and Tracey and Heidi, my daughters. I cannot soon forget the various services they rendered, especially their valuable clipping service. But most important was the support, encouragement, and love that only a family can give, and for this I am truly grateful.

Overall, my hope is that the great indebtedness I have incurred to so many in the course of this project will be more than repaid through the messages that flow from the pages that follow. Despite these many and diverse supports, however, in the final analysis I alone am responsible for what is recorded here, including the errors which invariably survive no matter what.

Lucius J. Barker
Washington University

Introduction

Our Time Has Come is an interpretive account of Jesse Jackson's campaign for the 1984 Democratic presidential nomination. But it is much larger than Jesse Jackson's story: it begins before Jesse Jackson announces his candidacy and does not end with his presidential campaign. It is a story that illuminates an unyielding determination to realize the dreams and goals of Martin Luther King and the civil rights movement. At bottom, it is a story that describes the most broadly based and courageous attempt ever undertaken to achieve the objectives of that movement through electoral politics rather than through protests and demonstrations. But it is also a story that describes how Jackson attempted to go beyond that movement—to apply its principles to the full range of domestic and foreign policy issues and to unite diverse individuals and groups into a Rainbow Coalition. Obviously, then, Jesse Jackson's candidacy for the 1984 Democratic presidential nomination is a subject about which social scientists will write for some time to come.

But to understand more clearly its essential nature and meaning, we must look at the Jackson effort from a number of vantage points, including observations from those actively involved in that campaign. We must also share these observations, not just with scholars and students of history, but with the widest possible audience. In this way both present and future generations, as well as scholars, will be able to more fully appreciate the impact and influence of the Jackson campaign. My hope is that the story told here will prove helpful in that regard.

However, this is not the usual scholarly or journalistic account of an election campaign, though it undoubtedly reflects elements of both.[1] Rather, it is a diary-like, chronological description and analysis of Jackson's historic campaign. This format allows utilization of materials and information from a number of sources, including those gained from my selection and service as a Jackson delegate to the 1984 Democratic National Convention. It also allows me to draw on life-long background and experiences as a Black American as well as my training and research as a professional political scientist. I believe that this blending process permits us to discern insights and perspectives about the Jackson campaign that might not otherwise be put forth and that could serve to enrich our understanding of that campaign.

When viewed in broad perspective, the central thrusts of Jackson's effort hold important implications for our politics and society and could well determine the kind of future we will have as a nation and as a people. Hence, it behooves us to see what we might learn from the Jackson experience. But how much we learn and the lessons we draw depend largely on how well we are able to capture its basic meaning and significance. This book is one effort in that direction.

Dimensions of Jackson's Candidacy

Jackson's campaign represents a watershed in our presidential politics and in American politics generally. The Jackson candidacy illuminated vividly our problems and progress as a nation. It proved once again that problems of discrimination and poverty continue to suppress and limit opportunities of women, blacks, and minorities. In very concrete ways, it illuminated both internal and external problems facing these groups. It pointed up problems of forging viable coalitions, both among these groups themselves and between them and other interests in the Democratic party. At the same time, however, the Jackson candidacy illuminated the progress that has been made in overcoming the "American Dilemma" of race, sex, and poverty. It showed clearly the dramatic increases in black voter registration and turnout, in the number of black officials elected to public office, and in the general socioeconomic progress of blacks. In fact, Jackson's campaign profited from the political advances and breakthroughs these groups had already made, especially at local and state levels; it was just such progress that gave the Jackson candidacy a credibility and vitality that otherwise it would not have enjoyed.

Jackson's effort dramatically expanded and galvanized this growing movement on the part of blacks and minorities to make maximal use of electoral politics to achieve their political objectives. Further, he brought into sharp national focus the political potential of these groups and outlined plans to convert this potential into actual power through his Rainbow Coalition. Throughout his campaign Jackson warned established politicians, in a language well understood, that the time had now come when these groups would no longer be taken for granted; that their needs and concerns must be dealt with fairly and effectively, just as those of other Americans; and that these groups themselves must be more directly and adequately represented in that dealing process. Moreover, the entire Jackson effort made it demonstrably clear that blacks, women, and minorities are interested in matters that go beyond their own particular problems and concerns. They too have definite opinions about how this country should be run, what kinds of domestic and foreign policies it should have, and how those policies should be implemented. And as the first Black American whose candidacy for a major party presidential nomination had to be taken seriously, Jackson demonstrated dramatically that the time had come when blacks, minorities, and women could no longer be overlooked when considering those who were qualified to occupy the presidential office. In general, the Jackson campaign suggested that "politics as usual" may never be the same again.

Understandably, Jackson's candidacy generated interest, excitement, and controversy. Some viewed it as a wonderful and plausible strategy, altogether needed to dramatize the continuing concerns and problems of blacks, women, minorities, the poor—all those who have been "locked out"—and to spur their political development and give them a more effective voice in the resolution of their own problems and other problems as well. But others saw Jackson's candidacy as a divisive force that would seriously jeopardize racial progress, including important advancements that could be made by helping Democrats recapture the White House. Still others viewed it as an unnecessary irritant that held too many damaging possibilities just to satisfy the ego of an overly ambitious person. Whatever the viewpoint, however, there was broad agreement that Jackson's candidacy was one of untold dimensions. This agreement was well based.

The story recorded here tells us about much more than Jesse Jackson himself. It is a story that Jackson correctly perceived as being about people at the grass roots, about their problems and frustrations, their long-suppressed yearnings and aspirations, and about what they thought of Jackson's effort and how they expressed their thoughts. It is a story about people participating, many for the very first time, in presidential primaries, in nomination caucuses, in politics of any kind. It is also a story that tells us much about the problems and opportunities facing our two major political parties and about the political-social dynamics of American politics and society.

The Participant-Observer

At another level, it is a very personal story, a story of how I myself participated in Jackson's campaign and in the process was converted from a cloistered scholar to an open activist delegate willing to go all the way for the Jackson cause. However, the story told here is more than a mere description of my own participation and impressions as a Jackson supporter. It is informed by my life experiences as a Black American and by my training and research as a professional political scientist. My participation in the campaign allowed me to experience firsthand many of the very things about which I have taught and researched as a university professor over the past thirty years. Thus this volume offers an assessment of the Jackson campaign and its impact that blends my practical experience and knowledge gained in the campaign with broader personal and theoretical observations.

I recognize, of course, that there are certain risks and pitfalls in the participant-observer's recounting of events, and I have attempted to remain alert to them. One has to be constantly mindful, for example, not to become so immersed in causes, personalities, and issues that they obscure or modify the description of what *really* happened. But I also recognize that this very immersion gives a *distinctive originality and authority* to the views of active participants, adding valuable perspectives and insights that might otherwise be neglected or overlooked in the historical record.

My role as a citizen participant also allows me to make observations about Jackson's campaign at every level—at the grass roots (township), the congressional district, the state convention, and the national convention, where I served as a fully accredited, elected Jackson delegate. To be sure, the national convention provided the most visible forum for the Jackson effort, but it is far from the whole story. To be more fully appreciated, the story must be told from the bottom up, not from the top down, and that is what I propose to do.

A Preview of What's to Come

Insofar as possible, this book is organized chronologically. Chapters 1 and 2 set the stage and describe the context out of which the Jackson candidacy developed. Chapter 1 opens with a glimpse of the initial caucus of Jackson delegates at the 1984 San Francisco Democratic National Convention and then reflects back to trace the dynamics and outcome of the early lively debate among black leaders over whether or not there should be a black presidential candidate. That outcome, of course, was inconclusive and eventually led to Jesse Jackson's decision to enter the race for the Democratic presidential nomination. Chapter 2 describes the formal announcement of Jackson's decision to enter and comments on various factors in the political-social environment that gave rise to and stimulated Jackson's candidacy. It also gives a summary overview of how my increased study and activity led first to my support of the black presidential strategy and eventually to my decision to actively support Jesse Jackson's candidacy itself.

After a brief overview of the nature of the Jackson campaign, chapter 3 looks at how the decision of some key black leaders to support Mondale and the release of Lt. Robert Goodman from a Syrian prison camp conveyed mixed signals about the potential of Jackson's candidacy, including its capacity to affect our politics and public policies at home and abroad. Chapter 4 considers low points in the campaign—Jackson's "Hymie" remark, Minister Louis Farrakhan's involvement—and how these and other factors affected Jackson's standing in the Jewish community. It attempts to look at these factors in the broader perspective of black-Jewish relations over time. An interpretive account of Jackson's participation in the presidential debates and primaries is the focus of chapter 5, which describes the style and substance of the overall campaign. It discusses the nature and impact of the "rules of the game" as well as the role and influence of media coverage, looks at the flaws in the campaign, and ponders "the campaign that might have been." It also looks at the successes of the Jackson effort and comments on the persistent strength and appeal of Jackson, especially in the black community, despite certain obstacles and barriers.

The dynamics of my selection as a Jackson national convention delegate is the thrust of chapter 6, which gives a rather detailed personal account of my conversion from a detached scholar-observer to an "attached" scholar-participant. This chapter also comments on my experiences as a national convention delegate-elect from the time of my selection until the beginning of the San Francisco convention.

Chapter 7 offers diary entries and commentaries on the 1984 Democratic National Convention in an attempt to set the stage and capture the flavor of the convention environment. It describes the Jackson delegate caucuses, the political situation facing Mondale, Jackson, and Hart as the convention began, and the keynote address of Governor Mario Cuomo of New York. It describes in some detail how the Jackson campaign came down to just one day (Tuesday, July 17, 1984) when we Jackson supporters had to finally come to grips with the *realities* facing us in the convention situation—i.e., the almost certain defeat of key issues embodied in certain minority planks and the strong support Mondale enjoyed among certain prominent black leaders. Particular attention, of course, is given to Jackson's one-hour-long, prime-time, nationally televised speech. The chapter ends with a brief overview of the aftermath of the convention.

Chapter 8 attempts to discern the lessons we might draw from Jackson's campaign—guides for 1988 and beyond—including the need for blacks to develop a common unifying strategy, the factors that could stimulate blacks to take more aggressive stances within the Democratic party, the failure of Mondale and party leaders to achieve a real unity in the convention and the importance of such unity in mounting a successful campaign, the role of the media in the campaign, the influence of the rules of the game on the outcome of political conflict such as presidential nomination contests, the capacity and limits of electoral politics, and the things that Jackson, or a Jackson-type candidate, *must* do in order to mount a more effective campaign. Finally, this chapter attempts to capture the deeper meaning of Jackson's overall effort.

Let us now begin our story of Jesse Jackson's quest for the 1984 Democratic presidential nomination.

Our Time Has Come

1

On the Right Side of History

So Happy Tonight

The day was Sunday, July 15, 1984, the eve of the official opening of the Democratic National Convention in San Francisco; the time, about 8:15 P.M.; the place, the Hyatt Hotel on the Square, the Jesse Jackson headquarters; the occasion, the initial caucus of some 400 Jackson delegates who, together with media persons of all types, jammed every nook of the meeting room to hear from the candidate himself. In the meantime, however, the speaker was Mayor Richard Hatcher of Gary, Indiana, national chairperson of the Jesse Jackson for President Committee. Hatcher captured well the sense of the occasion and set the mood for us all: "I am so happy tonight! I am so happy that years from now when my children and grand-children study the history books and say to me, 'Grandaddy, tell me about this man Jesse Jackson. Where were you when he ran for president? Did you help him?' I am so happy tonight because I will be able to look my children and grandchildren squarely in the face and say, 'Yes, I know Jesse Jackson. I stood right with him and did all I could to help in his great crusade.' I am so happy that I will not have to equivocate, hem and haw, and give excuses. Yes, I will be proud to tell my children and grandchildren that their grandaddy was on the right side of history. And I know all of you will be able to do the same."[1]

The roar of the delegates was deafening; words simply cannot describe the excitement that swept the room. Fortunately, I was one of those 400 delegates, a participant in and eyewitness to this history-making event. Like Richard Hatcher, I too felt a sense of pride and accomplishment and joy that I could someday tell my grandchildren—as well as my two daughters—that I had been "on the right side of history." There was no doubt in my mind that Jackson's campaign for the 1984 Democratic presidential nomination provided one of those pathbreaking developments which our children and grandchildren will study in order to understand *their* present. However, on that Sunday night in San Francisco, as I listened to Hatcher and then to Jesse Jackson, I began to wonder how such a study would look, how history would reflect Jackson's effort.

Thus, quite naturally, I began to reflect upon my own experience, on just when, why, and how I became involved in Jackson's campaign. For me that involvement began in early 1983 as I began to tune in on the debate among black leaders about whether a black should run for the Democratic presidential nomination.[2] The situation facing Black Americans in 1983 was one with which they had become quite familiar over the years. While hopeful signs of progress abounded, the evidence of pain remained all around. Being black in America was still a frustrating experience. This situation provided the backdrop for the proposal to run a black for the Democratic presidential nomination.

As a professional political scientist interested in American politics in general and in black politics in particular, I found the debate opened fresh vantage points from which to view political matters. As a Black American I found the debate reflected the continuing everyday frustrations and experiences of blacks. I found it so encompassing, so intensely personal, that it was clear to me that few Americans, especially Black Americans, could ignore or escape its implications. It was in theory and fact a debate over the very role and status of blacks and minorities in the American political-social order. On the one hand, it raised again the unfinished goals of Martin Luther King and the civil rights movement. It embraced not only the plight of blacks but also the plight of women, the poor, the elderly, the weak, the powerless—all the disadvantaged in our society. On the other hand, the debate evoked the progress and achievements brought about by the civil rights movement. It re-

flected the creation of an environment that made possible the shift
from protest politics to electoral politics. Thus I yearned to join the
debate both as a political scientist and as a Black American. It became
increasingly difficult to divorce the professional from the personal,
for they are obviously both part of the same person. At one time or
another, one or the other self seemed to dominate, but there was
little doubt that one was informing the other.

Something More Must Be Done, But What?

The debate about whether there should be a black presidential
candidate *never* posed a dilemma for me as a professional political
scientist or as a Black American. I was not so much wedded to the
idea of a black presidential candidacy *per se,* but I did believe very
strongly that only a new, dramatic, overall strategy could deal with
a painfully increasing stalemate in civil rights progress and with the
continuing plight of blacks and minorities. In fact, before the subject
was aired, the idea of running a black person for the presidency in
1984 had not crossed my mind. Nor had I been preoccupied with
any other particular strategy. I only knew that something more needed
to be done, that something more was needed to address the problems
of hunger, of poverty, of chronic unemployment, all of which hit
blacks and minorities especially hard. Though in absolute terms more
whites than blacks live in poverty, the stark fact is that about one-
third of all blacks remain in poverty. Additionally, unemployment
rates run twice as high among blacks as whites, with unemployment
among black youths, eighteen to twenty-four-year-olds, hovering
around a tragic 40 percent.[3]

To be sure, a few scholars and others, including blacks, suggest
that class rather than race now mainly account for these differences.[1]
But given the history of the black struggle in America, I find that
the class factor fails to explain satisfactorily the continued discrimination and deprivation felt by blacks at all levels of the class structure. Time and again blacks at all levels are tersely reminded of the
truth in the view that, regardless of achievements or wealth or status,
blacks in America "can never be sure." Certainly I myself, and many
other blacks who cut across socioeconomic class levels, can fill vol-
umes recounting instances of outright insults and discrimination unfortunately still suffered daily just *because we are black!* Attempts

to explain such deprivations mainly on the basis of individual constraints are also unsatisfactory.

No doubt there are individual and class effects, but racial bias affects blacks regardless of individual or class differences. We must never forget that many of today's so-called individual shortcomings are but reflections and indeed consequences of the many shortcomings that blacks as a group have suffered for generations. I remain horrified and impatient with the miserable existence in poverty that is the lot of more than one-third of all the blacks today and of many whites as well. Of course no one in the richest country on earth should have to live in poverty! And the fact that blacks suffer disproportionately in this regard cannot be ignored. Casual observation and concrete data are too strong. For example, a 1983 study by the Center for the Study of Social Policy concluded that "despite the fact that Black Americans have made some gains since the civil rights movement of the last two to three decades, the economic gap between blacks and whites remains wide and is not diminishing. On measures of income, poverty, and unemployment, wide economic disparities between blacks and whites have not lessened or have been worsened since 1960."[5]

To be sure, blacks have made such great gains in education during the past two decades that it is difficult to account for differences in income on the basis of educational attainment. Nonetheless, despite such progress, blacks still find a different system of financial rewards based on education than do whites. To put the matter starkly, "the income distribution of black families whose heads have completed four years of college parallels the income distribution for white families headed by high school graduates."[6] These gross inequities have been documented and analyzed time and again in scholarly studies and reports by government agencies and other groups. But while these data are being studied, I cannot help but remember that those who are subjects of such studies still live daily with frustration and despair. Apparently, however, too many of our leaders, including a few blacks, would rather ignore the overwhelming problems that remain, and accentuate the few positives. Certainly, many of us would like to have "successful" and "happy" endings to our problems. This is human nature. But the many inequities and deprivations that blacks and minorities still encounter simply cannot be ignored, nor can they be allowed to continue to fester.

I also thought that some new, dramatic strategy was needed to counter the attitudes and actions of the Reagan administration toward blacks, women, members of minorities, the poor, and other disaffected groups. This factor, perhaps more than anything else, is a vivid reminder to blacks and minorities how the actions of the president can directly affect their everyday lives. During the administration of Lyndon B. Johnson we saw how a president can positively support the interests of blacks and minorities. Of course, Johnson's actions, as well as those of other governmental institutions and officials, were spurred by the impetus of the civil rights movement. But during his first three years in office, President Reagan clearly showed that he had no sympathy or consideration for such groups. Budget cuts and policies with respect to various welfare programs, school lunches, social security, medicare and medicaid, legal services, and the enforcement of civil rights laws indicate clearly that the interests of blacks, women, minorities, the poor, and the elderly were not among the priority interests of the Reagan administration.

What made Reagan's policies and programs in these areas particularly devastating to blacks and minorities was the persistent, increasing high unemployment that these groups suffer. By almost any yardstick, the jobless rate among blacks and minorities indicated a tragic situation whose consequences, as the 1960s taught us (we so easily forget), can affect more than just those who suffer. However, there was little indication that either the Reagan administration or even Democratic party leaders were disposed to push these concerns on the eve of a presidential election year. Even more tragic, of course, is the fact that the very policies and practices of the Reagan administration were perpetuating these conditions and, if anything, making them worse.

Perhaps most damaging to blacks and minorities were the very negative attitudes and actions taken by the Reagan administration toward the basic human rights laws and policies which constitute the very foundation upon which our entire legal system is based.[7] Blacks and others who fought so hard during the civil rights movement to put basic laws on the books—such as the Civil Rights Acts of 1964 and 1965—surely expected that such laws would at least be adhered to by a country supposedly devoted to the rule of law, to justice and equality for all. But the actions of the Reagan administration reminded blacks and minorites that the struggle for equality and justice is continuous.

Blacks, and others as well, certainly remember that through the Supreme Court, the Justice Department, and eventually the federal government they were able to make important advances in overcoming centuries of oppressive, intolerable racial segregation and injustice. And quite naturally, it was these agencies to which blacks and minorities looked—perhaps somewhat naively—to continue to safeguard and promote their interests. Since the 1950s, for example, the Justice Department has been generally viewed as a positive force in civil rights progress. Under the Reagan administration, however, it has become a foe of such progress.

The Reagan administration also managed to considerably damage the U.S. Civil Rights Commission, the premiere symbol of the nation's commitment to civil rights. The administration took bold, unprecedented, highly visible, and largely successful steps to reshape the commission by removing, without cause, certain "unfriendly" commissioners and replacing them with "friendly" ones.[8] The commission, originally set up in 1957 to study the state of civil rights problems and progress and report its findings to the Congress, has become a sort of watchdog and potent symbol of our civil rights efforts. But that watchdog and potent symbol was severely damaged when President Reagan was able to make changes in commission personnel that brought about changes in commission policy, making those policies more congruent with those of the president and his administration.

But perhaps the posture of the Reagan administration toward civil rights was most vividly demonstrated by the president himself at a press conference in October 1983. When the president was asked about the charge that Martin Luther King had been a Communist or Communist sympathizer, he equivocated and vacillated in his response and left viewers with the impression that the charge might have been true.[9] Swift negative reaction by the press, civil rights leaders, and others led the president to make an "explanatory" call to Mrs. King indicating that his answer had been misinterpreted. Even so, the president's call only served to highlight his insensitivity to (and perhaps lack of knowledge about) the goals and aspirations of the civil rights movement. Ironically, this incident obscured the determinative role and deep significance of the president's eventual support for federal recognition of a holiday in memory of Dr. King. It certainly minimized whatever political benefit might have accrued to Reagan for his support, without which the King holiday legislation might never have passed.

Overall, I found these developments disquieting, reminders of a harsh political reality—i.e., that those who have benefited for so long and in so many ways from the deprivations and injustices suffered by blacks, minorities, and the poor do not give up such benefits easily. Thus I became strongly wedded to the view that Black Americans especially needed some new, highly visible strategy to counter both special problems posed by the Reagan administration and long-established injustices—the continuing devastating problems of poverty and unemployment. As I viewed it, we have become too accustomed to repeating mechanically that almost one-third of all blacks live in poverty and too willing to be consoled by such quarterly statistics that unemployment among black youth had indeed "dropped" from some 42 to 36 percent. Big deal! It has become too commonplace to complain loudly—for too short a time—about how the Reagan administration has scuttled social programs and wreaked havoc with civil rights enforcement generally.

It has also become too commonplace for universities and many other institutions to succumb to the changed political climate in which affirmative action is no longer an important consideration. Shunning the plight of blacks and minorities has become legally condoned and popularly acceptable, even among those who still suffer such injustices. We are just simply becoming too comfortable, too adjusted, and too tolerant of *intolerable* conditions! We have embraced the status quo, and it has dulled our capacity to feel anger or sense injustice. This bothers me deeply.

I was concerned that the widely publicized symbols of black achievement—e.g., the election of some big-city black mayors—was somehow concealing the pain and problems that too many blacks and minorities still suffer, not as *individuals* but as *blacks and minorities*. I knew such things would not disappear on their own and that only something extraordinary and creative could force Americans to face such persistently thorny issues as poverty and unemployment, no matter how much some might want to ignore or evade them.

But where would we find the necessary force and leadership to bring forth that something extraordinary and creative? Civil rights organizations such as the NAACP were experiencing trouble; funds and memberships were becoming more difficult to garner. Some were beginning to question their very reasons for being—for continuing to exist. The black church, still an influential force in the black community, was not equipped by function, role, or resources to deal with the manifold problems that still plague the everyday lot of blacks and minorities. Black elected officials, though still a highly visible presence in black politics, were finding that they were not able, in the main, to achieve expected goals and objectives. Overall then, by 1983, frustration was growing among black masses and leaders over the current state of things. Most agreed that something more needed to be done to deal with problems and to stem the retrogressive mood of the country. But they disagreed over what that something else should be and how it should be done.

Even so, as I looked over the situation, I found a measure of comfort in the fact that, despite outward appearances, a remarkable degree of consensus and unity remains in the black community with respect to policy interests and goals. Public opinion researchers consistently find that blacks are and remain the most "distinctively liberal" group in America and have an unusually high level of agreement on both civil rights as well as non-civil rights issues. However, on occasions such as that in 1983, I have found it frustrating that since Martin Luther King there has been no unifying focal point around which blacks and civil rights forces could rally. Some, of course, suggest that the many points of black leadership and access today, unlike King's day, obviate the need for such a unifying force. A sign of maturing political development, they suggest, is that the black community is not monolithic but speaks with many voices from many leaders in many positions.

And there is a great deal of merit in this view. But given the situation that prevailed in 1983, my view was that the voices of blacks in the political-social order were not sufficient in number or influence to promote and protect their interests. Thus I saw the need for a strategy that could unify and rally these black leaders so their voices could speak with a unity similar to that with which the black community still speaks. Even more, I thought the time had come to think of national strategies that could appeal to others who were being hurt too by policies and actions of the Reagan administration. Clearly, many others share with blacks common economic interests that are not being addressed by the Reagan administration or faced squarely by the Democratic party. And clearly, coalition politics had been at the heart of the civil rights movement, which brought about monumental social and economic change. I realized, of course, that developing such coalition politics would pose difficult problems, but the possibilities, I thought, were well worth the try.

I saw the idea of a black presidential candidacy, viewed in context, as an exciting and potentially rewarding strategy, one that could penetrate the many layers of the political-social order in ways that few other strategies could. It could not help but strike a responsive chord among blacks and *could*, with skill, ingenuity, and adequate resources, be made appealing to similarly disaffected groups and interests as well. It could prove a unifying voice and structure similar to that provided by Martin Luther King and the civil rights movement. To me, whether Jesse Jackson was the candidate was somewhat beside the point. The strategy, I believed, could fill a leadership void and meet the concerns of blacks as well as the needs of other groups and interests who also wanted to overcome the harmful policies and practices of the Reagan administration.

A Black Presidential Candidacy: A Viable Strategy

But my strong support for the black presidential strategy did not come full blown; it did not develop overnight. I came to it only after careful consideration, study, and writing on the subject. Indeed, until the matter hit newspapers and television, the idea of a black person running for the Democratic presidential nomination in 1984 did not seriously cross my mind. The more I thought about the presidential strategy, however, the more intriguing it became and the more I embraced the notion. It was indeed a sort of transformation process in which I moved from *concern* (the need to do something more) to *study* (an assessment of costs and benefits) to *full support*. The real transformation came as a result of my writing for a professional conference a paper that sought to assess the benefits and costs of pursuing such a strategy. A similar, though not identical, transformation led me eventually to become a fully committed supporter

of Jackson. In fact, support for the idea made it first very difficult
and finally impossible for me to remain neutral, "above the battle."

As the discussion continued, my background, training, and research interests as a political scientist immediately led me to think
about how a scholar might usefully (and professionally) contribute
to the public debate on this issue. To be sure, I thought of the
scholarly debates and contributions which informed the most important legal breakthrough in civil rights history—the 1954 school
desegregation case.[10] And I could not help but remember how scholars, through their expertise and as citizens, continue to enter our
public debate on many major public policy questions.

By early 1983 it was clear to me that the debate about whether
there should be a black presidential candidate involved matters that
were too important to be left solely to members of the "black leadership family" or to any other select group of leaders. The debate
was certainly too important to be left to columnists and journalists.
For, as I saw it, the debate involved matters of the highest order,
all rolled up in the question of how best to combat the Reagan administration's blatant attempts to disrupt the national consensus and
reopen the national debate over questions about the basic rights of
blacks and their socioeconomic status. I believed that these questions
should be studied by professional scholars, especially black and minority scholars whose unique backgrounds and life experiences could
add perspectives and insights which otherwise might not come to
the fore.

Accordingly, as president-elect and program chair for the 1983
annual meeting of the National Conference of Black Political Scientists (held in Houston in April 1983), I organized a roundtable
discussion on the question of whether there should be a black presidential candidate. Surely, I thought, an organization of predominantly black scholars, many of whom study and write about black
politics, ought to have something to say about this important issue.
Joining me on the roundtable were professors Marguerite Barnett
of Columbia University–New York; Ronald Walters of Howard University, later to become deputy national issues director of Jesse Jackson's campaign; Mack Jones of Atlanta University; and Paula McClain
of Arizona State University. We all shrouded our remarks in the
academic jargon appropriate for a conference of professional political
scientists. Some of the participants (Barnett and McClain) appeared

to hold fast to the position that objectivity required analyses that brought insights and information but that did not take a stand for or against the proposition. However, while bringing insights and information, others in the roundtable took clearer and more definite stands on the question. Ron Walters and I were obviously for the idea and argued on its behalf. On the other hand, Mack Jones remained quite skeptical of the whole idea, expressing doubt that a black presidential candidate could have genuine effect on the real problems of blacks and minorities.

The 1983 NCOBPS conference also included a roundtable discussion focusing on blacks and mayoral races, especially the April 1983 victory of Harold Washington of Chicago. In fact, perhaps more than anything else, Washington's success in Chicago's mayoral race now fueled the black presidential idea.

Obviously, the achievements, promise, and potential which electoral politics held for the continued progress of blacks and minorities evoked excitement, interest, and much discussion at the 1983 NCOBPS meeting. However, for a host of reasons, what academics discuss seldom penetrates to the outside world. This is perhaps even more true in the case of black academics, who find it difficult for their policy views to reach almost any outside audience, even that of white academics. Fortunately, however, in this case the quarterly news and notes journal of the American Political Science Association (*PS*) was anxious to share with their readers (primarily professional political scientists) some of the major topics of interest discussed at the NCOBPS conference. I was invited to serve as guest editor for this *PS* issue and immediately began to solicit manuscripts and suggestions. Eventually, due to *PS* space limitations and current interests, we decided to highlight black electoral politics, focusing specifically on Harold Washington's election and the debate over a black presidential candidate. Major excerpts from each of the participants' discussions were published in the August 1983 issue of *PS*.[11] As a result our views did reach a nation-wide academic audience of political scientists. Otherwise, however, with the noted exception of a David Broder column, not much public attention was paid to our discussion.[12]

Opposition, Frustration, Adaptation

By the end of 1983 the boomlet for a black presidential candidate seemed to have run its course. Time was running out for anyone who really wanted to be taken seriously as a candidate. I became increasingly disappointed and frustrated as first one black leader, then another, indicated skepticism or outright opposition to the idea. It was becoming increasingly clear that the black leadership family would be unable to reach a decision on the issue other than to agree to disagree. For whatever reasons, older as well as recently established black leaders such as Andrew Young, Julian Bond, Coretta Scott King, Wilson Goode, Coleman Young, Benjamin Hooks, Richard Arrington, and Tom Bradley were not ready to join the move for a black presidential candidacy. In addition, by mid-summer 1983 it was clear that the two major and oldest civil rights organizations— the NAACP and the Urban League—or at least their leaders were also opposed to the black presidential candidate idea.

Even more frustrating to me were the apparent reasons some gave for their reluctance or outright opposition. Some argued that now is not the time, or that a black presidential candidate cannot win, or that Mondale stood a better chance of winning, or that it was not the right time to fool around with symbolic politics since only through actual politics can one feed the hungry or provide jobs to the poor. Some reasoned that a black presidential effort would dilute or drain resources from local- and state-level black candidates who would have more realistic chances of winning.

To be sure, these were all plausible reasons. However, they did not seem to counter the benefits and potential of the black presidential strategy. As I weighed the matter and discussed it with others, the whole thing seemed almost tailor-made—a relatively low-risk, no-lose strategy with potentially high and far-reaching benefits. "Why all the fuss" was the refrain that crossed my mind time and again as one after another reputable black leader expressed skepticism or opposition to the strategy. In fact, I began to wonder whether their stated reasons—although plausible—were actually their *real* reasons. I wondered whether they were reacting to the *idea* itself, or to *Jesse Jackson*, who seemed most likely to emerge as the candidate, or to a combination of these and other factors. In any event, I recognized that black leaders—not unlike others—probably have varied reasons for their positions, some of which can be stated for the record, others perhaps not.

Simultaneously, I also recognized that no matter how attractive I found the strategy it was obviously not the *only* road to the promised

land. But to me the road that these leaders were disposed to follow—
support for the most sympathetic white candidate with the best chance
of winning—had been trod in the past and had resulted in many dead
ends. Why not try another strategy, one that was new, different, and,
I believe, much more promising? Despite my wonderment, however,
there could be no denying that those who were skeptical or outright
opposed to the black presidential strategy were an impressive and
highly reputable lot. More than this, some of them held important,
highly visible elective positions; their weight could be felt. Whether
or not I agreed with their position or reasons, like any other ordinary
citizen I had only the information they gave, to weigh and use the
best way I could. I thought the overall situation, and the gravity of
the issues involved, "required" me to somehow become a bit more
actively involved—how I did not know.

Thus it was that I found myself in the spring and summer of 1983.
My entire life had been devoted to scholarly activity, which was now
reaping some rewards and recognition—an endowed chair and ten-
ured professorship at one of the predominantly white elite universities in the nation; chairmanship of a department of political science
ranked in the top twenty in the nation; and the presidency of the
largest major regional political science association in the nation, the
Midwest Political Science Association. At the same time I had also
been honored by my fellow black political scientists and was serving
in 1983 as president of the National Conference of Black Political
Scientists. It was quite obvious, given the many requests for my
opinions from the media and others, that these roles lent credibility
to my views on the idea of a black presidential candidacy. What was
and is not so obvious is how the expectations and requirements of
these roles influenced my own views and behavior and, of course,
the views of others toward my posture on this matter. Certainly
American politics and black politics have long provided the major
thrusts of my research, and clearly I considered the role of blacks
in the 1984 presidential election as an area quite ripe for scholarly
study.

Almost simultaneously, however, through a sort of transformation
process, I had become strongly supportive, even committed, to a
black presidential candidacy even as the overall strategy debate was
taking place. To be sure, I was somewhat sensitive to (but not much
bothered by) the perennial quest for scholarly objectivity, detach-

ment from the political battles of the day lest one's personal biases and views interfere with scholarly objectivity and analysis. In my own thinking, however, I considered support for the idea to be still somewhat removed from ordinary "battles of the day." I saw an important distinction between support for the idea and support for a particular candidate. Some, of course, might view this as too much of an abstract, artificial separation, but it is nevertheless how I viewed the situation. Accordingly, I adapted my thinking to it as best I could.

As I saw it, the idea of a black presidential candidacy would affect issues that I believed far transcended ordinary issues of the day, including the Democratic presidential nomination contest itself. Even so, I clearly recognized that by coming out squarely in favor of the strategy, no matter the evidence or academic objectivity used in reaching this decision, I risked becoming involved, perhaps *more directly* than I would care for, in the actual dynamics of the controversy. But based on my study of the matter, as well as on my strong personal views of the larger issues involved, I thought it was an issue on which I could remain neither neutral nor uncommitted. It would have been equivalent to remaining neutral in the civil rights movement of the 1950s and the 1960s, and this, from my point of view, would be unconscionable. In any event, given my past research and teaching interests and my own personal views, I do not believe that my ultimate strong position supporting the idea of a black presidential candidacy came as a surprise to those who know me well—my professional colleagues and other close friends. On the contrary, I believe there would have been great surprise had I not shown intense interest and concern in what loomed as a development of historic proportions.

Thus from both a professional and personal standpoint I was determined to see the issue through. At the time I thought there was not much I could do to help the idea become a reality. However, I thought the issue had already developed sufficiently to provide useful vantage points from which to pursue my continuing research interests in American politics and black politics, and I tried to console myself by plunging into the professional world of research and analysis. But the halls of ivy did not provide sufficient satisfaction or escape from reality. If anything, they only served to fuel my pent-up feelings on the issue. Indeed, my continuing research and analysis on the issue affected me in two important ways. First, it reinforced strongly my view that, in terms of improving the lot of blacks and minorities, a black presidential candidate as a political strategy was both feasible and very timely. Second, because the strategy carried such low risks, I found it increasingly difficult to understand why a number of important black leaders were either opposed to the idea or reluctant to support it.

In general, I thought that a black presidential candidacy could not help but strengthen the role and influence of blacks and minorities in the cold hard world of everyday practical politics. This, in fact, was the thrust of my views that I presented to the 1983 Houston conference of the National Conference of Black Political Scientists.[13] In my opinion, it was just too plain for argument that, in return for their support and help over the years, blacks and minorities had for too long been shortchanged and overlooked by the Democratic party. It was clear to me that traditional clientage—i.e., black clients dependent on white patrons—had not worked and that a black presidential candidacy offered the kind of dramatic, creative, yet low-risk strategy which I believed the current overall situation and time demanded.

More positively and directly, the practical political benefits of a black presidential strategy seemed clearly apparent. For one thing, a black presidential bid "calls for a level and kind of political mobilization among Black Americans that has not heretofore been experienced in American politics." If recent black mayoral victories, such as that of Harold Washington in Chicago, had shown anything, it was that a black candidate could spur and energize black voter registration and turnout. A black presidential candidate could provide the same kind of focal point around which blacks and minorities could rally at the national level.

Further, I believed that a black presidential candidate would spur increased political interest and activity at local and state levels, including generating more black and minority candidates for political office. Overall, given the overwhelming disposition of blacks and minorities to vote Democratic and given the small margin by which Reagan won several key southern states in the 1980 election, the Democratic party would stand to benefit greatly from a black presidential candidacy. At the same time, the increased political interest and activity among blacks and minorities would give them increased influence in the Democratic convention and the general election, and of course in the ensuing Democratic administration, should the Democrats win. Put more directly, I believed that such a development, especially if done in unity among blacks and even more so among minority groups generally, could give these groups more bargaining power in presidential politics than they had ever experienced before.

In addition to stimulating voter registration and turnout, a black presidential bid could fashion for the first time a campaign structure that would identify and bring together leadership and specialist cadres from among the "locked out" (e.g., blacks) that have "heretofore been largely dormant, untapped, and underdeveloped or underutilized." I believed that "the sheer identification of such resources, and the kind of expertise and experience gained through a national campaign could not but help to enrich black and minority political development." Indeed, I reasoned that such an effort in 1984 might well bring nearer the day when a black presidential candidate will have a greater chance to win both the nomination and election.

Moreover, a black presidential candidate could utilize fully and effectively the opportunity for political education that election campaigns are supposed to provide in a democracy. Aside from the presidential election itself, contesting for a major party nomination offers a forum (or classroom) for political education that is unmatched in American politics. I thought that a black presidential candidate was likely to bring knowledge, insights, and perspectives on issues that heretofore have been largely underdeveloped, brushed aside, or ignored altogether. And I thought it was important that Americans should get insights and perspectives on major policy issues from a person such as Jackson who has actually shared a common life experience and background with those whose interests he seeks to represent. But as time passed, it became increasingly clear that a number of black leaders apparently did not believe that the *benefits* of a black candidacy would outweigh the *costs*.

Obviously, I saw the world differently than did these black leaders, but I very much wanted to understand their positions more clearly. I also wanted to see blacks pursue a united strategy to maximize their influence in the Democratic party. If not a black presidential candidacy, I thought, then what was the alternative strategy? Backing Mondale because he was likely to win the nomination—*without telling us something more*—was hardly a full-blown strategy. How much influence would blacks have in the Mondale camp? What issues was he prepared to back? In short, in *exchange* for black support what would be the likely payoffs, what were the likely "wins?" It struck me that the black presidential strategy was being subjected to this kind of scrutiny, but I did not see the same scrutiny or standards being applied to what I saw as an emerging Mondale strategy alternative. This bothered me.

As the 1984 presidential race approached, President Reagan and his policies were clearly proving the most effective stimuli and catalysts that the "cause" has had since the civil rights movement itself. Opposition to the president provided a unity among blacks that had not been seen since the movement of the fifties and early sixties. This, more than any other single factor, provided both the substantive and symbolic incentives from which Jesse Jackson (or any other minority presidential candidate) could launch a bid for the top elective office in the nation.

But despite these incentives and no matter the arguments or lessons of history, the cold, realistic situation was that some very visible and influential black leaders continued to speak disparagingly and discouragingly about the strategy of nominating a black presidential candidate.

It's Up to Jesse, and He Does It

As time wore on, it became abundantly clear that only one major black leader could give the strategy life-and-blood reality—the one leader who had kept the issue alive—Jesse Jackson. And in the end, this is what happened. With a good number of black leaders at his side but some highly visible black leaders standing on the outside, Jesse Jackson took the plunge into the virtually uncharted seas of Democratic presidential nominating politics. On November 3, 1983, Jackson launched his bid for the Democratic presidential nomination.

On both professional and personal grounds, I was elated. But this was only the beginning of an exciting and enriching experience, albeit one that had its peaks and valleys. Thus some eight months later (July 15, 1984), as I joined with other Jackson delegates in our initial convention caucus, I could not help but reflect on the story about how all this had come about. Sitting in that jam-packed meeting room of the San Francisco Hyatt Hotel, with television cameras and news-people swarming all around, one could not help but feel like an eyewitness to the making of history. I also felt a sense of accomplishment and satisfaction. However, what pleased me most about our Jackson delegates was an obvious, infectious sense of dedication and determination that made us vow to continue fighting for the principles and policies our candidate represented—a common bond that created the sort of unified and devoted commitment to Jackson that any candidate would envy.

Perhaps more than anything else, this common bond made an already history-laden atmosphere even more exciting and electrifying. Thus, just like Mayor Hatcher, I too could feel the excitement and pleasure of being part of a much larger historic struggle, one that could not be stopped no matter what the outcome of the 1984 Democratic National Convention. In short, by his decision to run for the Democratic presidential nomination, Jesse Jackson had provided one of those rare opportunities for his delegates (and many others) to be "on the right side of history," and I was honored to be among them.

2

Jackson's Candidacy and the Best of Both Worlds

A New Leadership: Jackson's Formal Entry

I never shall forget the Jackson announcement. To most seasoned observers Jackson's entry was expected. He would hardly use the Washington Convention Center to announce he was *not* running, and he would hardly have attracted a large media following to such an event. But even though expected, Jackson's announcement and entry provided signals of the excitement, the hope, the pride, and the responsive chord Jackson's candidacy was to find among blacks. Undoubtedly, the scene in my household must have been similar to that in many others. I will always relish the memory (with appropriate appreciation to Rev. Jackson) of how my fourteen-year-old daughter shrieked with joy while giving me a love-gripping hug. "Daddy, Daddy," she screamed, "he's in. He's running. Jesse Jackson is running for president." It was a day we as a family and as Americans, particularly Black Americans, will always remember.

I was ecstatic over Jackson's announcement, which I believed signaled a phenomenon of historic proportions in the making. To me, his entry was indeed a revival and extension of the civil rights movement; but this time it was not in the streets, it was in the electoral process. My only disappointment was that I failed to see the unity among black leaders which I believe the historic occasion demanded. It was beautiful to see Shirley Chisholm, Marion Barry, Richard Hatcher, Walter Fauntroy, and many others—some prominent but most not so prominent—rally to Jackson's call. But noticeably absent were other black leaders to whom I had long looked as among those willing to take *risks* for noble causes.

Certainly some risks were involved, but from my vantage point the potential benefits were so much greater than the costs that I thought it would be difficult, even for Jackson's critics, to oppose his candidacy. As a political scientist I realized that while Jackson's announcement would stimulate pride and enthusiasm among many blacks, his candidacy and the goals of his campaign would pose persistent and awesome challenges, not only for him and his supporters, but for the Democratic party and for American politics in general. But as a professional student of politics I also know that such is the stuff—the encounters, the struggles, the disappointments—from which historic progress comes. Thus Jackson's candidacy was a bold, courageous move which even with limited success would certainly effect fundamental change.

The change Jackson envisioned grew from his awareness of the feelings and frustrations in the black community and in many other communities where people—whites, Hispanics, others—continue to feel left out. His was really a politics of inclusion, of caring, of sharing, and his campaign was more than an ordinary campaign for the Democratic presidential nomination: it was a call to the locked out to use their newly won political power, gained through the Voting Rights Act, to finally throw away the many locks that still imprisoned the influence, hopes, and aspirations of these groups. Jackson's words portray well how he envisioned this moment in history would bring "hours of change" into the lives of many.

> I embark upon this course with a sense of inner confidence. I offer myself to the American people, not as a perfect servant, but as a public servant. I offer myself and my service as a vehicle to give a voice to the voiceless, representation to the unrepresented and hope to the downtrodden. . . .
>
> Lest there be confusion, let the word go forth from this occasion that this candidacy is not for blacks only. This is a national campaign growing out of the black experience and seen through the eyes of a black perspective—which is the experience and perspective of the rejected. Because of this experience, I can empathize with the plight of Appalachia because I have known

poverty. I know the pain of anti-Semitism because I have felt the humiliation of discrimination. I know firsthand the shame of bread lines and the horror of hopelessness and despair because my life has been dedicated to empowering the world's rejected to become respected. Thus, our perspective encompasses and includes more of the American people and their interests than does most other experiences. Currently, America rejects and excludes more people than it accepts and includes. Accordingly, I would like to use this candidacy to help build a new rainbow coalition of the rejected that will include whites, blacks, Hispanics, Indians and Native Americans, Asians, women, young people, poor people, old people, gay people, laborers, small farmers, small business-persons, peace activists and environmentalists. If we remain separated, we will forever remain poor and powerless. But if we come together around our common economic plight and a humane political agenda, we won't be poor and powerless anymore. Together, the old minorities constitute a new majority. Together we can build a new majority. . . .

We offer a new leadership that is deliberate but decisive. We offer a new leadership that will not just follow public opinion polls, but will mold public opinion. We offer a new leadership that will challenge corporate America, challenge the trade unions and challenge the Democratic Party to negotiate new covenants with us to make room for the locked out. We offer a new leadership that will defend the poor—those who have borne the national burden in the heat of the day.

We offer a new leadership that will take calculated risks as we confront the problems of this world in search of peace and justice. We offer a new leadership that is willing to take positions on issues that are neither political nor popular, but that are right. Might is not necessarily right, but right is always might. Our convictions must play an important part in our politics. We offer a new leadership that will reach out to the people of the world and define strength in healing, not in killing; and see power in liberation, not in occupation. We offer a new leadership that will reach out for a compassionate and ethical standard for measuring greatness.[1]

Jackson's "new leadership" did indeed emcompass a bold, broad, and all-inclusive agenda—a clear extension of the goals and objectives of Martin Luther King and the civil rights movement. The whole setting—the words, the religious and ecumenical flavor, the lead character himself, and even the uncertainty and promise—were all reminiscent of the earlier movement.

The Immediate Aftermath

Now that Jackson had entered and the idea had been given life, I thought I could once again settle down to the more quiet, reflective role of the academic professional analyst. But Jesse Jackson's announcement had indeed changed all this. Because of my teaching and research interests as well as my life experiences, media people and many others reminded me through their inquiries that I was in a good position to comment on Jackson's candidacy. Indeed, our own university public relations office, one of whose functions is to showcase the resources and talents of the Washington University faculty, led the way.

On November 4, 1983, the feature service of the university public relations office released a rather detailed article outlining my views and reactions to Jackson's candidacy. The title of that article, "A Black Presidential Candidate: Worth the Risk of Losing," captured well my strong belief that the strategy embodied far more benefits than costs and could not help but advance the important, unfulfilled objectives of the civil rights movement. While many persons, especially academics, might put things a little differently from journalists and public relations people, my overall impression was that the W.U. article capsulized my views rather well, at the time at least.

A Black Presidential Candidate: Worth the Risk of Losing
by Regina Engelken

Even if Jesse Jackson loses the Democratic nomination for president in 1984, blacks stand to win.

That's the opinion of Lucius Barker, president of the National Conference of Black Political Scientists and chairman of the political science department at Washington University in St. Louis. He is co-author of one of the leading college texts on black politics, *Black Americans and the Political System* (Little, Brown Publishers, 1980).

Increased black involvement in national electoral politics is the best way to speed up improvements in the political-social status of blacks, says Barker. That status has improved little since the 1960s, he adds.

"A black bid for the presidency is the most concrete way to demonstrate that blacks want a more direct voice in determining how the federal government addresses important issues," he says. "That more direct voice must include shaping the political agenda, which is crucial to achieving black goals.

"And in American politics, the president effectively sets the agenda." Barker says blacks stand to gain increased political consciousness and experience through a black presidential candidacy. More blacks will register and vote, and the spinoffs of the political mobilization could be enormous.

More blacks will be stimulated to seek congressional, state and local offices, Barker says, and that increased political know-how could influence long-term policy direction.

Barker says these are the realistic objectives of a black bid for the White House, and Jackson fits them to the letter.

"In the present context of American politics, Jackson could well be the best possible black candidate," Barker says. "And I think he is going to appeal to many people—not just blacks—who are disenchanted with American politics."

Whether Jackson actually stands a chance of winning the nomination is another question.

"All sorts of reasons indicate that it would take a miracle," says Barker. "Miracles happen infrequently, but they do happen.

"Jackson's charisma and personality will be very important assets. His entry means that this will be more than a 'politics as usual' campaign."

One of the loudest arguments against a Jackson candidacy is that it could hurt white candidates who are sympathetic to black causes, and more likely to win.

It is always true that certain candidacies might hurt front-runners, Barker says. "For example, one might suggest that the candidacies of Gary Hart and Alan Cranston are more likely to hurt Walter Mondale than John Glenn. But who would suggest that they not run because of this possible consequence?

"Why should a black presidential candidacy be treated differently? Because black interests can be better represented by
another candidate? Because they should depend on less direct
means, such as positions on staffs or advisory committees, to gain
access to particular presidential nominees? Because now is not
the right time?

"In short, that a particular candidate might affect the fortunes
of other candidates—sympathetic front-runner or not—must be
viewed as part of a general problem inherent in electoral politics,
especially presidential nomination politics, and cannot in itself
determine long-term political objectives.

"Jackson's entry is going to create considerable uncertainty
for the Democratic nomination process, and established politicians—whatever their color—don't like that," Barker says.

"A lot of politicians will be watching carefully how Jackson's
campaign develops and many will be hedging their own moves
accordingly," he says.

If Jackson succeeds in turning out large numbers of blacks to
register and if he continues to attract crowds and generate excitement, leading Democratic contenders will have to handle
the whole situation very carefully, Barker says.

Jackson's candidacy could help the Democrats because he is
focusing on groups that are more likely to vote Democratic,
Barker adds.

Some political observers criticize Jackson for lack of follow-
through on projects he has initiated as head of Operation PUSH
(People to Save Humanity), the civil rights group he founded in
1971.

Barker provides perspective. Jackson's follow-through appears good where it counts, he says. Jackson has succeeded in
getting some large corporations to increase black employment
and capital.

"The job of a leader, especially a civil rights leader, is to
facilitate, to create interest, to set the tone for change. If he
appears to jump from one topic to another, it's because he has
a wide range of topics to cover—education, employment, information, voting.

"Jackson comes into town one evening and speaks. His job is
to make the people want to register to vote, not to actually
register them himself."

Jackson's pledge to select a woman running mate is politically good, says Barker. "It will increase his appeal to the groups he is targeting. But he should perhaps look to someone other than a black. Of course, this is consistent with Jackson's 'rainbow coalition' concept."

Barker edited a special section on black electoral politics in a recent issue of *PS*, the quarterly publication of the American Political Science Association.

In his own *PS* article, "Black Americans and the Politics of Inclusion," Barker says many whites like to believe that minorities now are sufficiently included in the political system.

"Although the 'politics of inclusion' has made some important strides, many blacks and other minorities see only an 'illusion of inclusion,' " Barker says.

"Only since 1954 have blacks been legally guaranteed the treatment, recognition and respect that American law and practice always have accorded to whites. But a political-social order so long engaged in racial discrimination apparently finds it difficult to translate these legal guarantees into everyday practice.

"For example," he says, "it seems clear that the basic issues of the 1960s—such as overcoming inequities in resource allocation and rearranging the nation's priorities—remain the basic policy objectives of blacks, minorities and others.

"But to capture and maintain attention in the current political climate, a black presidential candidate who articulates the issues of the 1960s must do so with the rhetoric and in the context of the 1980s."

A More Active Life:
The Howard University Conference

As the Washington University feature service article circulated in the nation's press and word spread about my work and interest, I began to receive more calls from local and national media. This sudden and unaccustomed attention can prove traumatic to cloistered academics, and I must confess that initially I received such interview requests with some anxiety and reluctance. The workways and socialization of academics do not prepare them for on-the-spot reactions. Academics respond only after considerable study, reflection, and hindsight. Journalists and media people, responding to the requirements of their audiences, do not usually enjoy such luxuries. However, I decided that I could best contribute to this history-making event by sharing my insights and perspectives, even if they had to be given hurriedly. This decision was made easier by the fact that I had decided long ago to study the black presidential candidacy idea, and had been collecting and analyzing data and writing on the subject for some time.

After Jackson's announcement my involvement in research and speaking on the Jackson candidacy and campaign picked up noticeably. On November 18, for example, I joined several other speakers at an all-day conference at Howard University in Washington, D.C. The conference, sponsored by the political science department of Howard and the National Conference of Black Political Scientists, focused on the implications of a black presidential bid. Obviously, Jackson's November 3 announcement gave new importance to the Howard conference. Though basic theoretical arguments and perspectives remained the same, these arguments now had concrete bases for application. But the questions and reactions from the audience gave real life to the papers and to the conference.

Jackson's remark that, should he lose the Democratic nomination, he would not run as an independent stimulated much discussion. Jackson believed his loss would not prove a disincentive to continued black participation. The *New York Times* quoted Jackson as saying, "I have absolutely no fear of blacks being destabilized by the possibility of a loss at one level that they will not be able to adjust to the reality of the general election."[2] Some at the Howard conference saw this as Jackson's way of signaling certain black leaders who were opposed to or reluctant to join his candidacy that, should they decide to support him, he would not lead the black community into an independent movement, which many believed would almost certainly guarantee Reagan's reelection. However, others at the conference thought that Jackson's aim should be to maximize his leverage in future bargaining with the Democratic party's leaders for the goals of blacks and minorities and that by renouncing in advance a possible independent candidacy Jackson was giving up too much, too soon, without reciprocal benefits. To these, the independent route was perhaps Jackson's main bargaining chip.

Still others at the conference, including me, saw Jackson's denunciation of an independent candidacy as very clever. We reasoned that he was trying to strengthen his own support among both blacks and party leaders and that, should Democratic party leaders show gross disregard and unresponsiveness to black and minority objectives, he would still have time enough to opt for the independent route. In short, these conference participants reasoned that Jackson's entry into the Democratic contest brought party leaders face to face with a central political fact: they did not know whether they could count on the votes of blacks, whose support is widely considered almost indispensable for Democratic victory in the presidential race. Indeed, many attending the Howard conference urged Jesse Jackson to take full advantage of this fact; for the first time in history blacks now had a wonderful opportunity to show "them" that blacks cannot be taken for granted.

Further, I remember well that, though not large, the audience at the Howard conference was very lively and altogether supportive of Jackson's bid. To be sure, some speakers cautioned blacks and others to temper their enthusiasm with a little practical wisdom, since realistically Jackson had little or no chance to win the nomination. But even at this early stage, Howard students and others at the conference were not about to let words of restraint dampen their enthusiasm and imagination. I remember vividly that when one participant commented that now that Jesse Jackson had announced the press would subject him to closer scrutiny, which would reveal any skeletons that might be in his closet, a student quickly countered, "I'm from Chicago, and when they put out all kinds of stories and rumors about Harold Washington it only served to make him stronger in the black community, and the same thing will happen in Jesse's case." At the time I did not recognize what an accurate assessment this was, but as primary after primary election results clearly show, criticism of Jesse Jackson and of his troubles did not lessen his strong support in the black community.

Also attending that Howard conference was a representative from the Democratic National Committee. Her role was to explain the rules and procedures for the selection of delegates and for the national convention itself, and her presentation was very clear. However, when discussing rules and procedures, especially those relating to super delegates (those that would ensure selection of party leaders and public officials), I asked her to comment on whether and how such rules might advantage or disadvantage various constituencies in the party. Not unexpectedly, her answer described in detail how the rules were drawn up (by the Hunt Commission) and designed to be fair to all interests. Hence, as she saw it, the only job for the National Committee was to make certain that the rules were explained to and understood by all concerned.

I recognized that from her vantage point this was an expected and reasonable response to my question, especially in a general audience context. But, as a political analyst, I never let pass an opportunity that might reveal how so-called neutral and "fair" rules in fact work to advantage certain interests and disadvantage others. I do this across the board, from the rules embodied in local housing codes to the rules embodied in our Constitution itself. However, I recognized that this was not the time or place to push the matter further. Jackson's candidacy would provide other opportunities just as it had given our many conference discussions an excitement, reality, and meaning that otherwise would have been lacking.

That evening I attended a fund-raising reception—art auction sponsored by and for the benefit of the graduate assistance program of the National Conference of Black Political Scientists. After a long day's conference I looked forward with great relish to both the reception and the "informative informal" conversations which I had long understood took place in Washington. I was not disappointed. With many of the day's conferees in attendance, much of the conversation naturally focused on Jesse Jackson and his campaign. Moreover, it was still one of the hottest topics in town.

As part of the evening program, two members of the Congressional Black Caucus, George Crockett of Michigan and Walter Fauntroy of the District of Columbia, were presented special NCOBPS awards. (Crockett was unable to receive his award in person, but Fauntroy did.) In his remarks acknowledging the award, Fauntroy spoke of the significance of Jackson's candidacy and its broad implications. His remarks added fuel to the informal discussion of Jackson and his candidacy.

A few expressed great concern for Jackson's safety because they had heard that when he entered the campaign the D.C. police department had received more threats on his life than anything comparable they could remember. And as a consequence they had heard that Secret Service protection had been extended to Jackson immediately—comforting news since naturally all expressed the hope that nothing would happen to Jesse. Actually, threats to Jackson were such that Secret Service protection was given to him beginning November 10, 1983, more than two and a half months before other candidates were scheduled to receive such protection.[3]

Additionally, much conversation centered on the black leaders who were not supporting Jackson. Reactions to these leaders that I heard were uniformly *very* negative. And these were reactions from academics and other professionals, some of whom were not so sure about Jackson but reasoned that one did not have to like him in order to support what he represented. They had long viewed a black presidential candidacy as involving objectives rather than any one personality. However, all realized that a live candidate was needed to give these lofty goals content and meaning. And since Jesse Jackson was the only one who would run, blacks of course should unite behind his candidacy. Indeed, I heard this theme expressed time and again.

None of these reactions surprised me. Instead these informal conversations reminded me that many others, professionals just like me, shared my own strong views about the black presidential candidacy. So in general, the Howard conference and fund-raising reception were very good for me, reinforcing my analysis of the situation and my spirits. At a party following the reception, a very close friend told me how delighted he was to hear about my strong support of the black presidential candidacy. In fact, my friend told me, in the presence of several other very close friends, "Lucius, you are coming along well. Someday you may even wear a dashiki." At this, everybody laughed.

Time for Perspectives: The Challenges Ahead

Overall, it was indeed a happy and exciting time. I was absolutely overjoyed that Jackson had given life and reality to the black presidential strategy, focusing attention on the persistent problems that continued to hurt blacks and expressing outrage at how these problems were being exacerbated by a Reagan administration whose politics and practices struck at the heart of newly forged civil rights law that provides the fundamental legal-political basis for protecting the rights and opportunities of blacks and minorities.

In addition, I thought the black presidential candidate strategy—now Jackson's candidacy—of inestimable symbolic value. I believe symbolism is one of the most important areas of our political life. Symbols do much to influence people's minds, guide their behavior, and thus shape the political environment in which the practice of practical politics takes place. People love, hate, fight, and even die for symbols—e.g., flag, country, constitution, "our way of life." Symbols also include the political institutions, myths, rituals, and language that hold a society together. But many tend to minimize the importance of symbols in politics, especially in Jackson's candidacy. In fact, one of the repeated criticisms made by some persons, such as Mayor Coleman Young of Detroit, was that Jackson's candidacy was "merely symbolic" and would do nothing practical to feed the hungry or provide jobs for the poor. Of course, Jackson's candidacy was "symbolic" but it was much more than "merely" symbolic. In fact, symbolism gave Jackson's candidacy an importance far beyond that of most candidacies for the presidency.

Politics is both symbols and substance; the two are inextricably linked. Jackson's candidacy would affect the symbolic value structure within which the substantive allocation of resources takes place, and astute observers and political leaders, including Jackson, clearly understood this. What Jackson's candidacy symbolized gave it far more impetus and credibility than would be suggested by an actual accounting of traditional resources (e.g., available organization staff and personnel, money, pledges of support from important persons). Some criticized Jackson because he was not adequately prepared in terms of such resources to launch a creditable candidacy. Ironically, however, had Jackson been able to marshall such resources, the substance and appeal of his candidacy would have been considerably lessened. Bold political initiatives are rarely started by persons who possess such resources. Indeed, the reverse is often the case. The scarcity of resources has never thwarted leaders of important political-social movements in the past, including Martin Luther King and the civil rights movement,[1] and there was no reason to believe that such movements could be thwarted now. The main criterion for the launching of such movements has been the essentiality of their causes and objectives.

Of course, given its likely objectives, especially in context of the times, a black presidential bid was almost certain to take on "movement" character. Jackson recognized this and fashioned his candidacy accordingly, challenging not only current policies of the Reagan administration but, more importantly, very fundamental structures and beliefs which undergird our political-social order.

In many ways Jackson's candidacy was spurred by the continuing gaps between the symbolic side of politics (goals, myths, aspirations) and the substantive side (resources, benefits, privileges, and rewards). It focused attention on the structures and processes (e.g., voting registration procedures) by which influence and benefits are achieved. As a black presidential candidate, Jackson posed threats and challenges at several levels and to many people, black and white— to those who have prospered in and have been accustomed to, or who have accommodated themselves to, the practice of a practical politics that *does not fully include and respect* the rights of blacks, women, and minorities. By seeking the highest elective office the country has to offer, Jackson called attention to the deep concerns and aspirations of the locked out, who want to be treated as fully worthy members of the American community, not as objects of condescension or as outsiders wanting in; who want to share in power, not because votes force reluctant power holders to make concessions—although this is true—but because fair and equal treatment ought to be accorded to all. *Full* citizenship in a democracy requires nothing less. We continually strive to meet these natural human yearnings and aspirations; however, the extent to which we succeed directly affects whether people feel happy, frustrated, enraged, or dispossessed. And the effects of these feelings on political participation and political behavior are obvious.

Jackson's candidacy questioned directly certain myths, beliefs, norms, and rituals to which many Americans are strongly attached— principles embodied in our constitution and laws that claim that all persons, regardless of race, creed, or color, can expect to be treated fairly in our courts, in our electoral process, and in our bureaucratic and legislative institutions. It challenged Americans to live up to the oft-heard statement that any person—even a black or a woman—can be president and that all persons should be accorded every opportunity to reach their full potential. Specifically, Jackson's candidacy questioned certain myths that cast blacks, minorities, and women in a negative light, including the belief that blacks do not have high aspirations, that they are not articulate, that they are not informed about or interested in issues other than civil rights or minority issues. It challenged all Americans to consider "what they fear, what they regard as possible, and even who they are," and articulated much of what is left unspoken and unexamined in American political life.[5]

Certainly I realized, as did others, that the challenges posed by a black presidential candidacy could turn out to be an uncomfortable exercise for many; yet I strongly believed that it was both necessary and timely. Ultimately, I firmly believed that a black presidential candidacy could help us achieve our highest potential, paving the way for future generations to proceed with practical politics in an environment much more sensitive to the need to adhere to the highest possible ideals of American politics and society.

Could Jackson Meet the Challenges?

The black presidential strategy, now Jackson's candidacy, stood to affect many aspects of our political-social life. And a number of persons liked the strategy but wondered whether Jesse Jackson could meet the challenges involved, whether he was the right person to carry out the strategy. Personally, I believed that Jackson possessed certain qualifications that fitted him well for this particular role at this particular time in history. Politics as usual might look for candidates with more traditional qualifications. But as a Black American I did not view this as a politics-as-usual period. I certainly hoped that the present was not the norm of the future. Consequently, I thought a situation like this might well call for someone with *nontraditional* and *unusual* qualities. And I thought Jackson's charisma, oratory, and message could appeal to those who, for one reason or another, have strayed from or never been attracted to the political system. This was particularly true of a large number of blacks whose vote and political participation could prove important.

Additionally, I believed that Jackson could provide the sort of symbolic appeal that could capture the attention of the American people, and, of course, getting attention in political campaigns is indispensible. Symbols (such as Jackson's candidacy) can be used as a way to get people to vote their interests. They may provide the way to reach persons who are typically not motivated, and these are exactly the people that Jackson needed to reach. To be sure, I was reminded by colleagues and others that symbolism of this sort could prove demogogic, and there is a danger of overpromising. But somehow I wanted to believe that if Jackson were successful in activating large numbers of persons, he and other Democratic leaders—in both their self-interest and more long-term civic interest—could adequately deal with any kind of "overpromising." At the time, some black leaders and others criticized Jackson for not appreciating the hard, cold fact that he could not win the Democratic nomination and that the resulting disappointment and disillusionment could in fact turn off large numbers of black and minority voters. But I found such arguments unconvincing. I thought that in time leadership could well deal with such problems. In any event, I was willing to take the chance.

But others were not so willing. While sold on the black presidential strategy, they were not too sold on Jesse Jackson. Soon after Jackson's announcement, I met two black friends, both relative newcomers to St. Louis (one from Chicago, the other from Philadelphia), both well educated (MBAs) and clearly successful in the corporate world. Early in our conversation it became clear that we all strongly supported the idea of a black presidential candidacy but we disagreed rather sharply over Jackson the candidate:

LUCIUS: I'm glad Jackson announced. For one thing, it means that we now at least have a chance to reap some of the benefits we all agree could come out of such a strategy, and I believe he will do a good job. And I certainly intend to find out since I plan to do research on Jackson's campaign.

JOHN (not his real name): Lucius, I know you're interested in the research angle; you damn academics are always writing something. I just hope people like me will be able to read it; you know I've read some of your stuff (laughter). But let me get serious. I agree with all you say on why we should have a black presidential candidate; but I really have some real qualms about Jesse. I'm from Chicago, and you should hear what they say about him there. Read Barbara Reynold's book. Jesse's out for himself. He ran Operation Breadbasket, now PUSH, with an iron hand. He likes to hog the publicity and the headlines. Sure, Jesse's sharp and can really speak. But I'm not so sure he's what we need for this. Let some of those guys with more experience run.

Rod (not his real name): I agree. The strategy is great but I don't know about Jesse. He strikes me as too visceral, and a person who likes to appeal to people's emotions rather than laying out the arguments in a more rational manner. We need somebody who really knows the issues and can help people understand what's going on.

Lucius: I hear what both of you are saying. John, I don't know what happened in Chicago, and frankly it doesn't bother me. Don't get me wrong; I'm not saying that Jesse's the ideal candidate, but he's the only one who had the guts to announce, and under the circumstances, he might very well be the best person to get people to listen and make the Democratic party stop taking blacks for granted.

Rod: I agree that we need somebody to do those things but I'm still not certain Jesse's the right person. And Jesse's personal traits John alluded to earlier really don't bother me either. I suspect all or at least most politicians suffer, if you want to call it that, from super egos and want to hog as much publicity as they can get. But what really bothers me is that in addition to what I said earlier, Jesse just simply has not had the experience in dealing with the big, tough political issues. We need someone who can really explain these issues and let people know what's happening.

John: And I don't believe that Jesse can or will. I agree with you, Rod; Jesse will stir up people's emotions and leave them dry when he doesn't win. I'm just not convinced: he might prove me wrong and I kind of hope he does, since actually he is the only one who is out there, but I still have doubts. However, one thing is true, Lucius; Jesse will give you and everybody else lots to write about! (laughter).

So went our conversation in November 1983. Eventually John did come around to support Jackson, just as I and others did. In the main, however, his transformation was a rather slow process; it came only after the primaries, convention, and additional reflection. John's transformation resulted from Jackson's much-better-than-expected success in the primary campaign and the continuing need for a voice like Jackson's. Indeed, in a conversation in November 1986, John said that he's "absolutely convinced that what Jesse did and is about is altogether worthwhile and needed. We need a player like Jesse in today's politics, and if he runs again, I'll be out front! Definitely." But Rod is a somewhat different story. He continues to see the need for the strategy, but he is not convinced that Jackson is the right person to carry it out even though the convention speech (at San Francisco) "showed clearly that Jackson had grown and developed." In short, Rod is not ready to commit himself; he prefers to see how things develop next time around.

But not everyone enjoyed the luxury of time that my friends and I had to make up our minds, to become converted or transformed. Sheer practical politics helped some to see the light. In early March 1984, for example, one writer commented that "many black elected officials, especially in those states with early primaries in the South and North, have come over to Jackson's camp as he has gained in the polls and garnered positive news coverage." "Some admit frankly," the writer continued, "that they have moved in Jackson's direction for fear that opposing him will hurt them locally, [and] many others insist they now believe Jackson has tapped some energy among black voters that can be used later."[6] Whatever their rationales or explanations, these various conversions and transformations become much more understandable when viewed in the context of what made Jesse run. To this subject we now turn.

What Made Jesse Run?

What made Jesse run proved intriguing fodder for all kinds of analysts and gossips.[7] At base, however, the explanation may not be all that intriguing or complicated. A rather obvious—and perhaps the most plausible—explanation may be found in a careful, rational assessment of the overall political-social situation in 1983. Gross socioeconomic inequities, based on race, sex, poverty, and minority status, persistently threatened the life chances of many Americans despite some enactment of favorable policies and increase in the number of minority elected officials. Further, the attitudes and actions of the Reagan administration had direct, visible, and widespread negative impact on particular groups—the poor, the elderly, blacks, women, and minorities. Ironically, this Reagan administration posture, more than any other single factor, focused new attention and interest on the continued socioeconomic inequities suffered by these groups.

However, in contrast to the early days of the civil rights movement, in 1983 no single group was in a position to overcome these inequities without a broad base of support from all such affected groups. The black leadership family simply did not command the resources or the authority to deal with the nature and scope of the problems facing all minority groups. Consequently, they could not in 1983, nor can they today, conclusively determine what strategies should be used, including whether a black should run for president. So the most viable route to success for these groups in electoral politics appears to lie in their coming together to maximize their political strength.

This necessarily includes the fundamental tasks of unearthing new voters and reactivating old ones—grass-roots efforts aimed at the masses, not at leaders or the elite. These efforts require some magnetic, energizing focal point that can attract the attention and interest of these groups and stimulate discussion of common interests. This discussion must take place in a forum that offers the best possible chance to achieve stated objectives. In American electoral politics that forum is the contest for the presidency, the one forum that commands all the vast and sophisticated resources of the media and information industry and the rapt attention of the entire nation and the world.

To reap the full benefits of this forum, the concerns and objectives of these disaffected groups must be put forth directly by one of them, not by a surrogate. This single act, more than any other, would dramatize the fundamental human aspirations held by all persons regardless of race, color, sex, or station in life, including the very human desire to be accorded the respect, dignity, and opportunity necessary to reach one's full potential, even if one does not succeed. Jesse Jackson's qualifications could reasonably impel—indeed, require—him to fill this role. Consider the causes he has championed throughout his adult life, most recently through PUSH; his personal attributes and appeal; and his past success in gaining media attention—especially important in modern presidential campaigns. It seemed particularly logical for him to run for the Democratic presidential nomination since he had almost single-handedly kept the issue before the public. No other viable black or minority leader—elected or otherwise—came forth to offer his or her candidacy. The field was thus open for Jackson to offer himself for this role, and *he did*.

This single decision to try for the presidential nomination gave Jackson and his supporters the opportunity to achieve many important goals and objectives, some of which were strikingly similar to those of the civil rights movement. In his Rainbow Coalition he attempted to join not only blacks but many others, including whites who are poor, elderly, and unemployed—an effort very like Martin Luther King's attempt to expand the civil rights movement to include the nation's poor and those who were opposed to the Vietnam War. To be sure, I thought Jackson's dream would be very difficult to achieve, but his goals were altogether lofty, worthy, and noble and strongly consistent with the spirit and goals of the American Dream and the Constitution. I thought this congruence sparked interest in Jackson's candidacy.

Jackson's candidacy also struck me as congruent with deep cultural strains in the black community. A professional colleague and good friend of mine, Matthew Holden, describes these cultural traits with enviable sensitivity and clarity.[8] They include a "hope for deliverance," "the wish for defiance," a high value on "moralism," and "cynicism and fear." As I saw it, Jackson's candidacy both benefited from and reinforced these deep cultural strains.

Some blacks certainly viewed Jackson as God's instrument of deliverance, helping blacks overcome years of suffering and deprivation, defying the white power structure for its pervasive insults and humiliation of past and present by telling the white man where to go and what to do and making him go and do it. This wish for defiance is buttressed by a belief in the capacity of blacks to endure, no matter what.

I also believed Jackson would benefit from the strong attachment in black culture to "moralism," to the protestant view that "men ought to do right." Blacks see themselves, in contrast to whites, as possessing a "greater sensitivity, a greater humaneness or (in one version) more soul." "That 'the white man is dirty' and 'does not care about you,' " says Holden, "is so often advanced (among blacks) that it is quite striking." Blacks also impose high moralistic demands on their own leaders, expecting them to "approach perfection *in their heroism*, and the more clearly they do so the more their other failings can be excused. . . . But the absence of heroism," concludes Holden, "activates the bitter cynicism and the almost paranoid fear of being sold out."

This raises the aspect of cynicism and fear in black culture, where in their "hope for deliverance" and "wish for defiance" blacks are simultaneously *cynical* of their prospects for success and *fearful* of trying. Holden suggests that most leaders are unable or unwilling to demonstrate the sort of heroism needed to "go the uttermost distance commanded by the wish for defiance and deliverance." Failure to demonstrate this *heroism* can pose problems for black leaders. However, Jackson met these cultural expectations and therefore profited from an "in-built" appeal to the black community. Thus I thought that Jackson's candidacy, viewed in total context, could not help but strike a responsive chord among blacks and similarly disaffected groups, providing that unifying focal point similar to the role performed during the civil rights movement by Martin Luther King, filling the leadership void, and meeting the needs of those who felt that something more needed to be done.

It is ironic that most established black political leaders—those with the practical experience of elective public office—were unable or unwilling to seize the opportunity so graphically presented by the political situation described above. As a result, some black leaders found themselves in the awkward position of criticizing the one person who, for whatever reasons (courage, ego satisfaction, etc.), decided to undertake one of the greatest political challenges ever tried by *any* American. Jackson's candidacy insured that the nomination contest would command the greatest political coverage and attention that has been given to any battle for the Democratic nomination, at least since John F. Kennedy's successful effort in 1960 overcame the religious barrier.

Soon after Jackson's announcement, Eddie Williams, president of the Joint Center for Political Studies, summarized well the effect of Jackson's entry on black Americans: "The only question facing Black voters at this point (and white Democratic voters as well . . . is whether Jesse Jackson's candidacy will help or hinder the effort to defeat Ronald Reagan. The other question—is Jackson the right man to represent their hopes—is simply irrelevant: for Jesse Jackson . . . has now become the man."[9] Nonetheless, a closer look at Jackson the man might help us to better understand what made Jesse run.

Jackson demonstrated, in clear and unmistakable terms, that he possessed the sharp political instincts as well as the sensitivity to articulate issues and concerns that would strike a responsive chord among the groups he hoped to reach. Moreover, Jackson clearly knew his strengths (personality, style, and charisma) and how to use them in appealing to these groups and in attracting media coverage.

His alleged weaknesses (lack of follow-through and poor organization) certainly did not come through in his early trial run for the candidacy: if anything Jackson's "pre-campaign" was very skillfully and effectively carried out. For example, I thought his performance in the Mike Wallace interview on "Sixty Minutes," just prior to his formal entry, was impressive; it reflected the kind of thorough briefing and careful preparation which few political candidates would be able to match. Further, the management of his formal entry also reflected careful planning and preparation. In fact, throughout his pre-campaign for the nomination, Jackson effectively contradicted criticisms about his lack of careful planning and follow-through.

Jackson has tremendous courage and self-confidence (critics call it egotism). This was exemplified clearly by his ability to persist in his presidential effort despite criticism and dissuasion from friends and some well-known, established black leaders. Indeed, as I saw it, this too reflected Jackson's political wisdom: he was willing to fight against the odds—the establishment. And it is well known that the underdog role is not the worst role one can have in American politics.

Jackson's speech formally announcing his candidacy indicated clearly the factors that gave rise to his candidacy—the plight of poor people and minorities, the hostile attitudes and actions of the Reagan administration, and Jackson's hopes and strategies for improving the lot of the "downtrodden and dispossessed" through his candidacy for the Democratic nomination. In sum, what made Jesse run may be explained simply and straightforwardly, without latching on to "hidden agendas" or more intriguing theories that could well obscure the simplicity of some rather noble causes, obvious and clear to all who care to look. To me that was the appeal of the Jackson campaign, a campaign that I awaited with excitement, enthusiasm, and hope.

The Best of Both Worlds

Despite the appeal of the Jackson campaign, however, I was not ready to endorse Jackson as a candidate. I held to my position of supporting the strategy without committing myself to the candidate who sought to implement it. In late December 1983, however, my attachment to this view was put to the direct test, and in the end I had to face the issue directly. As in the transformation that led me to support the strategy, a "triggering" incident made me go the next step and support Jesse Jackson, the candidate.

Shortly before the Christmas holidays, a well-known black political scientist, a friend of mine from out East, asked me to serve on a national policy advisory committee for Jesse Jackson. I immediately demurred, offering the view that coming out squarely for Jackson— serving on one of his committees—could hamper some of my research. But my friend was persistent and persuasive. "Lucius," she said, "you and others like you were quite vocal and instrumental in supporting the idea, and now that the 'brother' is out there, we can't let him down. I think he could use us." My friend reminded me of the contribution I had made to the APSA news journal symposium (*PS*) on "Should There Be a Black Presidential Candidate," and now, she said, those of us who do research in the various policy areas must help Jesse to develop good policy papers. She identified, at my request, some political scientists and others who were being asked to serve on the committee, and it was an impressive group. Nonetheless, in keeping with the penchant of academicians for "further reflection," I asked my friend to give me a bit more time to consider the invitation and I would call back.

For the next few days I did go through a rather agonizing appraisal of my overall position with respect to Jackson's campaign—a timely and necessary appraisal. As I became more attracted to Jackson's campaign and what it stood for, I found it increasingly difficult to remain neutral and detached. The time had come, I thought, to express openly my innermost feelings on the matter, and in the end I decided to support Jackson. So I called my friend and accepted her invitation to serve on the committee. Ironically, however, my friend told me she had just learned that a similar group was already functioning and that there was no longer any need for her efforts or mine in this regard. Nonetheless, I very much appreciated the push given me by my friend's phone call: it spurred my predestined decision along and gave me the best of both worlds: I could continue to study the Jackson campaign with the focused eyes and ears of the political scientist-observer and at the same time work for its causes with the energy and efforts of the fully committed partisan participant.

3

The Campaign Opens with Mixed Signals: Mondale's Black Supporters and Lt. Goodman's Release

Soon after Jackson's announcement for the Democratic presidential nomination, Harvard psychiatrist Alvin Pouissant captured well the possibilities of Jackson's candidacy—the hope offered to blacks, women, and the poor, "neglected and hurt" by Reagan administration cutbacks in social programs and "angry, frustrated, and even hopeless"; the response of disadvantaged black and Hispanic youths to Jackson's "I am Somebody" chant; the "assertive 'Yes, I can' role model"; and the short-sightedness of those who viewed Jackson's candidacy as "merely symbolic," overlooking his "opportunity to nurture a spiritual rebirth among the forgotten and the powerless equal to the dream of Dr. Martin Luther King, Jr." Pouissant concluded that "Jackson's bid for the Presidency is much more than participation in a contest; it is an act of inspiration for those who have for too long been excluded from sharing the wealth and power of this nation."[1]

I too saw Jackson's candidacy as an act of inspiration and was excited about its possibilities. But almost from the very beginning, there were mixed signals as to the campaign's impact on black politics particularly and Democratic politics generally. Despite Jackson's entry into the nomination battle, a good number of very well-known black leaders held to their earlier declarations and continued to support Vice President Mondale rather than Jackson. This undoubtedly diminished the potential strength of Jackson's candidacy and suggested it was in trouble from the very start. In some ways it was. In addition to its admittedly late start, or perhaps because of it, Jackson's campaign lacked certain key resources, including money, experienced personnel, and organization. Now it also suffered from a wide division among the leadership of the one group (blacks) from which he was expected to win strong support. On the other hand, Jackson's negotiation of the release of Lt. Robert Goodman from a Syrian prison camp gave an important and timely boost to his developing campaign. A daring, highly publicized, and controversial venture, its eventual success gave Jackson's candidacy a high measure of sorely needed credibility. These two situations illustrated clearly the potential and limitations of Jackson's candidacy to affect our politics and public policy both at home and abroad.

Mondale's Black Supporters

Prior to Jesse Jackson's announcement for the Democratic presidential nomination, Walter Mondale was the most preferred candidate among black leaders and blacks generally. Naturally there was much interest in how Jackson's entry would affect Mondale's standing among blacks. As might be expected, Jackson's candidacy won prompt and widespread support in the black community. At the same time, however, a good number of the established black leaders clearly indicated they were not about to abandon Mondale and close ranks behind Jesse Jackson. As a political scientist, I found the whole situation intriguing—the kind of laboratory political analysts are eager to explore.

Consider the sequence of developments leading to Jackson's candidacy: the debating and skirmishing, especially among key black leaders, over the strategy of a black presidential candidacy and the eventual acquiescence to the idea by the black leadership family without any clear commitment to the implementation of the strategy; the persistent drive of Jesse Jackson, aided by good media attention that created a growing enthusiasm and support for the idea in the black community, and Jackson's anything-but-surprising entry into the contest. The resulting division among black leaders mirrored generally their positions in the debate over the idea of a black presidential candidacy: certain highly visible, established black leaders (e.g., big city mayors) supported Mondale; less visible and newly emerging leaders (e.g., state and local officials) supported Jackson.[2]

Clearly, an analysis of this split can tell us much about black politics and the American political system.

Although as a political scientist I was intrigued by the division among black leaders, as a Black American I found this split very frustrating and disappointing. I thought the negative impact of the Reagan administration's actions on blacks as a group called for a clear, forceful, unifying strategy from black leaders. Those leaders who opposed the strategy, a good number of whom backed Mondale, were an impressive group. During the debate over whether or not there should be a black presidential candidate but prior to Jackson's formal entry, leaders of the two oldest, most established civil-rights organizations, the National Association for the Advancement of Colored People and the National Urban League, opposed the idea. And even after Jackson announced his candidacy, Andrew Young, Julian Bond, and Coretta Scott King in Georgia; Richard Arrington and the Alabama Black Democratic Conference; Mayor Wilson Goode of Philadelphia; Mayor Tom Bradley of Los Angeles, Mayor Coleman Young of Detroit; and Congressman Charles Rangel of New York remained loyal to Mondale.

To be sure, the cold, hard political considerations that militated against the idea of a black presidential candidacy in the first place did not magically evaporate when Jesse Jackson decided to run. Given the current nature and operation of American politics, anyone who believed that Jackson or any other black person could win the Democratic presidential nomination, much less the presidency, seemed foolhardy. Moreover, those who opposed the black presidential strategy (now given life by Jackson's candidacy) could well reason, as some did, that this was a time for realism, not symbolism. Symbolic benefits simply could not substitue for substantive, long-term benefits, the carefully developed and nurtured access and influence points that could be jeopardized by a long-shot candidacy, which Jackson's surely was. This access had won for established black leaders and their constituents benefits that they were understandably reluctant to give up and that were much more likely to continue and even increase under established arrangements. Parenthetically, one might well ponder the real nature, quality, and impact of these benefits. Undoubtedly, this entire matter should be subject to more rigorous scrutiny and analysis. In any event, the very political success of these established black leaders had been due in important ways to persons and groups who now were calling in the expected IOU's of electoral politics. Moreover, even if one wished to take the risks, why do so with such a high risk candidate with little if any practical, hard-based (i.e., public office) political experience?

To be sure, there seem to have been little if any major policy differences between Jackson and other black leaders, including those who supported Mondale, but they differed openly about how best to achieve these goals. For example, there have been and apparently still are differences among various civil rights organizations over the use of direct-action protests and demonstrations to achieve particular goals. In fact, on various occasions such differences seemed to threaten the unity of the civil rights movement and had to be meticulously overcome through the persuasive intervention of Martin Luther King and others.

The 1963 March on Washington, certainly one of the most dramatic and effective demonstrations ever mounted, was threatened by such divisions. In the end, however, King and others were able to persuade the reluctant others (e.g., the NAACP and the Urban League) to join the march and similar direct-action efforts that could supplement more traditional, less confrontational methods such as litigation, which has been strongly pursued by the NAACP. Specifically, direct-action methods add a level of commitment and urgency which more traditional methods might not give to the achievement of certain objectives which otherwise might be snuffed out, given the overarching incrementalist nature of American politics and policy making. When viewed in this context, the black presidential strategy was essentially a difference over means, not ends.

But in my view Jackson's candidacy was a means that could make a lot of difference in practice. While the choice of means can certainly affect both the pace and nature of change, it can also affect the process of change. I want my bread, my job, my money as much as or more than anyone else, but it matters a great deal to me how I get that bread, that job, that money, and how these various goods are allocated. I believed that a black presidential candidacy would help to democratize this process and place it on a more permanent footing. I do not wish to perennially rely on the sufferance and whims of whites or on the most sympathetic white who just might happen to turn up in the race for the Democratic presidential nomination. When the chips are down, those who rely on such sufferance and happenstance are likely to be shortchanged or left out all together. By this time blacks, more than any other group, should be painfully aware of this fact.

On the other hand, established black politicians and Black Americans generally would like to respond to events and opportunities just like any other political leaders and any other persons. I share this longing too, but as I see it, blacks in America cannot as yet enjoy that luxury. We are still fighting for basic representation that could lead to more direct power sharing rather than indirect power paring, wherein others (mainly whites) circumscribe the parameters within which blacks might operate and control.

Understandably, we sometimes get tired of fighting and feuding: it is clearly debilitating and energy draining. And natural inclinations to live in peace and harmony make it easy to exaggerate progress, attaching undue importance to initial successes or modest increases, as in the election of black officials. To be sure, we all should feel a sense of pride in these concrete signs of progress. But although visible symbols of progress can lead to complacency and toleration of the status quo, invariably other factors come along that jolt us out of such apathy. For example, the hostile policies and actions of the Reagan administration reminded blacks of the fragility of racial gains and focused attention on the need to develop *political* strength to achieve and keep these gains.

I strongly believed that the renewed and persistent threats to black *group* progress must again and would be met best through group unity. Through such unity important advances had been made in the past. But my reasoning about Jackson's candidacy finally had to give way to reality: neither the black presidential strategy nor Jackson's candidacy had led to the sort of unity among blacks that I thought necessary for any *broader* coalitional activity. The division among black leaders persisted as one after another voiced his support of Vice President Mondale.

Perhaps the most common argument made by Mondale's black supporters was that Jackson had no chance to win the nomination and become president and that Mondale did. Coretta Scott King thought that in the final analysis Jackson's candidacy had to be "evaluated in light of the probable outcome," notwithstanding the fact that his campaign could "raise the level of interest in the 1984 races and create greater political involvement (e.g., voter registration and turnout) in the black community." "In terms of the end result," Mrs. King concluded, "one thing is clear: he will not win the nomination, and he has little chance of being elected president."[3] Similarly, Richard Arrington, in formally announcing his support of Mondale, said that although Jesse Jackson was a good friend, he had decided to support Mondale because "he stands an excellent chance of winning." "At this point," said Arrington, "the priority is to win the White House."[4] Not incidentally, the Alabama Democratic Conference, the largest black political group in the state, also endorsed Mondale while giving a faint nod to Jackson as vice president. Slating Jackson as vice president may have been viewed as a compromise by some, but I found it to be the height of irony that blacks themselves would now succumb to traditional racial patterns and once more relegate blacks to second place.

But Jackson's detractors continued to speak. Charles Rangel, congressional representative from New York, endorsed Mondale because "I'd like to see someone who can get the Democratic nomination." Hazel Dukes, New York state president of the NAACP, said that although she understood the symbolism of Jackson's candidacy she could not "symbolize this one out." "It might mean another four years of Reagan."[5] Similar comments came from other leaders such as Mayor Coleman Young, who criticized, even seemingly ridiculed, Jackson's candidacy and his chances for winning the nomination or the presidency.

Still further, Georgia state senator Julian Bond disparaged Jackson's effort, stating that Jackson had shown "little interest in political affairs in his early career." Indeed, Bond related an incident that he stated occurred in 1972 when he and Jackson were campaigning for Senator McGovern during the California Democratic presidential primary: "He asked me how much work I was doing for McGovern," recalled Bond; and "I said that I was making five speeches a day. He told me I was foolish to make that many. . . . He said I should be doing what he was doing—make one for the noon news [on television] and one for the evening news. He said, continued Bond, "I should spend time around the swimming pool [at the campaign hotel] so that reporters could find me."[6] I found it more than ironic that what Bond apparently viewed as a flaw I saw as a great plus. To me it showed that even as early as 1972, Jackson apparently had a very keen, perhaps even prophetic, sense of the increasingly important role of the media in modern political campaigns and in our politics and society generally.

Bond's assessment of Jackson in 1972 differed radically from mine. In 1971 I was so impressed by the accomplishments and leadership potential Jackson showed in Operation Breadbasket I decided he was one of the few persons possessed of the vision and resourcefulness required to effectively carry on the work of Martin Luther King in contexts consistent with the changing nature of American politics and society. Accordingly, I nominated him for an honorary doctor of humanities degree from Washington University, an honor which, I am pleased to say, was bestowed on him in 1972.

Jackson's Critics: Misreading American Politics and History

Of course I realized Mondale's black supporters were following traditional behavioral patterns typical of established elites, regardless of color or race. Conscious of Jackson's strength in the black community, they carefully acknowledged the benefits of Jackson's effort while simultaneously claiming that Jackson's candidacy would serve to hurt Mondale's chances for capturing the nomination, that blacks who voted for Jackson in primary elections would otherwise be likely to vote for Mondale, whom they clearly preferred to any other white candidate. This could deny the Democratic nomination to the most sympathetic white candidate who had the most realistic chance of defeating Ronald Reagan, clearly a high priority for an overwhelming majority of black voters.

However, to me, certain criticisms of Jackson's candidacy simply did not square with the lessons of American politics and history. Nor did they square with the deeper meaning and significance of Jackson's candidacy. In fact, I felt impelled to write an "Op Ed" piece analyzing more systematically the reservations that apparently led certain black leaders to support Mondale rather than Jackson.[7]

Take, for example, the "he can't win" criticism, so damaging to any candidate regardless of color. Similar criticisms had been made of Martin Luther King and the civil rights movement and other such path-breaking initiatives. Leaders, black or white, did not need to remind voters, black or white, that no black candidate would win a presidential nomination or election under the conditions prevalent in 1984. That's what Jackson's candidacy was all about: changing these conditions. Winning necessarily had to be restricted to increases in black political consciousness and, hence, to increases in black voter registration and turnout and in the number of black and minority candidates standing for and winning local, state, and congressional office. Of course I recognized that these wins, though very important, did not hold the immediate excitement or the tangible benefits that go to those who win the presidential office. Nonetheless, in this context the decision of some black leaders to endorse Mondale rather than Jackson became somewhat more plausible, reflecting the strength of current symbols, prevailing patterns of influence and political access, and standard political practice.

Somehow I thought that we had once again reached another of those points in the history of what I might call the "black struggle" where I expected our black leaders to go against prevailing norms and to practice uncommon politics to achieve their objectives. I was wrong. Nonetheless, no matter how politely or how thoroughly they attempted to explain their positions, Mondale's black supporters were unable to overcome the powerful symbolism of the Jackson candidacy. Nor were they able to overcome, as I saw it, what Jackson's candidacy suggested about the inability of past strategies (which their very endorsements of Mondale now perpetuated) to materially alter the wretched socioeconomic conditions under which blacks, more than any other group, continue to suffer.

Other criticisms of Jackson likewise reflect misreadings of the nature and dynamics of American politics and history. Consider also the "now is not the right time for Jackson or any other black person to run for president" ploy, the perennial argument used against those who launch major initiatives that portend fundamental change in the status quo. My reading of American politics suggests clearly that those who wait for the right time might find themselves forever on the sidelines. Thus, it is important for black leaders to remain alert to the lessons of politics and history, especially those of the civil rights movement. One has to fight to bring about the right time, and this fight can be waged more effectively by those who go out, develop their resources, and use them. As I saw it, this was what Jesse Jackson's candidacy was all about. It could not help but make the right time come sooner rather than later.

Moreover, consider a privately, but seldom openly, expressed criticism held by some whites and blacks—that Jackson is not qualified to run for president. This, of course, does not refer to constitutional qualifications which he obviously meets, but to Jackson's lack of experience in public office, elective or appointive, which many believe is necessary to run for president. I viewed this whole matter of qualifications as misplaced, since it assumes that there are indeed special qualifications, over and above the constitutional ones, that one must meet to make a good president. It may well be, as some scholars suggest, that nothing can really prepare a person for the presidency. Indeed, history clearly shows that some presidents rise to the occasion and others do not. Dwight D. Eisenhower, whom some might still rate as a great president, is a prime example of one who had no special qualifications in terms of experience in elective public office.

Another criticism levelled against Jackson—that his candidacy was merely symbolic and would do nothing to feed the hungry or provide jobs for the poor—made me wince over and over, even as I heard Jackson supporters respond, "So what?" Symbols and forms help to guard and promote certain interests and demote other interests. In this sense, Jesse Jackson's candidacy was certainly symbolic, but so was Mondale's, Glenn's, Hart's, and Ronald Reagan's. (Reagan is a master in the use of symbolism to achieve his political objectives!)

Important political actions—such as running for president—simultaneously promote both symbolic needs and material interests. Mondale's candidacy represented established interests, reassuring them of their continued influence in the party. Jackson's candidacy, on the other hand, reflected the concerns of potential and aspiring interests and thus suggested to established interests in the party and the country generally that their influence might decline should Jackson's candidacy take hold. Thus, given the historical context of the black struggle in America and the symbolism of Jackson's candidacy, it was not at all surprising that Mondale considered his endorsement in December 1983 by the Alabama statewide conference of Black Democrats a great victory, and it was. However, the symbolic benefits of that endorsement, rather than its actual benefits, were most important to Mondale's campaign. It sent signals to many other blacks (with the help of Mondale's campaign staff) that Mondale is "all right." Conversely, it stood as a symbolic barrier that Jackson had to overcome if he were to unite the black community and forge his Rainbow Coalition. The whole episode shows once again the important role of symbolism in American politics—a role that certain

of Mondale's black supporters attempted to minimize by charging
that Jackson's candidacy was "merely symbolic."[8]

Overall, I was not satisfied that the rationales discussed above fully
explained the persistent divisions among black leaders. The rationales were much too general, commonplace, and not well grounded
in history. Nor were they directly responsive to the larger issues in
Jackson's candidacy. But the mere fact that they were used indicates
clearly that some saw such reasons as both relevant and sound enough
to justify or explain their positions. And it is likely that a conbination
of factors, not any single one, led to the division over Jackson's candidacy.

Nonetheless, I wanted to understand the situation more fully, so
I continued to push for explanations. Might it have been that some
of these leaders, such as black mayors, have different institutional
concerns and bases of power within black America and the wider
society, and reasoned that their interests could be better protected
and promoted through Mondale's candidacy than through Jackson's?
To be sure, black mayors do have city budgets and federal grants to
consider. Could it be that some black leaders really have policy
differences with Jackson? Could it be that black people want diverse
leadership and black leaders have the right to be diverse? Or might
it be that class divisions are more salient among blacks than some
might like to believe or admit and that some black leaders might
truly represent different interests of the different classes? After all,
there is increasing discussion about how class and underclass factors
affect the opportunities of individual blacks.

Could it have been, in fact or perception, that Jackson didn't do
the homework to get black leaders' support to the extent that the
Mondale forces (who expected less automatic support from blacks)
did? Or might it have simply been that some black leaders had committed themselves to Mondale long before Jackson's entry, even in
advance of the debate over the black presidential strategy? Certainly
it is not easy for people, even politicians, to renege on a commitment
once made. To be sure, there could have been good reasons for
Jackson's late entry, not the least of which was his trying to find
more accord among black leaders for his candidacy, but the lateness
of his entry not only cost him the support of some black leaders who
had made earlier commitments but also affected his fund-raising, his
staff recruitment and development, and the time available to organ-

ize an effective national campaign. More established black leaders, especially elected officials, might have clearly foreseen these developments and accordingly discouraged Jackson's candidacy.

In addition, the division among black leaders over the black presidential strategy and now over Jackson's candidacy could have also involved certain personal and interpersonal factors. Might it have been that some black leaders simply had far closer personal ties to Walter Mondale than to Jesse Jackson? These and similar factors were pointed up succinctly by an anonymous reader who reviewed this manuscript for the University of Illinois Press: "With respect to the split among black leaders over Jackson, is it possible that these other leaders—who had had a lot of contact and experience with him— didn't trust him, or like him? Politics can get awfully personal sometimes, and the "leadership family" may be subject—because of their very closeness—to some very deep-seated squabbles centered around past experience, future ambition, etc. Was Jesse more ambitious than all the others? Who were the other most likely possibilities? Any? Why didn't they try? Any idea? Would you have been enthused about any black candidate? Only Jesse?"

Naturally, these comments and queries spurred me to consider the situation further. Over the years, of course, there have been some friction and factionalism among black leaders and black organizations.[9] However, such factionalism and friction are hardly unique to black leaders and black groups. It is quite true that "politics can get awfully personal sometimes" with current decisions being influenced by "very deep-seated squabbles entered around past experiences, future ambitions." Some books on Jackson discuss these disagreements,[10] and similar discussion appeared in news columns such as that which suggested that "the questioning of Jackson's ability to win has served as a convenient cover for frequently bitter in-house fighting that separates Jackson from those who lay claim to Martin Luther King, Jr.'s throne, guarded vociferously by his widow, Coretta Scott King."[11] Overall, I fully appreciate that such personal dimensions are obviously embroiled in the passions and practice of politics and it is certainly difficult to disentangle them. However, the more I reflected over this entire matter, the more I was convinced of two things: (1) that more personal considerations at times must give way to more general, fundamental considerations and interests; and (2) that Jesse Jackson's candidacy offered blacks a rare opportunity to enhance their standing and influence in the Democratic party.

Let us consider first the matter of personal considerations giving way to more general, fundamental interests. Jackson has been critized for his penchant to "hog" publicity, his super ego and boundless ambition, and his very personal style of politics and organizational management. I do not know whether or not these are fair or accurate characterizations of Jesse Jackson. But even if they are, Jackson would be far from unique among politicians, for in the hurly-burly world of politics such personal factors are not necessarily damaging liabilities; they can prove valuable assets. In my view, the far greater and broader interests served by a black presidential candidacy made such personal considerations pale into relative insignificance.

This kind of calculus would have allowed me to support any one of several black leaders as presidential candidates, even though I might have viewed them as lacking in certain personal characteristics—e.g., a forceful presence and charisma, and an ability to persuasively articulate the spirit and interests of blacks and minorities. Thus, I certainly could have supported, and in the end did support, a candidate who did not possess everything I would like to see in a presidential candidate. This is the nature of politics: it is difficult to find the perfect candidate. Thus whether Jesse Jackson was more ambitious than others became relatively unimportant in the broad context in which I considered the matter. To be sure, his very candidacy indicated that he is far from short on ambition. Ordinary people with ordinary ambitions do not ordinarily and actively seek the presidency.

Nor do I know whether I would have been as enthused about *any* black candidate as I was with Jackson. That obviously would have depended on who that candidate was and how he or she developed the ensuing campaign. But my enthusiasm for important general interests served by a black presidential candidacy would have strongly disposed me to support a black presidential candidate from among those prominently mentioned, even though my *personal* dispositions might not have led me to initially support the particular candidate that emerged. In fact, several of my close friends supported Jackson— some actually gave financial support—because of the larger issues involved, despite the fact that, as one friend put it, "Jackson is not my first or second choice."

As matters turned out, however, I was very pleased with Jackson's entry into the nomination battle. I strongly believed that, given the circumstances and context in which I viewed the situation, Jackson would make the strongest possible black candidate. Among the really crucial considerations for me were which of the potential candidates could best identify and articulate the interests of blacks and minorities, mount an effective campaign and attract media attention, turn out and maximize the vote in the black community so as to go to the convention with widespread black popular support and a relatively large number of black delegates, and do *all* of this with a minimum of the requirements deemed necessary in presidential campaigning— e.g., money, staff, organization. Jackson, to me, fitted the bill.

In fact, so well did Jackson fit the bill that at one period during the campaign, after the freeing of Lt. Goodman but before the "Hymie" incident, I came to more fully appreciate what I have long observed and what some of my politician friends have long told me— that in politics hope somehow springs eternal. For a few fleeting moments—especially during this period—thoughts (dreams?) of Jackson pulling off some miracle wins or at least some unexpected high primary showings (e.g., in New Hampshire) really did "invade" the privacy of my *personal* desires. And if this happens, I thought, who knows what might happen in subsequent primaries or even in San Francisco? But my professional training and experience managed simultaneously to balance these fleeting personal hopes and to remind me that a serious black presidential candidacy in 1984, be it waged by Jackson or someone else, could not help but speed the day when a black could actually be nominated by one of the major parties and have a more realistic chance of being elected president.

The Jackson Candidacy and a Divided Black Leadership

Perhaps most of all I was concerned that the division among black leaders might somehow blur the larger issues represented by Jackson's candidacy and thus obscure its deeper meaning and significance. I was concerned that this division among black leaders essentially over means (Jackson's candidacy) might signal to some a greater division in the black community over ends (policy concerns) than is actually the case. Despite signals to the contrary, the black community continues to speak, on both racial and nonracial policy issues, with basically one voice—a voice which in the past has been far different from the voice of white America.[12] And I believed that Jackson, more than Mondale or any other candidate for the Democratic nomination, would give life to that voice in content, language, and style that better represents the concerns and excites the interest of the black community.

Public opinion data suggest that, on both racial and nonracial issues (foreign policy, economic welfare, size of government, etc.), blacks exhibit a "degree of liberal attitude constituency" that is more "distinctively liberal" than any other group in American society.[13] This finding makes it clear why blacks tend to vote for black candidates, and many black political leaders, including those who now supported Mondale, have profited greatly as a result. Clearly, Jackson would, and indeed did, benefit in the same way, for blacks (and many whites as well) understand that much remains to be done before we achieve a color-blind society. Although notable progress has been made on a number of fronts, common sense, objective evidence and everyday experience demonstrate vividly that a color-blind society is not close at hand. In fact, clear and disturbing signs indicate that important programs needed to bring about equal justice and opportunities for blacks and minorities are no longer given high priorities by our national government or our two major parties.

Restoring these high priorities was a central focus of Jackson's candidacy, a focus that captured the hearts, heads, and votes of the black community. And this support made it more difficult for Mondale's black supporters to convince black voters that they should support Mondale rather than Jackson. Nonetheless, the fact remained that Mondale had the support of an impressive group of black leaders whose opinions commanded respect and attention. Clearly this division in the black leadership would raise questions about Jackson's campaign, not only among whites, but in the black community as well, and certainly would not help Jackson as his campaign began.

Lt. Goodman's Release

Great Risks, Great Opportunities
Like many other Americans, I was aware that Lt. Robert Goodman had been shot down in a reconnaissance flight on December 6

over Lebanon and was being held in captivity in a Syrian prison camp. And undoubtedly like others I was beginning to regard this type of news as commonplace. Jesse Jackson, however, changed all this when he decided to go to Syria and negotiate directly for the release of Lt. Goodman. This certainly caught my attention: I found it difficult to overlook how Jackson's mission might affect his presidential nomination bid.

Jackson insisted that his was a humanitarian, moral mission and should be viewed in that much broader context. Even so, however, Jackson found little encouragement. The media and others looked askance and even ridiculed the venture. He found no sympathy from the White House; in fact, President Reagan did not return his repeated phone calls. But despite such discouragement, skepticism, and even outright opposition, Jackson remained undaunted; he was determined to try to win the release of Lt. Goodman, an act that he thought would help to break the "political-military deadlock" between Syria and the United States. "Lt. Goodman," said Jackson, "should not be used as a trade-bait or war-bait." Jackson maintained that the moral appeal to President Assad of Syria would have an impact and that the "mission is not nearly so much a challenge to President Reagan as it is to President Assad."[11]

The Jackson mission did vent a feeling among some Americans that the administration was not giving enough attention to the prisoner issue or to U.S.–Arab relations. But the White House and others remained aloof and skeptical of the Jackson mission. Indeed, White House spokesman Larry Speakes cited official efforts to win release of Lt. Goodman and said that although they believed Jackson's trip was "certainly well-intentioned" it could nevertheless be "counterproductive." In this connection, Speakes also mentioned the Logan Act, which makes it illegal for private citizens to carry on diplomatic functions, and said that Jackson "cannot and would not engage in such activities." Thus the overall atmosphere was anything but encouraging as Jackson pressed his humanitarian mission to free Lt. Goodman. The media and others seemed poised to pounce on any misstep in the Jackson venture, building up to what many, including some sympathizers and supporters, saw as an almost impossible mission.

But once Jackson went to Syria and started negotiations, the day-to-day waiting for developments held the rapt attention of all—Jackson's friends and foes and, of course, the media.[15] Like many others, I believed the outcome of Jackson's mission would hold serious implications for the future of his campaign, and as a growing Jackson partisan, I was hoping for the best. When the news came that Jackson had won Goodman's release, the scene in my household was reminiscent of that which followed Jackson's announcement to seek the Democratic nomination—ecstatic and thankful. I could not wait to see the reactions of those who had disparaged Jackson's effort—particularly President Reagan and the White House and the *New York Times* and the *Washington Post*. Again, the key consideration was the effect on Jackson's presidential campaign.

Successful Action, Mixed Reactions

Reactions came quickly. Jackson's arrival at Andrews Air Force Base on Wednesday, January 4, 1984, was well orchestrated to maximize all the possible benefits for the Jackson campaign. Crowds, bands, and speakers all boosted Jackson's image and credibility as a presidential candidate. Of course, Jackson himself was not unaware of the political benefits that could accrue to his campaign. In his remarks at the airport welcome, Jackson reflected openly on the political risks involved in his mission: "Narrowly conceived, this mission was a political risk. But it was the right thing to do."[16]

Overall, the ceremony at the airport, full of thanks for Goodman's release and praise for Jackson's efforts, was a great testimonial for Jackson, but this was Jackson's crowd, his friends, his supporters. How the mission would play in other contexts remained to be seen. Much attention, of course, was focused on the official reaction from the White House, which was not long in coming.

Later that same morning Goodman and Jackson were invited to the White House for an official welcome. And in fine character, President Reagan seemed once again to have risen to the occasion. He now found a way to become part of Jackson's success story. In a brief private meeting before the Rose Garden public ceremony, the president told Jackson that he did not return four telephone calls prior to Jackson's trip because of his "initial misgivings" about the trip and because he thought Jackson's trip "had 'the best chance of success' if he 'kept hands off' and made it clear that the minister [Jackson] was not an emissary for the United States."[17] Then as expected, in his official public remarks welcoming Jackson and Goodman home, the president praised the "qualities of leadership and loyalty" exemplified by Goodman. But he also praised Jackson: "Reverend Jackson's mission was a personal mission of mercy and he has earned our gratitude and admiration."[18] For his part, Jackson took full advantage of the praise and the forum offered by the president and the White House ceremony. Jackson not only thanked the president for not blocking his trip, but he also thanked President Assad of Syria for granting Goodman's release. It was vintage Jackson—articulate, charismatic, excellent media copy. But so was it vintage Reagan—the typically attractive and receptive political style that has become the envy of many a politician. The *Washington Post* referred to both men, excellent practitioners of political craft and skill, as the "Not So Odd Couple."[19]

Overall, the whole venture, officially crowned in success by the White House ceremony, provided Jackson a publicity and credibility advantage that would be the envy of any politician. As Senator Edward Kennedy put it, "Surely, . . . this personal initiative by Reverend Jackson will rank as one of the finest achievements by a private citizen in the history of international relations."[20] As to the effect of the Jackson trip on the Democratic campaign and black officeholders who had endorsed Mondale, one Democratic consultant put the matter this way: "He is now without question the most formidable black leader in America. I doubt that Andrew Young, Coleman Young, and Tom Bradley can deliver on major sections of their constitutencies. I'm not sure they should even try."

But despite its successful outcome, Jackson's mission continued to meet with faint praise and outright opposition from two of the nation's leading papers, the *New York Times* and the *Washington Post*. The *Times* was sharply critical of Jackson's mission and bluntly stated that "what's best for Lt. Robert Goodman is not automatically best for the United States." The *Times* editorial continued: "The Navy flier's release, though welcome, was achieved at the expense of President Reagan's authority in the midst of negotiations with Syria. By thus undercutting Mr. Reagan for partisan advantage, the Rev. Jesse Jackson has done nothing to enhance his own reputation as a diplomat. Neither has Syria's action made President Assad a humanitarian." The *Times* charged that Syria "joined in this publicity stunt" to "encourage agitation in America for withdrawal of the Marines from Lebanon" and because they want to make Lebanon safer for

Syrian domination. However, the editorial suggested that "it does not follow . . . anything Syria wants is automatically bad for the United States" and went on to offer suggestions that would allow the withdrawal of "those 1,800 troops who are more nearly hostages than Lieutenant Goodman ever was."[21] In commenting on the White House welcoming ceremony marking Goodman's return home, the *Washington Post* said they "loved" watching "pure [political] skill in action from two fellows who know what they're doing. "We loved it," said the *Post*, "much more than we love the loose cannon, ill-considered initiative of Reverend Jackson in the first place."[22]

A Political and Moral Triumph

When viewed in overall perspective, Jackson's mission was clearly an important political and moral triumph. He had defied the odds, criticisms, and doomsayers; achieved success that many thought impossible; and reaped the full political benefits of his mission. His mission showed a person of rare courage and skill, one willing to take grave risks to his own immediate political future to achieve particular objectives. Obviously, of course, Jackson (and many others) was not unaware that success from such risks could certainly serve as tremendous boosts to his political future. In short, Jackson was willing to assume the risks, and he won. And though criticism and cynicism abounded from many influential quarters, Jackson had done what no other person, including the president, had been able to do— win the release of Lt. Robert Goodman. As the president himself aptly put it: "You don't quarrel with success." And he won the attention, if not the respect, of many who had written his candidacy off as sheer opportunism, as sheer searching for ego-satisfaction. As a result, Jackson's image and credibility as a serious presidential candidate took on new meaning and excitement.

Of course, some disparaged what they considered Jackson's pro-Arab, anti-Semitic tendencies, and in this sense the Goodman release solidified this current of opinion. But given the sheer population and status of Arab nations in the complicated Middle East situation, our nation clearly needed leaders who could maintain effective relations not only with Israel but with her Arab neighbors as well. Our relations with Israel have been good and secure; with the Arabs our relations have been unsatisfactory and insecure. Indeed, past history of the region indicates that maintaining effective friendly relations with both the Israelis and Arabs can prove a difficult, if not impossible, balancing act for any political leader. And due to various common bonds, we have chosen to opt mainly for the Israeli position. Winning Goodman's release, however, meant that Jackson was at least willing to explore the mine-filled area and shore up relations with the Arab nations.

Thus, while Jackson's initiative may not have commended him to some, it did commend him to others, such as myself, who have for so long been looking for something and someone new and refreshing to alter our humdrum, politics-as-usual, military way of conducting our foreign affairs and international relations. I continue to believe that there must be a better way than continuous fighting and bloodshed to achieve peace in the Middle East. However, as the nomination campaign evolved, it became painfully clear to me that past and subsequent developments would make it especially difficult for Jackson to prove an effective broker between Israel and her Arab neighbors.

4

Jesse Jackson, Farrakhan,
and the Jewish Community:
Lowpoints in the Campaign

Seeds of Cooperation and Conflict

Within a few days of his announcement for the Democratic
presidential nomination it was clear that Jesse Jackson's relations
with the American Jewish community would be watched closely. This
was quite understandable. A long-standing sympathy between blacks
and Jews grew out of the fact that both groups had suffered gross
abuses and oppression of their human rights. Jewish involvement in
important causes to support civil rights and improve the plight of
blacks had long been commonplace. Indeed, during the civil rights
movement Jews were openly sympathetic and widely supportive of
the interests and concerns of blacks and Martin Luther King, and
this black-Jewish cooperation formed an important component of the
broadly based and effective civil rights coalition. Thus there was
justifiable reason to believe that a black presidential candidacy would
meet with a measure of friendly receptivity in the Jewish community.

However, since the late 1970s, black-Jewish relations have become somewhat strained over a number of issues raised during the
civil rights era, such as affirmative action, which was highlighted
during the debate in the widely publicized *Bakke* case.[1] But friction
points in black-Jewish relations involve much more and can be traced
back farther than the 1970s. Roughly from the 1920s through the
1940s, for example, southern blacks searching for a better life in the
North were considered by some to be easy prey for some Jewish

landlords and merchants who charged inflated rents and prices, knowing that blacks were trapped in the ghetto by discriminatory racial and economic barriers that prevented them from moving or shopping elsewhere. In a 1967 article entitled "Negroes Are Anti-Semitic Because They're Anti-White," James Baldwin describes with pungent clarity how he viewed the situation:

When we were growing up in Harlem our demoralizing series of landlords were Jewish, and we hated them. We hated them because they were terrible landlords and did not take care of the building. A coat of paint, a broken window, a stopped sink, a stopped toilet, a sagging floor, a broken ceiling, a dangerous stairwell, the question of garbage disposal, the question of heat and cold, of roaches and rats—all questions of life and death for the poor, and especially for those with children—we had to cope with all of these as best we could. Our parents were lashed down to futureless jobs, in order to pay the outrageous rent. We knew that the landlord treated us this way because we were colored, and he knew that we could not move out.

The grocer was a Jew, and being in debt to him was very much like being in debt to the company store. The butcher was a Jew, and yes, we certainly paid more for bad cuts of meat than other New York citizens, and we very often carried insults home, along with the meat. We bought our clothes from a Jew and, some-times, our secondhand shoes, and the pawnbroker was a Jew—perhaps we hated him most of all. The merchants along 125th Street were Jewish—at least many of them were . . . and I well remember that it was only after the Harlem riot of 1935 that Negroes were allowed to earn a little money in some of the stores where they spent so much.

Not all of these white people were cruel—on the contrary, I remember some who were certainly as thoughtful as the bleak circumstances allowed—but all of them were exploiting us, and that was why we hated them.

It is galling to be told by a Jew whom you know to be exploiting you that he cannot possibly be doing what you know he is doing because he is a Jew. It is bitter to watch the Jewish storekeeper locking up his store for the night, and going home. Going, with *your* money in his pocket, to a clean neighborhood, miles from you, which you will not be allowed to enter. Nor can it help the relationship between most Negroes and most Jews when part of this money is donated to civil rights. In the light of what is now known as the white backlash, this money can be looked on as conscience money merely, as money given to keep the Negro happy in his place, and out of white neighborhoods.

One does not wish, in short, to be told by an American Jew that his suffering is as great as the American Negro's suffering. It isn't, and one knows that it isn't from the very tone in which he assures you that it is.[2]

Such beliefs and conditions created tensions between blacks and Jews. And to some extent these beliefs and stories of the past remain part of black folklore that seeps in even today through casual conversation or wry jokes. However, in many ways these tensions were somewhat abated and even overcome by the era of common understanding and good feelings brought on by the strong support of American Jews during the civil rights revolution of the 1950s and 1960s. Blacks and Jews marched together, fought together, and died together.

But by the 1970s that togetherness had once again given way to friction, this time over such issues as affirmative action "quotas," which Jews had long feared. Thus party politicians and others were naturally concerned with how American Jews would react to Jackson's candidacy. Would it once again usher in an era of strong cooperation and good feelings toward one another? If so, two of the most supportive and loyal constituencies in the Democratic party could command major attention and perhaps bring about fundamental change in party politics. If not, then their disunity and friction could hold similar but more debilitating and devastating effects.

Obviously then, the whole matter of black-Jewish relations was a matter of major interest to party leaders and many others, a matter pondered during the debate over whether or not a black should become a presidential candidate. But what made the matter of especial concern was that Jackson was not just *any* black presidential candidate. He was one whose past positions on American-Israeli relations, on the Middle East, and on Jewish-Arab relations generally had created concern in the Jewish community. Of course, much depended on how Jackson himself would handle the situation. And

Jackson's relations with Jews soon received wide attention in the media.

Four days after Jackson announced his candidacy, the *New York Times* ran a news analysis, "Jackson and Jews."[3] This was the first such commentary on the topic that I saw after Jackson's announcement, and I gave close attention to every aspect of the story. Apparently what prompted the story and "dumbfounded some Jackson aides" was Jackson's decision "to keep a date with the American Arab Anti-Discrimination Committee on November 7, 1983." The story indicated that in the past Jewish organizations had attacked Jackson's position in favor of a Palestinian homeland and criticized his earlier visits with Arab leaders, including PLO leader Yasir Arafat.

Given this background, apparently some Jackson advisors thought that, rather than appearing before an Arab group, "a wise political strategy . . . would have been to appear before Jewish groups first." One such advisor, Ernest Green, acknowledged that "it wasn't the most politically wise thing to do" and said that "professional political campaign strategists would have advised against the appearance." However, Green continued, "those same professionals also would have told him he couldn't get as far as he has as a candidate." Hence, despite the risks Green, and apparently Jackson himself, thought that it was important for Jackson to hold to his views—such as support of a Palestinian homeland—for not to do so in the campaign would "make him no different from other candidates."

But a number of Jewish leaders and organizations viewed the situation, and Jackson's candidacy itself, quite differently. Indeed, the *Times* analysis made it clear to me that Jackson's candidacy would find rough going in the Jewish community. And these difficulties would come from more than the "militant Jewish Defense League," which now openly opposed Jackson. Jewish organizations no longer masked their concern in silence. For example, although saying that his group was nonpartisan and that he would not comment or offer an opinion himself, Nathan Perlmutter, executive director of the Anti-Defamation League of B'Nai Brith, left no doubt about his position on Jackson's candidacy or on the position he thought that his group or Jews generally should take. Said Perlmutter: "Jesse Jackson's image in the Jewish community is conditioned by more than his views on the Mideast. . . . Many of us remember that he is the man who is sick and tired of hearing about the Holocaust and that

he blamed 'Jewish domination of the media' for some of the news
coverage he has gotten. Considering these things, coupled with his
embrace of Yasir Arafat, I have no question that Jews, like most
groups who have a commonality of interest, will be listening closely
to what he says."

The *New York Times* story also reviewed Jackson's defense of Andrew Young (later mayor of Atlanta) after his resignation as UN ambassador when it was revealed that Young had held secret meetings
with PLO representatives, which was against U.S. foreign policy. It
recalled that, when Jackson opined that Young's resignation was
forced, "many were angered by the suggestion that Mr. Young was
forced out by pressure from Jewish groups or Israeli officials." The
story also recounted how black-Jewish relations, already strained
over such issues as busing and affirmative action, became further
strained when in 1979 Jackson and some other civil rights leaders
visited the "Middle East and talked with Palestinian and Arab leaders" and how "on this visit to the region in September 1979 . . . Mr.
Jackson was photographed embracing Mr. Arafat."

Moreover, the story noted that, although Jackson "visited Israel
before going to Arab countries, Israeli officials refused to meet with
him noting that he had already become 'prominent in the anti-Israeli
mood,' recalling that on this trip Jackson "expressed impatience with
frequent Jewish references to the Holocaust." "In comments on a
visit to an Israeli memorial," the article continued, "he said that he
understood the importance of a Jewish homeland, and 'the persecution complex of many Jewish people that almost invariably makes
them overreact to their own suffering because it was so great." It
also pointed out that at the time Jackson "coupled his insistence that
the PLO be recognized as the representative of the Palestine people
with insistence that the group refrain from violence."

In summary the *Times* analysis indicated that Jackson had "repeated these themes" in his November speech before the American
Arab Anti-Discrimination Committee. The news analysis concluded
by noting that, when asked after his speech if he thought he would
have an opportunity "to present his position directly to Jewish
groups," Jackson said: "We all have responsibility to remain open
to dialogue and we should not expect that Jewish groups won't want
to listen. My concern is that blacks, Arabs and Jews should begin to
talk to one another."

This particular *New York Times* news analysis disturbed me. To be sure, I was aware of Jackson's general position on the Middle East— a plausible position which I believed merited the attention of all parties, including both Israel and the United States. I was very pleased with Jackson's strong defense of Andrew Young; I thought that President Carter should have given Young more support. At bottom, I suppose, I abhor any policy that precludes talking with anyone, even your enemies. Understandably, of course, a chief executive has a right to expect that subordinates will carry out existing policies. Even so, I thought that, whether due to bureaucratic principles, the merits of the particular policy, or the stature of policy supporters or to any combination of these, Mr. Carter had overreacted by accepting Young's resignation. In fact, I was surprised that any of the above factors, individually or in combination, were strong enough to warrant such punitive action as Young's resignation.

Indeed, at another level, I immediately thought of the strong support that Andrew Young and other black leaders had given Carter at the time of his "ethnic purity" comment, at a point in his 1976 campaign when Democrat Carter very much needed help from black leaders lest he suffered erosion of the black support he needed to win the election. Thus, by accepting Young's resignation President Carter had disappointed me. I expected greater resistance to pressures, sensitivity to the symbolic and substantive importance of Mr. Young's position to black political development, and compassion from him in these particular circumstances. To be sure, given the dynamic character of American politics, I expect such resignations to continue to occur; nevertheless, I was disappointed by the Andy Young affair and pleased that Jesse Jackson had strongly defended him.[1]

Moreover, I was surprised and affronted when Israeli officials refused to meet with Jackson and other black civil rights leaders on their Middle East trip soon after Young's ouster. Whether they liked Jackson or not, he and the other black leaders did indeed represent a significant segment of the views of Black America and others as well. To me, Jackson was not just any person; he was one who commanded more respect and decency than Israeli officials accorded. And Jackson's reaction to this rebuff at the time seemed most appropriate. Jackson warned the Israelis that Black Americans represented a "political reality that Israel should not ignore. . . . We do

have 17 congressmen. We do have 15 million eligible voters. We
are the difference in presidential elections."[5]

Additionally, given my research and teaching in constitutional law
and civil liberties, I was keenly aware of strains and stresses between
blacks and some Jewish leaders over affirmative action and other
issues and was distressed by this estrangement. However, I continued
to believe that the important common interest in civil rights and
liberties among blacks and Jews would overcome these differences.
I hoped, perhaps naively, that Jackson's candidacy would be well
received in the Jewish community. I sincerely anticipated a heated,
though friendly, debate between Jackson and Jewish leaders over
his various policy positions. I thought that much good could result
therefrom in terms of curbing the continuous unrest and bloodshed
in the Middle East—one of the prime situations that I believe could
trigger World War III.

All these thoughts came to me as I read the *New York Times* news
analysis. As I viewed it, the analysis accentuated the points of friction
between Jackson and Jews in particular and, implicitly, between blacks
and Jews in general. Both the presentation and the interpretation of
the facts would invariably lead to the conclusion—even if not so
intended—that Jackson was against Jews, which I do not believe to
be true. As a result, I thought Jackson was (and still is) being criticized for positions on the Middle East, positions which I do not think
at all unreasonable. But despite my overall concern over the *Times*
article, I saw a ray of hope: Jackson thought that there was a need
for dialogue in which blacks, Arabs, and Jews "should begin to talk
to one another." It was this slight ray of hope, this kind of talk, which
I was counting on to allay Jewish qualms about Jackson's candidacy.

Hope Dims, Tensions Mount

However, I soon realized that I was seriously underestimating
the scope and intensity of Jewish feelings about Jackson, as well as
the schisms that had developed between Jews and blacks since the
civil rights movement. These feelings erupted in their most extreme
form soon after Jackson's formal entry into the Democratic contest.
On November 11, 1983, an advertisement placed in the *New York
Times* by a New York-based group called Jews Against Jackson made
shockingly clear the extreme depth and intensity of feelings held by

some Jews against Jackson. Under the caption Do you believe that any Jew should support this man? Should any decent American? the ad went on to read in large print, "We Believe that Jesse Jackson Is a Danger to American Jews, to the State of Israel and to America Itself. And We are Appalled at the Absolute Silence of the Liberal Community and, Most Importantly, of Jewish Leaders and Organizations!" The ad then cited what appeared to be excerpts from Jackson statements illustrative of his negative attitudes toward Jews. I personally found the ad revolting and was pleased to see that some leading Jewish groups denounced it.

Nonetheless, the whole developing atmosphere did cause me to think much more about black-Jewish relations in general, and I began to realize that Jackson's success in gaining Lt. Goodman's release, which I had considered a great *plus* for Jackson's campaign, could confirm Jewish suspicions of Jackson's "friendly" relations with the Arab world.

More than this, and perhaps of greater importance given its crucial role in modern political campaigning, I had seriously underestimated the in-depth attention the media would give to highlighting points of friction between Jackson and Jews, exemplified vividly by the next major news story that came to my attention during the campaign, about mid-February 1984. Even the caption of Rick Atkinson's article in the *Washington Post* mirrored friction and conflict: "Peace with American Jews Eludes Jackson."[6]

Reporter Atkinson began his story by stating how Jackson's desire to use "dialogue and diplomacy to calm the world's trouble spots" had eluded him in finding "peace on the home front with American Jews." The second paragraph in the article stated: "Nearly five years after embracing Palestinian leader Yasser Arafat, and five weeks after hugging Syrian President Hafez Assad, Jackson remains at loggerheads with many Jewish leaders over his ties to the Arab world. He has become a lightning rod in the center of an emotional ethnic triangle of blacks, Jews and Arab Americans." The article covered certain major points discussed in the earlier *New York Times* article— e.g., strains between blacks and Jews over affirmative action; Andy Young's forced resignation as UN ambassador and Jackson's defense of Young; Jackson's 1979 trip to the Middle East and his friendly relations with PLO leader Arafat, Jordan's King Hussein, and then Egyptian president Anwar Sadat.

In addition, the *Washington Post* article reported on a recent interview in which Jackson outlined his basic positions on the Middle East. To begin with, Jackson suggested that he had empathy with Arabs since, as a "Third World person" who grew up in Greenville, S.C., he had to "negotiate with a superpower . . . for the right to vote, for open housing, equal pay. . . ." But Jackson also indicated how he identified with the "Israelis because I understand persecution." "My people went through a holocaust, a sustained holocaust and suffering." Domestically, Jackson saw the need to "redefine" the "traditional alliance" between blacks and Jews since "many things have happened to both of us in the last 15 years." Jackson holds that blacks have a greater sense of reliance now and are "far more involved in politics now. We ought to be able now to relate to Arabs and Jews, and maybe even serve a role in expanding that dialogue in this country." In terms of foreign policy, Jackson suggested that "America's strategic alliance with Israel is 'inadequate' for the U.S. national interests because 'it excites one nation with 4 million people and incites 21 nations with 106 million people.' " An important way to help Israel, Jackson said, is to promote greater trade between Israel and the Arab world since "obviously the more trade Israel has, the less aid Israel needs." "Israel's sovereignty," continued Jackson, "is threatened by the amount of American aid and military weapons."

Additionally, the *Washington Post* article quoted Jackson as saying that "when we were in the Middle East in '79, when we met Arafat, in the Middle East people traditionally embrace. In Japan, they take their shoes off. Embracing Arafat was not embracing his politics. . . . We have not taken an anti-Israel's-right-to-exist policy. Never did." Nonetheless, the *Post* story told how Jackson stated that that particular gesture had brought a storm of outrage which included "heads of dead animals" being left on the doorstep of his home—actions which Jackson stated could have engendered "mass marches and stuff, (and) triggered some real black-Jews confrontation." Moreover, Jackson indicated that since the campaign had begun there had also been threats on his life, which he thought had come mostly and "paradoxically" from "Nazis or Jews." And even though Jewish leaders indicated that such actions did not represent them, Jackson thought that these leaders had not openly criticized such acts and thus "silence by the credible community gives comfort to those who are disruptive."

From Private Conversation to Public conflict:
The Hymie Affair

Atkinson's *Washington Post* article also reviewed a number of other matters, including an account of a conversation that was to prove a devastating blow to Jackson's entire presidential campaign and was certain to exacerbate his relations with Jews. Tucked away on a continuation page of the article were these two short paragraphs:

> In private conversations with reporters, Jackson has referred to Jews as "Hymies" and to New York as "Hymietown."
> "I'm not familiar with that," Jackson said. . . . "That's not accurate."

In my first reading of Atkinson's article, I saw the comment and thought the terms were derisive but had frankly never heard of them, much less heard of them being used to disparage anyone. Hence I paid little attention to the matter since in any case I did not believe that Jackson would knowingly give reporters anything that could damage his campaign.

But as I inquired and listened to a number of my professional colleagues and friends, a number of whom are Jewish, I became concerned and very frustrated about the report. I found out that Hymie is a shortened version of Hyman, a common name among Jews. To be sure, I know a person whose name is Hyman, (I call him "Hy"), but I never thought the name could be used in a derogatory manner. But clearly the term was offensive to many Jews; some suggested its analogy to terms that had long been used to disparage blacks—e.g., "Nigger." With this awareness, I found it even more difficult to believe that Jackson would knowingly use such a term even off the record, particularly in talking to reporters, no matter what color.

Simultaneously, I found it difficult to believe that if the remarks were off the record—and were indeed said to any reporter, again no matter what race or color—they would be reported, even anonymously. As a professional, I have indeed been told things that were "off the record" which I would have loved to use, but they were "off the record" and had to be treated as such. In any event, it seemed to me that it was just this sort of issue that would permit the media and others to plug away at the "moral idealistic cloak" which Jackson had wrapped around his campaign—a cloak which seemingly was serving Jackson well. It is not that the media had any hidden motive but rather that this issue might give a measure of credence to Jackson's alleged pro-Arab sentiments and to the charges of anti-Semitism some had levelled against him. Moreover, the mere allegation of Jackson's having made the remark was a serious charge and, whether true or not, tended to undermine the fundamental moral principles of the Jackson campaign.

From this point on, for the next two weeks or so, the Hymie affair and Jackson's denials colored television and news reports on Jackson's campaign. The incident triggered anew a rehashing of background information that had been reported on Jackson in earlier stories—e.g., his 1979 trip to the Middle East and his embracing of PLO leader Arafat. As one whose allegiance to Jackson was growing, I wanted to believe that the allegations were not true. But somehow I sensed that Jackson's denials were becoming increasingly soft.

At the same time, I was surprised and disturbed to learn that Milton Coleman, whom I've known for years, was the reporter who heard and reported the remark. While we were not personal corresponding friends, we know each other well enough to call either just to pass the time or to get information. I immediately thought of calling Milton, but fortunately my wife prevailed upon me not to do so. While I really wanted to know the facts, I had serious qualms with Milton for reporting what I understood to be off-the-record comments. But even if the remarks were not off the record, I still questioned whether Coleman should have made such disclosures in view of the many choices that all of us constantly make in our professional work.

To say that Coleman had an obligation as a reporter to make such disclosures is only the beginning of the problem; professionals of various sorts—especially reporters, research professors, public affairs analysts—are constantly engaged in sorting out what to report and what not. Sometimes this is a conscious decision motivated by a number of factors, some personal, some professional—all a consummation of our political-social background, professional training, ethics, and judgment. To be sure, I oppose racial or ethnic slurs, no matter their source. Yet I was frankly disturbed, as were most of my close friends, that Coleman decided to report what seems to have been off-the-record comments.

These personal thoughts aside, however, the basic question remained: did Jackson in fact make the remarks? The matter continued
to haunt Jackson because he had never definitely said, "I did not."
But after two weeks of what must have been pure torment for him—
it certainly was exasperating to me—on Sunday, February 26, just
hours before the New Hampshire primary, Jackson finally acknowledged that he had indeed used the terms attributed to him. He thus
reversed his earlier denials and claims of no recollection. Obviously
as a matter of strategic choice, Jackson decided to make his admission
before a Manchester, New Hampshire, synagogue audience of some
400 persons. Said Jackson:

> Even as I affirm to you that that term was used in private con-
> versation, I categorically deny that I am anti-Semitic.
>
> At first I was shocked by the press interest in private conver-
> sations apparently overheard by a reporter.
>
> (It was not used) in the spirit of meanness. (But) however
> innocent and unintended, it was wrong.
>
> I affirm to you that the term was used in a private conversation
> (in which) we sometimes let our guard down.
>
> An off-color remark has no bearing on religion or politics.[7]

Jackson told the audience that, since his trip to the Middle East
in 1979 in which he was photographed embracing Arafat, "there has
been so much pain, anxiety, and hostility, that I have not felt welcome
among Jews." However, Jackson reminded his listeners of the close
ties between blacks and Jews during the civil rights movement and
indicated that he "now . . . offered" his campaign as a "vehicle of
reconciliation 'for all minorities, including Jews.' "

The Conflict Continues:
The Farrakhan Intervention

But as much as Jackson and many others had hoped, the admission and apology did not end the controversy. Rather, it shifted
to another level—in apparent reaction to what many sincerely thought
had amounted to an overkill of criticism over the Hymie matter.
And, ironically, the seeds for the continuation of the conflict came
from one of Jackson's earliest and strongest supporters, Minister Louis
Farrakhan of the Nation of Islam. Indeed, the controversy now shifted

to Jackson's refusal to repudiate or disassociate himself from Minister Farrakhan. Appearing at a rally with Jackson only a day or two prior to Jackson's February 26 apology, Farrakhan "warned Jewish organizations that there would be retaliation 'if you harm this brother.' " Jackson defended Farrakhan's remarks and said that they "reflected black anger at the assassination of (black) leadership figures."[8]

Some of Farrakhan's most vituperative statements were clearly directed toward Milton Coleman, the *Washington Post* reporter who broke the Hymie story. In a March 11 radio broadcast, for example, Farrakhan is reported to have referred to Coleman as a "no good, filthy traitor" and indicated that "one day we will punish you with death."[9] "We're going to make an example of Milton Coleman," said Farrakhan. However, in a subsequent news conference Farrakhan charged reporters with "wicked and malicious tampering" with his comments, saying that they had taken his comments out of context and that the thrust of his earlier comments was to indicate that Coleman would be socially ostracized as a "betrayer" of his race. Farrakhan charged that the press had overlooked his remarks that he had wanted no physical harm to come to Coleman and had rather focused on his comment that "traitors would be punished by death." "I want the world to know," said Farrakhan, "that the lives of Milton Coleman and his wife and his family are sacred to me." However, Farrakhan did not back away from his strong criticisms of Coleman for reporting the Hymie incident and indeed viewed it as part of a conspiracy to discredit Reverend Jackson as the first black person to seriously contest for the presidency. "The consensus among the black masses," concluded Farrakhan, "is that Milton Coleman is a 'Judas' "[10]

Farrakhan's strong denunciation of Coleman apparently struck a sympathetic chord among many blacks, even among those who did not care much for Farrakhan or Jackson. Indeed, those conversant with the black community would have to agree with Dr. Alvin Pouissant, a black Harvard psychiatrist, who suggested that many blacks preferred to blame Milton Coleman as a traitor rather than blame Jesse Jackson for his naivete. Pouissant's view that feelings were running high in the black community, leading some to comment that "somebody should get that brother," referring to Coleman, also found support among blacks.[11]

Unquestionably, the incident had done damage to Jackson's campaign. One could sense the pressures mounting on Jackson to do something to extricate himself from an increasingly nasty and confused situation. To be sure, Jackson did disassociate himself from certain of Farrakhan's remarks made in the March 11 broadcast and indicated that he deplored both violence and the threat of violence. Additionally, on April 8, Jackson is reported to have said for the first time that Milton Coleman "had 'assumed his professional responsibility' in reporting his remarks and 'did what tough reporters do.' "[12]

But even as he disassociated himself from Farrakhan's remarks, Jackson refused to renounce Farrakhan or break ties with him. Obviously, Jackson was well aware that Farrakhan's views met with a great deal of receptivity in the black community, a community whose strong support Jackson certainly needed. Jackson's reluctance to break with Farrakhan was summarized well by attorney Thomas Todd of Chicago, who said: "Why should he renounce someone who is registering and turning out the vote for him to curry favor with white America when white America is not going to vote for him anyway?"[13]

However, the situation became even more troublesome for Jackson and worrisome to his supporters when it was revealed that in the March 11 broadcast Farrakhan had also referred to Hitler as a "great man," apparently in response to some Jews who had compared him with Hitler. Said Farrakhan:

> "Here, the Jews don't like Farrakhan, so they call him Hitler. Well, that's a good name. Hitler was a very great man. He wasn't great for me, a black person, but he was a great German, and he rose Germany up from the ashes of her defeat by the united force of all of Europe and America after the First World War.
>
> Now, I'm not proud of Hitler's evils against Jewish people. But that's a matter of record. He rose Germany up from nothing. Well, in a sense, you could say there's a similarity in that we're rising our people up from nothing. But don't compare me with your wicked killers.[11]

When questioned at an April 11 news conference about his Hitler remarks, Farrakhan stuck to his views: "I don't think you would be talking about Adolf Hitler 40 years after the fact if he was some minuscule crackpot that jumped on the European continent." "He was indeed a great man," continued Farrakhan, "but also wicked—wickedly great."[15]

Overall, the effect of Farrakhan's remarks was to keep Jackson on the defensive and exacerbate the anxieties of Jews and many other Americans, including some Jackson supporters. As a result, Jackson found it necessary once again to disassociate himself from these latest Farrakhan remarks. In doing so, Jackson said: "I find nothing great about Hitler and everything about him despicable. Hitler's greatness was great for some Nazis, but that's all. I find no pleasure in what he represented ideologically or what he did. He represents an expression of madness on the face of the human community."[16]

By April 12, with his campaign increasingly embroiled in controversy about Farrakhan's remarks, Jackson seemingly began to put some distance between himself and Farrakhan by saying it would probably be "more appropriate" to refer to Farrakhan as a "supporter" rather than a "surrogate."[17] Indeed, Jackson said he had also sought political support from Governor George Wallace of Alabama and former Governor Orval Faubus of Arkansas, two of the nation's most noted segregationists during the civil rights movement and Jackson's opponents during that struggle. Said Jackson: "I do not think it is fair to impose upon our campaign the views of a given supporter, ones that we do not hold ourselves. . . . Any candidate who becomes the nominee of the Democratic Party will have within that party strong extremes, the very hawks to the right, the very doves of the left, and all of those in between. It is that sense of delicate balance that I am concerned about." Despite this apparent backing away, Jackson still directly refused to disassociate himself completely from Farrakhan.

To one who had by this time become strongly committed to Jackson's cause, the whole situation was frustrating and disheartening. I found it nightmarish and I was ready for the nightmare to end. Here, I reasoned, had been a beautifully developing campaign that had been sidetracked by the candidate himself by the Hymie remark. I believed, however, that it was a wound that could be healed, even if not fully, by Jackson's belated apology, his subsequent actions, and by good practical common sense and wisdom, which I felt certain both black and Jewish leaders would in time come to exercise.

But this was not to be. In late June, the whole issue resurfaced with a fury. Once again, comments by Minister Farrakhan provided the fodder. Published excerpts of a radio speech by Farrakhan in

Chicago on Sunday, June 24, forecast clearly the reactions one could expect. Said Farrakhan:

> I'm not anti-Jew. I am pro-truth, but in this serious hour, the truth must be told so that the true people of God may come up into the view of the entire world. . . .
>
> I say to the Jewish people and to the Government of the United States of America: The present state called Israel is an outlaw act. It was not done with the backing of Almighty God nor was it done by the guidance of the Messiah. It was your cold naked scheming, plotting and planning against the lives of a people there in Palestine. Now you have taken the land and you called it Israel and you pushed out the original inhabitants, making them vagabonds in the earth. You have lied and said this was a promise made by God to you.
>
> What will you do today when the lie is uncovered and we show the world that we are the chosen people of that promise? We are the people who have no land that we can call our own.
>
> America and England and the nations backed Israel's existence. Therefore when you aid and abet someone in a criminal conspiracy, you are a part of that criminal conspiracy.
>
> Now that nation called Israel never had had any peace in 40 years and she will never have any peace, because there can be no peace structured on injustice, thievery, lying and deceit and using the name of God to shield your gutter religion under His holy and righteous name.
>
> America and England and the nations, because of their backing of Israel, are being drawn into the heat of the third world war, which is called Armageddon. Oh, America, you have blundered so and instead of recognizing the mistake you have made and making amends, you persist in your evil and so the consequences of evil must come.
>
> You hate us because we dare to say that we are the chosen people of God and can back it up. We are ready to do battle with you wherever you come from in the earth. It is the black people in America that is the chosen people of Almighty God.[18]

Farrakhan Denounced

As expected, reactions to news reports of Farrakhan's speech were swift and sharp. The most important reaction—the one most awaited and welcomed by many—came from Reverend Jackson himself. Though in Latin America at the time, Jackson issued a statement through his campaign office, sharply criticizing Farrakhan's statements as "reprehensible" and "morally indefensible":

My staff in Washington has now briefed me on Minister Farrakhan's comments in his most recent speech. I refer specifically to his comments describing the creation of Israel as an "outlaw act" and his assertion that nations that help found and now support Israel are "criminals in the sight of Almighty God."

I find such statements or comments to be reprehensible and morally indefensible. I disavow such comments and thoughts. I am a Judeo-Christian and the roots of my faith run deep in the Judeo-Christian tradition. This philosophy embraces Judaism, Christianity and Islam as monotheistic religions all founded in Jerusalem. Such comments are inflammatory in the context of the Middle East and are damaging to the prospects for peace there. Such statements and thoughts have no place in my own thinking or in this campaign, and I call upon all of my supporters to join me in speaking out in support of my stand.

Although most of the press has chosen not to note it, Minister Farrakhan has not participated in my campaign in recent months because I discouraged his participation. He is not a part of our campaign. That was a conscious policy which I intend to continue because our campaign is structured and disciplined and cannot have others perceived as spokespersons for the rainbow coalition.

I will not permit Minister Farrakhan's words, wittingly or unwittingly, to divide the Democratic party. Neither anti-Semitism nor anti-black statements have any place in our party. Having expressed my views on this matter as clearly as I can, I would observe that those who continue to attempt to use those statements to make an issue in the Democratic party are not working for the good of the party.

Finally, the problems these issues have raised are more troubling than any immediate political consequences that may ensue. They go to the very fabric of our national civility. I believe that we must begin a process designed to heal the wounds that injudicious words, relentless accusations and widespread publicity have opened within the Christian, Islamic and Jewish communities. To that end, I have asked my friends and associates to begin exploratory ecumenical meetings that would lead to serious discussions between these constituencies and others of good will who are committed to the elimination of misunderstanding from our national life.[19]

By this time I was a duly elected, fully committed Jackson delegate to the San Francisco convention, and quite naturally I was elated by Jackson's statement. It was straightforward, unambiguous, and well-crafted; it projected a depth of feeling, understanding, and sincerity which I had long believed characterized both Jackson and his campaign. In short, as a Jackson supporter, I felt both relief and a rejuvenated sense of pride in our candidate and the campaign.

Others were also pleased and relieved by Jackson's statement, especially Democratic party leaders and officials who undoubtedly saw Jackson's statement as tempering the increasing friction between blacks and Jews, two of the most important constituent groups in the party. Vice President Mondale, for example, who by this time loomed as the Democratic party nominee, seemed especially calmed by Jackson's statement. Said Mondale, "Mr. Farrakhan's obscene statements deserve to be condemned. I commend Reverend Jackson for making it clear that Minister Farrakhan has no part in his campaign. The only way to advance the cause of justice in America is to condemn bigotry and injustice wherever it appears."[20]

National party chairman Charles Manatt, in reactions made prior to Jackson's statement, called Farrakhan's statements "outrageous" and "obscene," and indicated that he wanted to meet with Jackson, leaving the possibility open, as the *New York Times* reported it, "that Mr. Jackson would not be allowed to address the Democratic National Convention in San Francisco if he did not disassociate himself from Mr. Farrakhan's remarks," a course of action some members of the House of Representatives had urged Manatt to take.[21] But some black leaders, including Mondale supporters, reacted angrily to this warning that would prevent Jackson from speaking at the convention unless he repudiated Farrakhan.[22] Georgia state senator Julian Bond, for example, called the action "ridiculous and foolish" and described "pressure from Jewish leaders and others . . . as 'blackmail of the worst kind.' " Bond said that many Jews had been drifting

away from the Democratic party for some time and had now "seized
upon the Jackson-Farrakhan thing to justify their natural inclination." "That's going to happen," concluded Bond, "when people
become affluent and comfortable."

The Farrakhan situation engendered still further reactions. In an
official statement, executive director Benjamin Hooks of the NAACP
placed the organization on record as deploring "the inflammatory
statements that are being made by Black Muslim leader Louis Farrakhan that labeled Judaism as a 'gutter religion' and cast Israel as
a criminal nation." Said Hooks:

> The N.A.A.C.P. is on record as rejecting all forms of racism and
> anti-Semitism.
>   The N.A.A.C.P.'s struggle historically has been against those
> groups and people who have sought to divide the nation along
> religious and ethnic lines. The N.A.A.C.P.'s philosophy, beliefs
> and programs are grounded in the constitutional principles of
> equality, liberty, and freedom for all people without regard to
> race, color, nationality, creed or sex. . . .
>   The N.A.A.C.P. rejects all statements and actions that are con-
> trary to its established policy.[23]

Vice Pesident George Bush said in a speech that "recent statements
by Louis Farrakhan have no place in America." "The President and
I," said Bush, "condemn in the strongest terms those who preach
hate, racism, and anti-Semitism."[24]

On June 28, at about the same time as Bush's speech, the United
States Senate adopted by a 95-0 vote a resolution that called on both
party chairmen to issue written repudiations of Mr. Farrakhan's statement. The resolution, in the form of an amendment to an appropriations bill for several cabinet departments (viz.: State, Justice, and
Commerce), read as follows:

> Mr. Louis Farrakhan, advisor to one of the presidential candi-
> dates, is reported to have referred to the Jewish faith as a "gutter
> religion."
>   Mr. Farrakhan has also accused the United States of being a
> "criminal" for our "aiding and abetting" role at the time of the
> creation of the Israeli nation and,
>   Mr. Farrakhan has even called the very existence of Israel on
> [sic] 'outlaw act' that it is therefore the sense of the Senate that—

(1) there is no place in our society, nor in our electoral process, for hateful, bigoted expressions of anti-Jewish and racist sentiments such as those reportedly being made by Louis Farrakhan, and all such vicious expressions must be condemned, and

(2) the leadership of the Senate is instructed to communicate with the Chairmen of the Democratic and Republican parties to request that they immediately repudiate in writing the sentiments and expressions of hatred reportedly made by Mr. Farrakhan.[25]

I was surprised and puzzled at the relatively little publicity and reaction that the Senate action engendered. But at least, as I saw it, there was one glimmer of hope: at long last the entire controversy might finally be put to rest.

The Hymie Affair in Perspective

Overall, as one who saw (and still sees) great benefits from Jackson's campaign, I found the whole Hymie affair frustrating and damaging. I understood how, in a private conversation, Jackson might have made remarks he would not have made in public. But it is best, especially for a public figure, not to say in private what cannot be said in public. On the other hand, I remain troubled by the whole incident and still wonder whether or not Milton Coleman did indeed breach professional responsibility by disclosing the remarks. This has nothing to do with the rightness or wrongness of the remarks as such: they were wrong. Rather, it has to do with the ethics of one's explicit or implicit pledge of confidentiality. This, as mentioned earlier, is a constant problem with which many professionals deal, and in the end, individual professionals (in this instance Milton Coleman) must answer that question for himself or herself.

Similarly, even if consistent with professional responsibilty, there is also the question, likewise common but as here at times difficult, as to the benefits and costs of divulging particular information. Again, the perceived benefits and costs might vary from individual to individual, but it is nevertheless the type of weighting or balancing which professionals—such as Coleman—might on occasion find it appropriate to go through. In context of the already grave concern expressed by Jewish leaders about what they considered Jackson's

pro-Arab or anti-Semitic leanings and given the foreseeable ramifi-
cations involved in divulging arguably off-the-record remarks, Coleman must have gone through some sort of weighing or balancing.
But I am not at all certain that, given the same situation, other reporters, just as dedicated and responsible, could not have come to
a different decision. In short, despite holistic preachments about
professional responsibility, I am not at all certain that Coleman did
the right thing, nor, of course, can I be certain that he did the wrong
thing. A decision with such far-reaching consequences cannot be
made solely (and mechanically) in terms of "professional responsibilities and requirements." Seldom, if ever, is there escape from
individual judgment and discretion, no matter how definitive the
professional ethical code.[26]

By the time the Hymie affair surfaced (mid-February), I was becoming an increasingly strong Jackson supporter. Naturally, I was
concerned and frustrated by the allegation and the harm it could do
to Jackson and the cause he represented. Additionally, after Jackson's
initial denial I remained disturbed that the press would continue to
focus on this rather than on the essence of Jackson's campaign. But
I was even more distressed to later find out that the allegation was
indeed true. To be sure, I was relieved with Jackson's apology, even
if belated, and hoped that he and we had learned from the experience
and that at long last the media could focus on the really important
proposals Jackson was making in his campaign.

But again I was disappointed. Once more the increasingly vituperative reactions of Minister Farrakhan diverted media attention
from the real essence of Jackson's campaign. Some of my friends—
and on occasion I myself—thought the media seemed to be looking
for something to discredit Jackson's campaign. But whether they
were or not is beside the point; Farrakhan gave the media and others
all the fodder they needed and more. Initially, despite the death-
threat talk, I sensed a real sympathy among blacks for Farrakhan's
reaction to Coleman. I must repeat time and again that I do not
believe many persons—including some important black and white
leaders, journalists, and professional analysts of all types—really appreciated the very deep attachment and support that Jackson's campaign enjoyed in the black community—an attachment and support
that cut across socioeconomic lines and approached religious fervor.
This religious fervor involved a "heavenly sense" of brotherly love

and nonviolence toward all persons—blacks, whites, poor, rich, Jews, Arab, etc. And this strong and deep religious tradition among blacks made it necessary for Jackson to eventually repudiate and disassociate himself and his campaign from Farrakhan.

Like many others, I found it puzzling that Farrakhan would continue to make statements, no matter how much he believed them to be true, that would have the obvious prospect of harming Jackson's campaign. At the same time, however, I appreciated why Jackson found it difficult to repudiate Farrakhan summarily. Indeed, one might suggest that Farrakhan represents or reflects an important strain of political thought in the black community—separatism—which all of us might do well to analyze and ponder even if we disagree with it. My hope at the time, however, was that Jackson would either distance himself from Farrakhan or convince him to moderate his rhetoric. The real damage of the whole Hymie-Farrakhan situation to Jackson's campaign could be capsulized in the following:

(1) Farrakhan's language was in fact repulsive to everything that the Jackson campaign represented—i.e., a healthy and decent respect for all persons; the promotion of love, justice, and equality; and the use of dialogue and diplomacy rather than violence to achieve these ends. Farrakhan's comments—especially after Jackson's apology for his Hymie remark—provided the fodder needed to keep astir fears of anti-Semitism in Jackson's campaign and to cast aspersions on Jackson and his overall effort.

(2) Although Jackson's Hymie remarks deserved criticism on their own and were exacerbated by Farrakhan's comments, they could be used as convenient cover under which those already disposed to criticize Jackson's candidacy could express their concerns more openly without jeopardizing their liberal or racial credentials. And these, in my opinion, included a lot of good people, mostly white but some black, who perhaps really thought that now is really not the time for the changes Jackson advocated or, more basically, for a black man to contest for the presidency.

Overall, to be sure, the Hymie-Farrakhan debacle was most damaging to Jackson in the larger American (i.e., white) community. For a host of reasons, it was not as damaging in the black community, in which this type of rhetoric still retains a measure of vitality and support. Although many blacks would not themselves use Farrakhan's rhetoric and would find it offensive, its use did not cause the stir among blacks that it did among whites. (Indeed, I did not find it surprising at all, as one writer apparently did, that a *Los Angeles Times* poll found that 47 percent of black delegates attending the 1984 Democratic National Convention held a favorable attitude toward Farrakhan. By contrast, an overwhelming majority of non-black delegates—76 percent—had an unfavorable attitude toward Farrakhan.)[27] Sooner or later whites must understand that this type of rhetoric and behavior has been fostered by their own ongoing maltreatment of blacks in the American political-social order. As long as such conditions exist, blacks understandably find themselves more receptive to many types of rhetoric and promises of deliverance than would otherwise be the case.

A second reason why the Hymie-Farrakhan situation did not engender too much stir among blacks is that Jackson's campaign was of paramount symbolic as well as substantive significance to blacks in a group sense. To many blacks, Jackson's running for president represented goals and aspirations they had longed for—that a black, just as a white, could indeed become president; that blacks, just as whites, must be treated with dignity and respect and must share all the benefits and responsibilities of the political-social order; and that government, especially the national government, cannot now shy away from its responsibilities and must perforce play a major role in bringing these changes about. These basic factors constituted the essence—or at least what many blacks believed to be the essence— of Jesse Jackson's campaign. Hence, it would take much more than a mistake by Jackson, for which he apologized, or the familiar, even though offensive, rhetoric of Farrakhan, or the condemnation by the white press, or a condemnatory resolution unanimously passed by a white United States Senate, or even condemnation from a moderate civil rights organization like the NAACP to temper the enthusiasm of the black community for the goals and objectives of Jackson's campaign.

If we consider the historical context, we will understand why certain actions and reactions against Jackson seemed to bolster and strengthen rather than dilute and weaken his support in the black community. For example, strong criticism of Jackson for not immediately and definitively denouncing Farrakhan revealed an obvious lack of knowledge and sensitivity, on the part of some, to black political thought and development. It also typified traditional white attempts to control or discredit emerging black leaders whose policies would fundamentally change, or at least disturb, traditional patterns of status and influence in American politics.

Although Jackson was wrong to describe Jews in stereotypical terms, even in private, Black Americans can't forget that such descriptions have been all too frequently used against them and acted upon by those who were in positions to legalize their feelings and prejudices, and that it took centuries of bloodshed and suffering—culminating in a civil rights movement led by blacks themselves—before such legalized prejudices and racism were overcome in our formal law. Nor can we forget that even today full and effective implementation and compliance with this new legal regime—instituted in the 1950s and 1960s—still encounters formidable opposition. In this context, the repeated criticisms of Jackson for his Hymie remark and the newsworthiness of the incident smacked of an arrogant hypocrisy and an attempt to impose "capital" punishment for a "noncapital" offense.

Similarly, one must also raise questions about the resolution passed by the U.S. Senate condemning certain offensive statements made by Farrakhan, who was referred to as "an advisor to one of the presidential candidates." Where did the Senate stand when Congress failed to pass antilynching legislation in the 1930s and 1940s, or when not only words but actual violence and repressive actions were openly directed against blacks (and their white supporters) in the 1950s and 1960s? Where did the Senate stand during the tortuous history of civil rights legislation during those years? Or where has this body stood in more recent times in terms of condemning and correcting the glaring socioeconomic inequities that continue to exist between whites and blacks and that hurt blacks and minorities so badly?

I viewed the Senate resolution regarding Farrakhan in this context and found the *Congressional Record* on this matter interesting. The *Record* is replete with statements supporting the resolution condemning Farrakhan, with senators rushing to cosponsor or express their abhorrence for Farrakhan's statements. Indeed, our senators exhibited an unusual unanimity of support for a resolution to which there seemingly was no question but that all members of the Senate would agree. The *Record* did show, however, that only one senator (Stevens of Alaska) questioned the wisdom of the "midnight" Senate action which occurred about 10:00 P.M. on June 28, 1984. Consider the *Record* entry at this point:

PRESIDING OFFICER: The Senator from Alaska is recognized.

MR. STEVENS: Mr. President, what is this resolution doing here?

PRESIDING OFFICER: The Senator from Alaska has the floor.

MR. STEVENS: Everyone says it is late, but sometimes I think we ought to stop and think a little bit about what we are doing. This has no business in connection with the State-Justice-Commerce appropriations bill. Are we here to play politics? What is this Senate doing tonight? I move to table that and I ask for the yeas and nays.

PRESIDING OFFICER: Is there a sufficient second? Is there a sufficient second?

MR. STEVENS: We ought to table it. We really ought to table this and just get rid of it. It is not a good precedent for the Senate.

PRESIDING OFFICER: There is not a sufficient second. The question is on agreeing to the motion to table.

The motion to lay on the table was rejected. A roll call vote then ensued on the anti-Farrakhan resolution and the Senate voted 95-0, with Senator Stevens joining in approval. Five senators were reported as "necessarily absent" (Goldwater, Arizona; McClure, Idaho; Cranston, California; Hart, Colorado; and Stennis, Mississippi).[28]

I viewed the Senate action with a strong measure of cynicism. To be sure, rhetoric like Farakhan's is not likely to create racial peace and harmony. But neither are the serious socioeconomic inequities that remain between whites and blacks. The appeal and vitality of the former is clearly related to our unwillingness or inability to deal with the latter. Thus I found the Senate resolution disturbing, for it appeared all too congruent with both the current conservative public mood as well as the more basic traditional propensity of white-dominated institutions to punish blacks more than whites.

In sum, the Hymie-Farrakhan events reminded me of an observation I made during the early debate over whether a black person should contest for the Democratic presidential nomination. I said at that time that a strong black presidential effort (such as Jackson's) could penetrate and threaten so many traditions, customs, and practices of our politics and society that it could bring out both the best in us and the worst in us. The Hymie-Farrakhan developments did indeed bring out some of the worst in us, and unfortunately, some of that worst spilled over, not on only one side but on a number of sides.

5

Vintage Jackson:
The Debates and Primaries

The Jackson Campaign: Style and Substance

My local newspaper hardly needed to remind me with the headline that "All Eyes [Were] on Dartmouth As Democrats Debate."[1] Sunday, January 5, 1984, was indeed an historic day. My family, friends, and many, many others had been looking forward to this first debate in which, for the first time in American history, a Black American would participate as one of the major candidates for the Democratic presidential nomination. The *New York Times* reported that there were seventy-one declared candidates for the Democratic nomination, but the organizers decided to limit the debate to the eight major candidates.[2] That Jackson was to be among this eight was in itself an accomplishment, and there was sheer ecstasy as well as nervous expectation in the Barker household.

We wanted Jackson to do well, to hold his own in the debates and in the primaries. Jackson, of course, is an articulate, attractive, sharp person with a strong and arresting personality. Whether one likes him or not, Jesse Jackson commands attention. He is indeed blessed with that rare but readily discernible attribute called charisma. And this made him stand out even more in a rather dull, unattractive field of Democratic candidates. Indeed, on April 19, near the end of the Democratic presidential primary season, the *Christian Science Monitor* captured well this enviable Jackson asset.

Only two persons in the political running in the United States this year have a touch of the indefinable but priceless quality called charisma. Ronald Reagan is one. Jesse Jackson is the other. Whatever one may think about Jackson's policies and behavior, he has a touch of that something that makes people listen to him speak even when they don't like what he is saying.

Jesse Jackson can rouse an audience as a Franklin Roosevelt or John F. Kennedy could. He has brought to the voting polls thousands of blacks who otherwise would not be there. He and he alone can persuade or induce thousands of new black voters to come out on election day, if he chooses to do so. Walter Mondale can probably get the Democratic nomination without benefit of Jesse Jackson, but not the presidency.[3]

A tall, powerful, athletically built, handsome man, Jackson has the kind of physical attibutes that make him stand out in the crowd. His sheer physical presence draws attention, evoking kisses and starry eyes from women and "so-what" glances and shrugs from men. More than this, however, Jackson possesses a powerful voice and enviable speaking skills. In short, he is what folks call a "spell-binding" speaker, which is what Baptist preachers had better be to survive, and Jackson is a *good* Baptist preacher.[1] To be sure, he was an attractive, articulate, and charismatic person. But the breadth of his appeal and the depth of his knowledge of issues was more unclear, uncertain.

His appeal and attractiveness to blacks, however, had been demonstrated time and again before and during his pre-campaign activity. Blacks understood him, he was one of them. And blacks constitute one of the largest and most loyal Democratic groups, having cast about one-fourth of the total Democratic vote in the 1980 election. Certainly any Democratic nominee would need such support. What was uncertain, however, was whether blacks would follow Jackson or whether they would follow certain other prominent black leaders who had reservations about a black presidential candidacy (and perhaps about Jesse Jackson as well) and had endorsed Walter Mondale, whom they now encouraged blacks to support.

Even more uncertain was how Jackson's candidacy would appeal to others he hoped to bring into his Rainbow Coalition—women, Hispanics, the poor, and generally the locked out. Jackson's message definitely held appeal for these groups. However, whether Jackson would attract broad support from these groups (e.g., white women) was more uncertain. But it was just this uncertainty that created the great interest in Jackson and his campaign. And it was just this interest that Jackson (and others) was counting on to spur his candidacy. But now that he had such interest, he had to hold it and use it. And the debates and primaries would give an opportunity to do so.

Fortunately, given his fast campaign pace, we did not have to wait long to see how Jackson would try to use this opportunity and how the nation would react. Indeed, we soon found out that this man of the cloth is also endowed with a keen knowledge of and sensitivity to the ways of the world. Time and again Jackson demonstrated that he had a rich, factual, analytical grasp of major policy issues, domestic as well as foreign. He was much more than merely conversant about issues such as unemployment and poverty. In many ways Jackson has been in the trenches; he knows first hand how life is in "boats stuck at the bottom." Thus his deep commitment to the poor, downtrodden, forgotten, excluded could be viewed as experientially as well as morally based. Pressures need not be put *on* Jackson to represent these interests; these pressures are already *in* him and are a part of him.

As the campaign progressed, Jackson's comments on the nature and importance of the federal budget and the budget process, revenues and expenditures, and the importance of budget priorities to policy making and policy implementation revealed that his grasp of issues went beyond those that could be directly linked to his life experiences. And his lack of direct involvement or experience in these matters was hardly a handicap; he was able to vividly describe the intimate relationship and importance of such matters to the quality of life and lifestyles that we experience daily. Moreover, Jackson appeared at home discussing the relative importance and interrelation of private sector development and prosperity to public sector policies and activities.

In addition, Jackson displayed a broad knowledge of and feel for matters relating to foreign policy and international relations—nuclear policy, the Mideast and Arab-Israeli matters, our policies toward South Africa, South America, and the third world generally. And the fact that his positions on these matters were usually different, and consistently forceful and clear, invariably pleased his supporters but infuriated his critics.

Even more, Jackson has a way with words. He has the ability to turn a phrase, to play on words (often with alliteration) and thus capture the attention of news reporters and excite and draw responses from audiences. This combination of personal and political traits—an imposing physical presence, a captivating oratorical style, a sharp mind, and an uncommonly distinctive and inclusive policy agenda—is somewhat commonplace in the black community, especially among black preachers, but rarely have they been used directly by one of them in a political campaign and never in a presidential campaign! Thus, Jackson's personality and campaign style, plus his stand on important policy issues, brought a unique and distinctive flavor seldom seen in presidential politics or American politics generally.

Jackson dramatically used the style and spirit of his campaign to convey the substance of his policy positions. A Jackson rally or speech engendered a range of emotions: from anger to love, confusion to peace, from despair to hope. It was the spiritual and moral tone of repetitive themes (freedom, justice, and equality for all); the power and choice of words; and the force and nature of the delivery that set the Jackson message and campaign apart from all others. Excerpts from Jackson's speeches recall vividly the force and fervor with which he said them.

—This is a poor campaign with a rich message.

—It's better to lose an election going in the right direction than to win going in the wrong direction.

—We'll utilize trained minds, not guided missiles, for world peace. We'll include Africa, Asia, and South Africa in our foreign policy.

—Facts and figures can be manipulated, but faith cannot be manipulated. Our time has come!

—My style is public negotiations for parity, rather than private negotiations for position.

—We're going to get some popular votes, some congressional districts. But most of all we're going to get our self-respect.

—We should not get trapped trying to color poverty. Poverty is not black, it's not brown, it's not white. Color poverty pain, hurt, agony, ache, necessity, desperation, destitution.

—We can't ride to freedom on Pharoah's chariot. It means self-respect, self-government. It means an ideology in the human rights tradition. Black, yellow, red and white, we are all precious in God's sight. It doesn't mean English or Spanish. A broken heart is the same language.

—The fact is, I look at the missing windowpane, that's the slummy side. Train that youth to become a glazier and let him in the union, that's the sunny side. Whenever I see a missing brick, that's the slummy side. Train our youth to become brick masons and let them in the unions, that's the sunny side. When I see a missing door, that's the slummy side. Train our youth to become carpenters, that's the sunny side. All this writing on the walls; let us become painters and artists and use our creativity. Just because it rains, you don't have to drown!

—Brown, black and white, we're all precious in God's sight. I AM SOMEBODY.[5]

Both the style and the substance of Jackson's campaign would be put to their most severe test during the presidential debates. This kind of debate, of course, was not the typical forum in which Jackson had experience; few Americans have. Indeed, neither Jackson nor any other Black American nor any woman had ever been in this particular situation, literally on the center stage in national party nomination politics. There was so much riding on how Jackson would do. The debates did indeed give Jackson untold opportunities, which otherwise he would be unlikely to have; they presented him with the type of publicity and exposure that were obviously beyond the reach of his limited campaign funds and gave his "poor campaign with a rich message" a great opportunity to get that message across to the American people.

Jackson's participation in the debates would dramatically call attention to the deep desire of blacks, women, and minorities to be treated fairly, respectfully, and to be fully included in all aspects of American politics and society. Very directly, Jackson's appearance could serve as an inspiration, as a role model for these long-deprived groups. His participation in the debates could also help to dispel lingering beliefs that blacks are uninformed, unarticulate, and unambitious. I thought it unfortunate that even in 1984 Jackson had to prove once again that blacks could hold their own and more with whites in any arena. Now he had an excellent forum in which to let Americans know, through his forceful and informed discussion of both racial as well as nonracial issues, that blacks and minorities are Americans too and have some definite, even if different, perceptions of how this country should be run and toward what ends. And Jackson had to do this in a manner that would guarantee his view would be considered seriously, not ceremoniously. But I also recognized that serious consideration of Jackson's views depended in large measure on his perceived or actual political clout—i.e., his ability to win votes and to speak for particular constituencies, especially for Black Americans. Party leaders certainly recognized the actual and potential importance of blacks to possible Democratic success in the presidential race. But they also knew of the split in black leadership over Jackson's candidacy.

So much symbolic and substantive importance was wrapped up in the Jackson candidacy that all except the most hardened must have wished him well in his efforts, especially those like me, members of groups Jackson represented. I realized that being the first in anything can be a high honor but can also pose awesome responsibilities—responsibilities that were even more onerous since Jackson sought the highest elective political office in the nation.

Thus the Dartmouth debates, and those that followed, were of utmost importance to Jackson and to many others. To be sure, no forum could handle effectively all of the concerns mentioned above. But the debates offered wonderful opportunities that could not be squandered, especially by one who had a "poor campaign with a rich message."

The Debates

With debate time—January 5, 1984, 2:00 p.m. CST in St. Louis—at hand, anxious questions arose in my mind. How would Jackson look? Would he appear nervous, uncomfortable? How would he match wits with the seven other candidates, all of whom had national-level political experience? Would Jesse's inexperience in national politics show? How would others treat him? How would the media interpret the debate, especially Jackson's participation?

Overall, I considered the Dartmouth debate something of a letdown. In the main, I thought the candidates, including Jackson, appeared somewhat subdued, and attention focused too much on the moderators, Ted Koppel and Phil Donahue. Even so, as I watched the debate, I admired not only Jackson's positions on the issues but particularly the way he stated his views—the choice of words that reflected a keen sensitivity to and awareness of the human dimensions of problems, and his depth of feeling and commitment to the positions he took.[6]

On putting a woman on the ticket. There is the need to involve the persons who in the past have been denied in the ways of justice within our society. Women are 53 percent of this nation. Seventy percent of all poor children live in a house headed by a woman. Our convention in San Francisco will be 50 percent female. So there's a basis for having equity. We now have women in Congress and the Senate, on the Supreme Court. Lastly, if indeed Mrs. Indira Gandhi can run India, a nation of 600 million people, if Golda Meier could run Israel in time of war, if Mrs. Thatcher can run Britain, a woman can run this country.

On the importance of face-to-face leadership contacts in foreign policy. We make progress in foreign policy through presidential initiative, not through isolated rhetoric or threats. It was Eisenhower going to Korea. The detail people followed. Kennedy going to Geneva. Nixon going to China. Carter convening Camp David. When it's all said and done, a group of academics can agree that we must freeze weapons that will destroy all of us. The leadership must take the risk for peace and make a difference. If you meet, if you talk, you act, if you act, you change things. So you must unthaw that relationship before you can begin to freeze, verifiably, the weapons.

On balancing the budget. It is important that unless we're going to challenge the corporations that pay their fair share of taxes and deal with the military budget, . . . we cannot reduce the budget.

The Republicans cannot sit home and enjoy this because they created this budget with their Reagonomic tax proposal. I would hope that before we finish today, it's not just enough for us to offer aid and programs for poor people. We must empower poor people to aid themselves. Now to that extent, so long as the Voting Rights Act of '65 is not enforced across the South, it means you'll not get equity amongst blacks, Hispanics, women and poor people in the Congress, in the Legislature, in the judiciary where these decisions are made—in fact, unless that Voting Rights Act is enforced, you'll never get the E.R.A. passed, and that's critical because 70 percent of all poor children live in a house headed by a woman. And unless that passes, you'll not end right-to-work laws so people get paid for the work that they do. See, I want some focus here on lifting the boat at the bottom. The blacks, the Hispanics, the women, the Asians, the locked-out must be empowered and not just embellished. . . .

We need to restate, in my judgment, some things basic. One, Reagan came with a $30 billion deficit and ran on a balanced budget agenda. It's now $200 billion and that needs to be stated for the record. From 30 billion to 200 billion under the Reagan Administration. No. 2, money in an economic system is like blood in the human body. Unless it travels in a circle, your blood, your body will die. A $750 billion tax break with no obligation to reinvest in this economy is like a hemorrhage of blood going that way. That contributed to the deficit.

Now, Democrats must challenge industrial integrity. These corporations that get our tax dollars and consumer dollars and kitchen funds have an obligation to reinvest, and if they do not they forfeit such an investment. On the other hand, the military budget, I said three or four times a day with no takers that 40 percent of this budget is going, military budget, to Japan and Europe's defense. Japan and Europe are now of age. They must pay their share of defense.

On the essence of Jackson's campaign. My campaign provides a live choice and another chance for redemption for this nation. It represents the ability to say America is not a broken piece of cloth, a blanket, it is indeed a quilt of many patches, many colors and many pieces and all of it fits somewhere.

A few other high (or perhaps low) points occurred in the Dartmouth debate, as when Mondale and Glenn stood shouting "gobbledegook" and "baloney" at each other. If this was indeed Mondale's way, as his aides suggested, of quieting "criticisms that he is too cautious," I found the exchange rather hollow and amateurish.[7] However, the episode did provide Jackson with the opportunity to remind both Mondale and Glenn (the two frontrunners at the time) that with "Democrats and the nation looking at us, we have to conduct the affairs of this business in a serious vein."[8] And in this connection, I very much agreed with the political analyst who indicated that the debate allowed the public to see "aspects of the candidates" not seen before—for example, "Mr. Jackson's ability to switch personas from pundit to prophet to statesman."[9] However, though Jackson had done as well as anyone else, I still had a let-down feeling, wishing that he stood out more, distinguished himself from what I considered a rather ordinary group of candidates.

Then as I read and reflected on several commentaries and heard observations from friends, I realized that Jackson should not stand out, not try to use his oratorical ability to overshadow his adversaries, which he surely could have done but which could have aroused spectors of his Baptist-preacher image—an image he surely wanted to keep under control. Instead, he had to portray the calm, poise, and confidence of an experienced professional, even though that experience was not gained in politics. In his very first debate, and the very first in which a Black American had ever participated, Jackson needed to make his points and distinguish his positions from others but otherwise to blend in with the flow, style, and substance of the debate. He did not make that grand or petit faux pas, as some might have expected or wished. He showed himself to be at least as knowledgeable and articulate as any of the others. In short, Jackson made it possible for Americans to see that a black person could indeed run for president, participate in the debates and primaries, and that nothing disastrous or untoward would occur as a result. But while I understood and appreciated this blending in, I still wondered whether Jackson could afford to hold to this style and demeanor and simultaneously avail himself of the wonderful opportunities presented by the debates to achieve his objectives.

The second debate took place in Iowa. Improvements in the format allowed candidates more freedom and even more time to express their views. This kind of setting allowed Jackson to come through better, and he clearly profited from the first debate and showed more poise and self-assurance the second time around. Beyond this, however, I thought there were striking similarities between Dartmouth and Iowa.

Just as at Dartmouth, Jackson was able to articulate his positions with clarity, sensitivity, force, and commitment. And this time he seemed able to state his positions more fully.[10]

On the unfairness of party rules in delegate selection. I think that when we structure in injustice and have two sets of rules we also structure a lot of anxiety and hostility and bitterness. There are four phases in this campaign: This is the exhibition season, then the conferences begin, you have the regular season, in San Francisco we have the playoffs, and then you have the Super Bowl between San Francisco and November.

And you'd better be careful and not lock people out of the playoffs that you're going to need in the Super Bowl. You want to play? In 1960, we won by the margin of hope and revived spirits. A hundred and twelve thousand votes beat Nixon. In '68, we lost by the margin of despair, 550,000 votes.

And so when you make the threshhold so high and so poor people can't reach it, then that's dangerous, . . . I hold fast to the one-person, one-vote provision so as to make everybody count: the peace activist, the environmentalist, the black, the Hispanic, the Asian, the American Indian, the women. These people must feel that they count somewhere.

Labor commandeers the money and gives it to one candidate and knocks seven of us off. I wish labor would have had a platform like this and not just a newspaper.

On improving education. There's a dual dimension in this educational pursuit. One dimension is adequate opportunity, enough money to pay teachers, enough money for scholarships. No child in this society who wants to go to college, has a mind to learn and a will to work ought to be turned away just because of lack of money. It's a much better investment in that child's mind.

But with all the talk about opportunity, there's a flip side we don't talk about very much, the crisis in effort, too. Our children are watching five hours of TV a night, choosing entertainment over education, and that's a crisis. The same kind of energy spent on developing our motor skills athletically is not spent on developing cognitive skills intellectually—the flip side of that. And unless parents assume their share of the responsibility—teachers give homework, the parents must have them home to do that work. Education is a partnership. The government cannot teach you against your will. So there must be a sense of a combination of opportunity and effort to really make education work.

On summing up the meaning of his campaign. We've heard crisis stated from several angles today. The question is what man, what men have the qualities of leadership to revive and redeem and reconcile the people. I have confronted corporations and governments and foreign leaders. Leaders must take charge and risk and make things happen. Whether it's Cuba or Nicaragua or Lebanon or the Soviet Union or Syria, leaders cannot wait until after the fact and follow opinion polls. Leaders must mold opinion, they must inspire youth—28 million young people between the ages of 18 and 24 are eligible, 17 million unregistered. They are the difference.

Leaders must motivate the party, not monopolize it. We must speak to the third world, where three-fourths of the people on earth exist. Leadership must be believable, it must reconcile the rural farmer and the urban consumer. The rainbow coalition is a way out for the locked out. We are reaching back to those who have been forgotten and rejected and despised. We must restore confidence in our national leadership.

We as a nation have the capacity to destroy the world. We also are so civilized and so moral, ultimately, that we will choose another way. We will choose to feed and clothe and heal; we will choose to freeze the weapons and not burn the people and freeze the planet.

We must choose a more excellent way. I'm standing here today as a member of this body of distinguished leaders. I've come from further back than any of them have come from. I intend to go further. I represent for this party and for this nation a chance and a choice. I'm not looking for a voter; I'm looking for a partner. Together we can make a difference.

Overall, I thought Jackson had done a better job than at Dartmouth in developing and distinguishing his issue positions from the other candidates'. And I now realized that he was able to state his positions forcefully and fully while simultaneously blending in well with the ebb and flow of the debate. Two Iowa residents who watched the debate commented on this. Said one: "I was much more favorably impressed than I thought I would be. . . . I liked his symbolism, his way of presenting his views. He speaks very knowledgeably and to the point without extra words." And the other Iowa resident drove the point home. "I'm kind of excited about him," she said, "he's really got me interested. I didn't see his color after a while, and if anyone would notice color, we would. We're not used to it."[11]

After Iowa I felt much better. I could see Jackson taking increasing advantage of the opportunities afforded by the debates. However, I should have known that, as politics would have it, things would not continue to go as they had at Dartmouth and Iowa. Each debate would reflect the changing dynamics and issues of the nomination campaign. For example, Jackson's successful mission in early January to seek the release of Lt. Robert Goodman from a Syrian prison camp measurably increased his visibility and credibility as a presidential candidate. And this in turn brought increased attention and scrutiny by the media and others and the revelations of contributions from Arab interests to People United to Save Humanity (PUSH). During the Iowa debate Jackson was asked to comment on contributions from Arab interests to "his civil rights organization" (PUSH) as they might relate to what some consider his strong pro-Arab positions. But the issue was not forced, and Jackson stated his position convincingly, saying that "what is at stake here is not a legal matter, not my integrity, but an organizational judgment," that of the PUSH Foundation, with which he had no "affiliation with at all."[12] Jackson reiterated his views of a Middle East policy which "must not just relate to Israel adequately but relate to other Arab nations properly, because as a superpower we must reconcile our moral, economic, political, geopolitical and military interest."[13]

But these were far from the last words Jackson would say on this matter. The report of Jackson's Hymie remark and the subsequent Farrakhan intervention fed the appetites of those who saw Jackson's Middle East policy as pro-Arab and saw him as anti-Semitic. Thus, rather than being able to pursue the positive opportunities which the debates offered, Jackson found himself often on the defensive, attempting to deny anti-Semitic charges or to explain his relationship with Minister Farrakhan. He was asked repeatedly whether or not he referred to Jews as "Hymies" and to New York as "Hymietown." Though I thought Jackson should have been more definitive in his denial, I grew tired of this persistent line of questioning, which gradually reminded me of valiant attempts to break down the witness in an amateurish cross-examination. Thus, whether Jackson did or did not make the comments was in my view being overshadowed by the seemingly hostile manner and tone of the questioning.

To be sure, presidential candidates must be circumspect about their every move and comment, especially those that could cast aspersions or reflect negatively on a long deprived or persecuted group. But with all the monumental issues which we face at home and abroad (e.g., hunger, poverty, unemployment, threats of nuclear war), I found the preoccupation with the Hymie matter most frustrating. The continued badgering in any one particular session came close to amounting to overkill and hence to arousing sympathy for Jackson. Obviously, repeated questioning did prod Jackson to "confess," but I thought the media—like our criminal justice system—must remain alert to the manner in which such confessions are elicited.

Similarly, in the Texas debate, Jackson faced repeated questioning about Minister Farrakhan's open denunciation of Jews and alleged threats on the life of Milton Coleman, the *Washington Post* reporter who first broke the Hymie story. Indeed, the Farrakhan situation became so salient that both Senator Hart and Vice President Mondale found it expedient to use the forum of the debate to directly criticize Jackson.

Mondale and Hart also strategically distanced themselves from Jackson's call for abolition of runoff primaries in the South, an issue that Jackson considered central to his campaign. A number of party leaders from the South (where runoffs are chiefly used) had strongly criticized Jackson's position; this included the chairman of the Texas state Democratic party. Rather than outright abolition, Mondale and eventually Hart called for state-by-state analysis to weed out runoffs that had racially discriminatory effects. This open and direct criticism of Jackson by his two rivals was noteworthy. Prior to this time, conventional wisdom was that white candidates were very careful about their criticisms and treatment of Jackson lest they alienate black voters whose support was considered crucial to Democratic victory in November. Nonetheless, by the time of the Texas debate (May 2) circumstances had changed sufficiently so that both Mondale and Hart found it necessary, and apparently worth the risks, to criticize and distance themselves from Jackson. Of course, their actions could also have been viewed in terms of what they perceived as the benefits—e.g., increased support from the Jewish community and the traditional proclivities of blacks to vote Democratic no matter what.

As I viewed the Texas debate, I found that the more Jackson was criticized, the more I was determined to support him, for overall, I believed that the bedrock of Jackson's campaign—the full inclusion of the locked out and all that implied—transcended by far the weaknesses and pitfalls to which Jackson himself had succumbed or for which he was otherwise criticized. I also considered this to be *the* fundamental issue on which the political leadership of both parties continued to falter. Overall, however, these negative aspects of the debates did not overshadow their many bright spots.

In general, I thought Jackson profited greatly from the debates, from the sheer television exposure which otherwise he surely would not have had. The American people were able to see for themselves, to assess his demeanor, to hear his positions first hand, and to evaluate his responses, rejoinders, and interactions with his fellow candidates. And during the final debate—when the field had dwindled to three— each candidate had more opportunity to show his wares, and each seemed to have profited, particularly Jackson. Soon after the New York debates (March 28), for example, the *Christian Science Monitor* headlined that "TV TURNS CAMPAIGN INTO 'FRITZ, GARY, AND JESSE SHOW'."[11] With respect to Jackson the *Monitor* said:

> The Rev. Jesse Jackson is the prime crowd-pleaser at debates. With pithy remarks, he cuts through a lot of the political rhetoric, and regularly gets the most applause from the audience.
>
> Through the debates, Mr. Jackson's personality and his way with words have caught the fancy of a sizable segment of voters, and have helped him raise funds and win a small but respectable number of white votes.

In the end, of course, the black vote proved crucial to Jackson's survival in the debates and the campaign. And while other aspects of his campaign (e.g., rallies, impromptu speeches) helped him to harness this vote, the TV debates undoubtedly helped to cement Jackson's hold on the black vote.

The televised debates (and television generally) helped Jackson in another important way. Near the end of the primary campaign, the media apparently were determined to play up the "two-man horse race" between Mondale and Hart, leaving Jackson as an also-ran. Even in the debates Mondale and Hart tended to talk to each other, ignoring Jackson, overlooking his comments, attacking each other. This kind of treatment seemed at times impolite and even downright offensive. But television and the televised debates proved Jackson's savior, allowing him to rescue and even benefit himself. Jackson simply refused to be short-changed or locked out.

The New York debate provided a good example. From the beginning, despite the moderating efforts of Dan Rather, Mondale and Hart clearly were going for the jugular. At times the two seemed to completely forget that Jackson and even Rather were there. But the experienced Rather and the vintage Jackson were not about to be upstaged by two mere politicians. Jackson, just like Mondale and Hart, had much to gain or lose from the debate, which was nationally televised and held just a few days prior to the crucial New York presidential primary. Hence, I delighted in watching Rather and especially Jackson, each in his own way, maintain their essential roles in what threatened to be a runaway debate between Hart and Mondale.

The burden for Rather, of course, was clearly defined: he had to effectively carry out his prescribed role as moderator, which he did. But Jackson's role as participant was much more uncertain and difficult. Indeed Mondale and Hart did not address their comments to Jackson and seemed to overlook any comments he made toward them. Nonetheless, Jackson rose to the occasion. At one memorable point in the debate, for example, Jackson decided to address his remarks directly to Rather. At the small table at which all were seated, Jackson sat directly across from Rather, facing him and the studio audience, between Hart and Mondale, who faced each other. With a wave of his arms, Jackson interrupted one of the many Mondale-Hart faceoffs and suggested to Rather that he might wish to stop their repeated arguments, since they really amounted to nothing more than a kinship struggle between two people going in the same direction. "Tomorrow the issue will be this rat-a-tat-tat," said Jackson. Speaking in the manner of a dispassionate analyst rather than an involved participant, Jackson observed that "the reason why they're having such a kinship struggle is there's such a similarity in policies."[15] This was vintage Jackson and drew the only applause from the audience of about 200 as they witnessed the proceedings in Columbia University's Low Memorial Library.

The New York debate sent a clear message: television is Jackson's medium. He knows how to use it and projects very well. Plus he is too articulate, too knowledgeable, too savvy, and just plain too charismatic to be ignored by a Hart or a Mondale or anyone else. Additionally, what Jackson symbolized in the campaign was just too great to be brushed aside. Black Americans and many others knew full well that Jackson represented their interests and concerns. Many had seen him in person long before the 1984 campaign, and now many more saw him on television.

Jackson's candidacy unquestionably engendered a deep sense of pride and inspiration and held a tremendous appeal for Black Americans. Consider, for example, comments made during a group interview of black voters arranged by the *Wall Street Journal* in late May 1984. "I plan to vote for Jackson," said one, "for the simple fact that he's inspired me. He made me feel good about a lot of things." Or as a school nurse put it, "Working with youngsters who have a poor self-image, watching him (Jackson) on television, it sort of like turns them around." Another voter said that when her friends were criticizing Jackson for his Hymie remark and giving her all sorts of arguments for not voting for Jackson, she found it necessary to "give them the bottom line." "I'm voting for Jesse Jackson," she said, "because he's black and he needs my vote." Additionally, when another black person was asked whether a black child had a fair chance in today's society, the *Wall Street Journal* reported that the entire group of blacks in the room broke out in laughter at what they considered a ridiculous question. But the black woman to whom the question was addressed apparently summarized well the mood of the group and many blacks generally when she said that a black child could not get a fair chance in today's society. "Society is not ready for that," she said. "They're not going to give you a fair chance. Why, I don't know. I think the majority of white people have a fetish against black people. They don't want to live next door to you and are not going to go to school with you."[16]

Making Society Ready

On the campaign trail, however, Jackson was doing his best to make society ready. He hit hard at civil rights issues: the Reagan

administration's tragic record with respect to enforcement of civil
rights laws such as the Voting Rights Act; the rules and structures
imposed by the Democratic party and government generally (delegate selection rules, at-large elections, runoff primaries) that inhibit
black political representation and development; and the obvious indifference to civil rights indicated by the increasingly conservative
trends in public opinion and American politics.

Despite opposition from certain key black leaders and his own
campaign mistakes, Jackson's candidacy increasingly maintained its
strong appeal among blacks. And the appeal went beyond racial pride,
self-esteem, and civil rights issues. Although Jackson obviously recognized the special appeal his campaign had for the black community, he conceived his constituency as being much larger. From his
initial entry, Jackson viewed himself as spokesman for those excluded
or disillusioned by current policies or by politics in general. Hence,
on the domestic front he aligned himself with women and minorities,
the poor, the homeless, the unemployed, the aged, the environmentalist, the small farmer, the "little guy." He pressed hard for the
bread-and-butter issues—for jobs, for decent education and housing,
for the elimination of poverty, for an economy where the least of us
could enjoy life with dignity and self-respect. And though supportive
of private enterprise, Jackson recognized government's necessary
role in assuring all persons a decent standard of life.

He also strongly advocated new directions in our international
affairs and foreign policy. Above all, he believed that the nation
should have adequate defense, but he advocated cutting in our military budget without endangering our defense needs. He was the
only candidate who proposed a flat 20 percent cut. He wanted new
initiatives in disarmament and nuclear policy, and advocated a verifiable freeze on nuclear weapons and pledged a no-first-strike policy.
He stated repeatedly his preference for the "human race" over the
"nuclear race." Moreover, in face of suspicion and outright criticism,
he boldly advocated a Middle East policy that would include the
entire region, considering the interests of both Israel and her Arab
neighbors. He wanted new policy initiatives toward Central America
and the Third World in general and a strong, unequivocal stand
against South Africa and its apartheid policies.

Jackson also proved a daring and courageous candidate, willing to
participate in actions or events that would invariably involve risks—

Table 5.1 1984 Democratic Primary Turnout (Selected Primaries)

State	1984 Turnout	1980 Turnout	Black Areas	Total Change 1980-84
Alabama	428,283	237,464	+ 87%	+80.4%
California	2,724,248	3,363,969	n.a.	−19.0
Florida	1,160,713	1,098,003	+ 38	+ 5.7
Georgia	684,541	384,780	+ 14	+77.9
Illinois	1,659,425	1,201,067	+ 19	+38.2
Indiana	716,955	589,441	+ 29	+21.6
Maryland	506,886	477,090	+ 33	+ 6.2
New Jersey	698,893	560,908	+ 82	+21.0
New York	1,387,950	989,062	+127	+40.3
North Carolina	960,857	737,262	+ 53	+30.3
Ohio	1,444,797	1,186,410	+ 36	+21.8
Pennsylvania	1,656,294	1,613,551	+ 32	+ 2.6
Tennessee	322,063	294,680	+ 58	+ 9.3

Sources: Turnout and Total Change: "Guide to the 1984 Democratic National Convention," *Congressional Quarterly* (CQ Press, 1984), p. 37. Black Areas (precincts in which blacks comprise 80% or more of the total population): Thomas E. Cavanagh and Lorn S. Foster, *Jesse Jackson's Campaign: The Primaries and Caucuses*, The Joint Center for Political Studies, Election '84, Report #2, p. 17.

the kind of risks which mainline candidates, such as Mondale or Hart, would be unlikely to take. Jackson, however, had little choice. Since his was indeed a poor campaign with a rich message, Jackson knew that, for that message to reach the voters, he must attract attention to get media coverage. And Jackson had the courage and flair to engage in such risky but also potentially beneficial activities, such as his trip to Syria to seek the release of Lt. Robert Goodman. Although subject to criticism and adverse reactions, this act did symbolize dramatically Jackson's strong belief that foreign policy crises should be settled through peaceful negotiations rather than military might.

Similarly, Jackson demonstrated his deep commitment to human rights and the poor by his repeated forays into the urban slums and ghettos, the barrios, the projects, and the homes of the poor, the disfranchised, the locked out. Such forays lent an authenticity and credibility to Jackson's campaign on behalf of this growing dispossessed sector of the party and the nation, demonstrating emphatically that Jackson really was with the "least of these" and giving depth

and meaning to his words. For example, after spending the night
with a family in the South Bronx (New York City), Jackson said at a
rally:

> They are living in the slum, but the slum is not living in them.
>
> There's another side of the Bronx, a family intact, a religious
> family, a man with cancer in his body feeding the hungry people
> of the area.
>
> Even though we stayed there to dramatize the plight, there
> are 180,000 families in New York in line to get into public
> housing, living on top of people. We are going to stay night after
> night right down bottom where the boats are stuck. We are going
> to be the conscience of this campaign.[17]

Of course other candidates had similar photo opportunities to identify with causes, but close and repeated identification with the poor
and the dispossessed of society has become less attractive to mainline
politicians—especially presidential candidates. Understandably,
members of the family were honored for Jackson to come to their
home, for they felt that in this way he could "marshal people and
help accomplish some of the things that are important." And a neigh-
bor of the family told Jackson: "Thanks for coming into the neighborhood. Mondale won't and Hart won't."

Jackson also symbolized and dramatized the plight of those he
represented by his strong and persistent attacks against both the
runoff primary in the South and the Democratic party rules governing the selection and apportionment of national convention delegates. Where no candidate receives a majority in the primary election, a second primary pits the two top vote-getters against each
other in a runoff.[18] Instituted about the turn of the century, the runoff
is deeply entrenched in Southern politics. Runoff supporters felt that
such a system has been necessary in predominantly one-party areas
to insure that the eventual party nominee represents a majority of
Democratic party voters. While this might have been true, Jackson
and his supporters felt the runoff allowed the South yet another
device to inhibit or prevent black political participation and representation and hence assure continued white dominance of the Democratic party and politics in the South. Invariably, Jackson con-
tended, if a runoff involved a white candidate against a black
candidate, strong white bloc voting would insure defeat of the black

candidate. To Jackson, therefore, the runoff operated just as at-large elections, literacy tests, and other devices that, though racially neutral on their face, nonetheless inhibit blacks and minorities.

For the same reason Jackson strongly attacked national Democratic party rules that he thought impaired the effective and full representation of blacks and minorities in the presidential nominating process, especially in the national convention. Specifically, Jackson attacked delegate allocation formulas such as those based on winner-take-all rules and on a 20-percent-threshold rule that required a presidential candidate to garner at least 20 percent of the vote in a given electoral area to be accorded any delegate representation from that area at the national convention. Further, Jackson attacked the superdelegate rule that guaranteed automatic selection of elected public officials and party leaders as delegates to the national convention. Jackson charged that these rules unfairly limited the delegate potential of his candidacy and hence the influence in the party of those groups he represented.[19]

Nor was Jackson mollified by party rules that required that half of the delegates be women and that minority groups (such as blacks) be represented in proportion to their presence in the population. In fact, these numbers were met by the Democrats in 1984, but Jackson was interested in more than mere numbers being present in San Francisco. Jackson and his supporters were concerned about the relative influence of black and minority delegates in the convention. Indeed, as I viewed it, the major thrust of Jackson's campaign was not that such groups be proportionately represented under the rubric of traditional party candidates or interests, such as Mondale or Hart or organized labor but that Jackson felt the delegate selection rules should permit these groups, if they so chose, to be represented through a new force (hopefully himself) at the bargaining table. But the very purpose of such party rules was clearly to prevent or at least impede the development of such a new force.

Jackson's attacks on the runoff as well as on Democratic party rules undoubtedly upset many persons. Some, of course, stated that, having entered the contest, Jackson was obliged to play by the rules of the game that were in place when the game started. But I saw this as wistful and extraneous thinking. The entire character of Jackson's campaign demanded that he raise such issues, attack rules and structures that, on close examination, would disadvantage blacks and minorities from full and effective participation in the political game.

Overall, Jackson's attacks on established electoral and party rules took advantage of opportunities which he could ill afford to miss to both symbolize and dramatize how the rules of the political game constrain blacks and minorities. His position forced all of us to remember that rules or structures are not neutral; they promote and safeguard certain interests and inhibit and hurt others.

Downsides and Flaws:
The Campaign that Might Have Been

Even as I celebrated the successes of Jackson's campaign, I could not help but see problems, some attributable to the candidate and some to others. Throughout it all, I thought of the campaign that might have been. For example, what might have happened if Jackson had not started his campaign so late, or had had more success in uniting black leaders and others for his candidacy, or had developed and instituted more systematic fund-raising activities during the early pre-campaign period? I wondered how different the campaign might have been if more time and resources had been put into the development and operation of the campaign organization and the consequent development of a more holistic campaign strategy. I wondered what might have happened if it had been possible to devote more time and effort to building the Rainbow Coalition, to push issues and programs that appealed in a real way to all or most of those locked-out groups that Jackson wished to bring into his coalition. I wondered what might have happened if there had been a more obvious systematic development of policy papers and more careful planning for concrete alternatives to deal with problems and conditions which Reagan was being criticized for exacerbating (hunger, unemployment, poverty). I wondered what might have happened if the Hymie incident had not occurred or if Jackson had immediately acknowledged his error in making such remarks. I wondered what might have happened if Jackson had had sufficient funds to mount an aggressive media campaign to compete with those mounted by other candidates. I wondered what might have happened if the media had not tabbed Jackson as a black candidate and repeatedly minimized his chances of winning and if media coverage of Jackson had not grown more negative as the campaign wore on.

And these were not just idle wonderments on my part. Time and again I encountered vivid examples that brought home the realistic dimensions of my concerns. During the campaign, for example, I had several calls from interested colleagues and friends who wished to give time, expertise, and even money to Jackson's campaign but did not know who to contact. And since they had seen me on local television or heard me on radio talking about Jackson, they thought I might be able to tell them what to do. When I suggested that they call either Jackson's local campaign office or his national campaign headquarters in Washington, they said they had done this, and that the phone number was not listed, or that there was no answer or the lines were always busy, especially at the national headquarters.

Stories abounded of poor planning, haphazard scheduling, on-the-spot changes—mostly by the candidate himself—and just plain confusion. I saw some inklings of this, as in the situation discussed in chapter 2, in which a political scientist friend of mine invited me to join a policy group to help Jackson and subsequently we learned that such a group was already operating and did not need us. Clearly I had no way of knowing how this confusion came about; all I know is what I experienced. To me this was a sign of poor coordination, poor planning, or at least a failure to utilize available resources. And I know of a number of other persons whose expertise and aid— including money—were not tapped at all or as fully as they might have been.

Another example. Before a campaign appearance in St. Louis in mid-April 1984, Jackson's people in charge of local arrangements solicited and received special donations (about $100 per person) from supporters who wished to join Reverend Jackson at a brief reception following his public speech. After the public event, special donors did gather in the reception room, awaiting the candidate's appearance. However, after some thirty or forty minutes of waiting, a local Jackson spokeman apologetically told the group that, because of fatigue (which undoubtedly was true) and an imposing schedule starting early the next morning (also true), Jackson would be unable to come to the reception as planned. Clearly I sensed that most everyone understood the situation, but just as clearly I sensed some disappointment, especially given the early buildup of the special chance to meet Reverend Jackson. Such last-minute changes and adjustments invariably occur in campaigning, but such disappointments as these obviously must be minimized as much as possible.

Similarly, the matter of issue selection and development also became crucial to Jackson's campaign, especially with respect to finding that common ground on which the locked out could be brought into the Rainbow Coalition. During the campaign, I did encounter some criticism of Jackson for making the abolition of the runoff primary in the South the litmus test issue—i.e., for determining whether particular individual leaders were *really* concerned about the plight of the locked out. I myself found the runoff issue appealing, since it reflected more broadly on how so-called neutral rules and structures might help or impede group progress, which I saw as one of the most valuable lessons of Jackson's campaign. Nonetheless, the runoff was certainly not the kind of issue that affected all or most would-be rainbow groups across the board and directly as would, say, problems of unemployment, underemployment, job training, and job loss to overseas markets.

Additionally, of course, the Hymie incident hurt Jackson. It occurred at a time when his campaign seemed to be catching hold, after his glowing success in winning release of Lt. Goodman from a Syrian prison camp and just before the New Hampshire primary. And Jackson's repeated denials only prolonged the agony. Perhaps most damaging to Jackson personally, the Hymie remark and resulting publicity undercut much of the liberal character and high moral tone which I believe Jackson's campaign projected much more effectively than any others along these dimensions. In the end, however, perhaps most damaging to Jackson's overall campaign is that his remark hurt both ways: it provided not only a valid basis for criticism but also a convenient cover for those who wanted to criticize or minimize the effects of Jackson's campaign without appearing racist.

Jackson and the Media: From Positive to Negative

Throughout the campaign I made every effort, with the aid of others, to watch Jackson's television appearances, to read what the print media had to say about him, to observe how the media reacted to and treated Jackson. Early on, the media helped Jackson by treating him as it would any other candidate running for the presidency. And in this context the fact that he was black illustrated the increasing openness and democratization of the system. It also demonstrated the increased use of electoral politics by blacks and others to achieve their political objectives. Thus, early on, media coverage helped to advance Jackson's candidacy. Moreover, the fact that Jackson was good copy helped him to gain free media attention, something that he very much needed in view of his limited resources.

But as I observed the campaign, I thought media coverage also hurt Jackson. Indeed, frequent repetition of the view that Jackson had almost no chance to win—even though accurate—did risk, as one study aptly put it, "taking on the quality of a self-fulfilling prophecy."[20] I thought this hurt Jackson badly; nobody (except perhaps the most committed) likes to back a person who has little or no chance of winning or of affecting the election outcome in a real way. And I thought this view clearly influenced the way Jackson's campaign was covered (see chapter 8).

More than this, considering how the matter of race has hurt blacks in the American political-social order, I became increasingly concerned with the media's repeated references to Jackson as the "black presidential candidate." I found one incident particularly disturbing. In a "Meet the Press" show, Marvin Kalb asked Jackson, "Are you a black man who happens to be an American running for the presidency, or are you an American who happens to be a black man running for the presidency?" The question puzzled and disturbed me, and I really was at somewhat of a loss at how to express my feelings. Jackson was not; his response was most appropriate and to the point: "You ask a funny, Catch-22 kind of question." And it was just that. As I read and reflected about this incident, my feelings were perhaps best captured by one study that suggested that "the dichotomy between blackness and Americanism implicit in the question can be interpreted as a casual slur on Jackson's patriotism, if not the patriotism of black Americans in general."[21]

In addition, I thought the media's coverage of the Hymie incident almost amounted to an overkill. Although Jackson had only himself to blame for the remarks and for failing to acknowledge his error in a timely and forthright manner, it did appear to me and to others that "the tone of the media coverage and commentary took a sharply negative turn." As two writers put it, "The media seemed almost relieved to be able to criticize a black candidate in the name of defending liberal values."[22]

Long after the heat of the campaign had subsided, I was relieved to find out that my observations and feelings about the media's treatment of Jackson were not without foundation. Indeed, after an obviously systematic, painstaking, and meticulous review of news clips and other data, one study concluded that on the whole the media did treat Jackson as a "horse of a different color."[23]

Overall, despite the opposition of some black leaders, the late start and limited resources, the problems of organizing staff and developing concrete policy proposals, the biased media coverage, and his own self-inflicted wounds, Jackson received consistent, overwhelming support from Black Americans throughout the primaries. He provided inspiration and incentive to those who have long felt forgotten, overlooked, or who have been treated unfairly, deprived of or restricted in the privileges and opportunities that should rightfully be theirs and that would help them develop to their full potential. These persons, especially Black Americans, supported Jackson because he supported them; he supported *their* interests. The campaign and television debates served to facilitate this mutual feeling. And this mutual feeling inspired me to become more directly involved.

6

The Making of a Delegate

Some Background Perspectives

April 18, 1984, was the date of the first official step in the Missouri caucus system for the selection of delegates to the Democratic National Convention—city and township caucuses. By that time, of course, I had realized that I could not remain neutral and uninvolved in the Jackson campaign—the scholar-researcher studying and analyzing the Jackson campaign, preserving scholarly objectivity—and had become firmly and openly committed to Jesse Jackson's candidacy.[1] Originally, I planned to do the kind of field-observation research usefully undertaken by scholars in a number of areas.[2] I thought research on Jackson's campaign would both clarify a number of matters in my continuous analysis of black politics and, specifically, unearth information and insights that could prove helpful in revising the 1980 edition of *Black Americans and the Political System*.[3] Accordingly, I set my research plans in motion.

In October 1983 I contacted Jackson's state coordinator in Missouri, attorney Charles Bussey, in order to discuss my research plans and to seek his cooperation. Although I had heard of Bussey, I did not know him. But I shall never forget my discussions with him. We met at a luncheon at the Washington University–St. Louis Faculty Club—Whittemore House, an elegant old mansion. At the appointed hour, I saw a rather tall, immaculately dressed, youthful black man enter the Faculty Club, and recognizing his inquisitive look, I approached him. (A friend of mine had given me a fairly good description of Bussey, thus I was not wildly asking any black man I saw whether he was "so and so," a practice to which I have been subjected and misidentified more than I would like to remember.) Bussey was articulate, obviously sharp, and impressive in appearance—and after our luncheon, I could also say that his representations and comments on behalf of Jackson were equally impressive—well considered and thought out.

Having requested the luncheon, I wasted little time in getting down to business. I told Bussey about my work in black politics, in constitutional law and civil liberties, and in American politics generally. I then mentioned my special research interest in the Jackson campaign and my intention to remain detached from the battle. Bussey listened attentively and appreciatively to my plans. In fact, he was most encouraging and indicated that he too would be pleased if black scholars would avail themselves of this opportunity. With my intended role in the Jackson campaign clarified, we then talked about ways in which my research effort could be aided—e.g., making one or two campaign trips with Rev. Jackson, attending meetings of Jackson groups at the state and local levels, setting up interviews with key people—in short, we talked about the research-analyst's central need for access. Bussey assured me that he would help in any way he could.

At this point I wanted to know more about the Jackson organization. And Bussey came prepared—brief case and all. The lawyer's penchant for planning and organization came through clearly. He explained in some detail his plans and hopes for the Jackson organization in St. Louis and Missouri. I was most impressed. As some would put it, Bussey really had his stuff together—outlined on paper, supplemented with charts, graphs, data—all a researcher's delight. Our luncheon lasted some two hours and in my view was altogether profitable: I had made a key contact and my research plans were on track.

Some two months passed before I talked to Bussey again. I was gathering background material on the Jackson campaign, making TV appearances, answering questions on radio talk shows, preparing papers for professional conferences and civic meetings—all devoted in one way or another to the Jackson campaign. However, the more I studied and discussed the Jackson campaign, the more difficult I found it to remain neutral, to remain uncommitted and above the battle. My close friends and family, even my two young daughters, were totally involved and openly and strongly supportive of Jackson. I too saw the Jackson effort not just as a political campaign but as the most dramatic holistic strategy that could be developed to remind us all of the unfulfilled objectives of Martin Luther King and the civil rights movement and to warn us that the movement's earlier gains were in danger. In my own area, for example, I could see the obvious lack of real attention and concern for increasing the number of black students and black scholars on our university and college campuses. Indeed, even the hallowed halls of the academy were not sufficiently thick to keep one from feeling the dwindling opportunities and resources so urgently needed to combat persistent racism and inequities. By his decision to seek the presidency Jackson obviously became the symbol for the reinvigoration, formulation, and implementation of something very much larger than himself.

Moreover, the Jackson candidacy finally gave me the first realistic opportunity to become an actual delegate to a Democratic National Convention. In this regard, I could not help but reflect on my life as a black person growing up in my small hometown of Franklinton, Louisiana, during the 1930s and 1940s. Not only there, but in the South generally, blacks were not accorded even simple respect and dignity as persons, much less fundamental rights as United States citizens. To think of going as a delegate to a national party convention—to help select a presidential candidate—would have been among the most ultimate of dreams.

Thus, I did not find "idle rhetoric" or "dramatic alliteration" in Jackson's oft-repeated comment that one may be "born in the slum but the slum need not be born in him." This Jackson comment was very personal and real to me. I remember all too well the hardships and indignities that my parents (though well educated) and we as a family suffered only because of our race and color! Likewise, I remember thinking—as I saw whites posturing in their roles as "superior persons"—how shallow and dense many of them were. Nonetheless, I knew very well that they were enjoying this higher status, this higher quality of life, simply because they were white and that law and tradition both accorded and protected them in this role.

Even so, I now remember with pride how my family and many other blacks endured, despite subhuman conditions and situations to which we were subjected: segregated and inferior everything—dirt and gravel roads, little food and meager housing, delapidated public schools. The "colored" schools, as they were called, were indescribably bad. Nonetheless, with no thanks to the white power elite, we were blessed with a few "colored" teachers who recognized that such conditions need not and must not retard our learning, inhibit our development, and generally tarnish our self-image. Fortunately, my parents recognized this too. Of course, these conditions made it awfully difficult for blacks to negotiate the pains and pitfalls of segregation and discrimination, and many, including some very good persons of my acquaintance, simply did not survive this vicious system.

My undergraduate college days at Southern University in Baton Rouge (the "Negro" college, as it was referred to in that day) were also reminiscent of the deprivation suffered by blacks. Black students could not even think of going to Louisiana State University, the white state university with all its facilities. But at Southern, just as in my hometown high school, I found some good teachers who were training us to be leaders and who constantly and proudly proclaimed—as I later found to be true—that despite obvious difficulties they were preparing us to compete with all persons, whatever their color or background. Because of one of these teachers, the late Dr. Rodney Higgins, I became engrossed in political science, in the whys and hows of politics and governments.

During my stay at Southern (1945-1949), I became intensely interested in the role and importance of national party conventions. The 1948 Democratic National Convention eventually nominated Harry Truman, but not without a deep split over the question of race and civil rights which resulted in the walkout of the Southern Democrats. This convention caught my attention, gave a measure of reality to my courses in American government and politics, and stirred me, from that time on, to become a convention watcher.

But it was not until 1960, long after graduation from Southern and a few years after acquiring my Ph.D. from the University of Illinois–Urbana that I was able to get a more proximate feel for Democratic nomination politics. As a young instructor at the then newly created University of Wisconsin–Milwaukee, I became active in the Milwaukee county Democratic party organization. Eventually, I became political action chairman (or some such title) of the county party. At long last, I was beginning to have the opportunity to engage in party politics in a real way, doing and observing firsthand things that previously I was only able to study from books or listen to on radio and later watch on television.

The politics of the approaching 1960 presidential election indicated clearly that the Wisconsin presidential primary of that year would be a crucial battleground for a heated and potentially divisive contest between Hubert Humphrey and John F. Kennedy for the Democratic presidential nomination. Kennedy, of course, was trying to become the very first Catholic to win the presidency; and Humphrey was well remembered not only for his crucial role in the 1948 convention in pushing through a strong civil rights plank but for his long support of the poor, the working man, the "least of these." Somehow, as this battle shaped up, everything began to come together for me. I wanted to study the Humphrey-Kennedy contest, to see close up what happens in a presidential primary and what happens in a national convention. My aspirations were high: I wanted to go all the way to Los Angeles, where the 1960 convention was to be held; and I wanted to do all of this—the study, the field observation, the research—while simultaneously retaining a measure of involvement so as to get as full a feel as possible for the presidential nomination process.

Fortunately, both the Humphrey and Kennedy organizations acceded to my request to tag along on several of their campaign trips with the hordes of media people who followed them around the state, and I did so.[1] And to cap things off for me, Wisconsin Democratic state party officials and the Eagleton Institute of Politics of Rutgers State University made it possible for me to follow my research interests all the way to the Los Angeles convention. Party officials gave the crucial "access" to delegate caucus meetings, and the Eagleton Institute gave me (and a number of other political scientists) the funds necessary to attend the convention and carry on my research project. All of this was great; I remember with pleasure the wonderful experiences involved and the publication which resulted therefrom.[3]

However, the experiences only whetted my appetite to become a full-fledged, accredited delegate. I did not want to observe again from the sidelines; I wanted to be actually involved. But, not unexpectedly, this appetite was tempered not only by time and inter-

vening professional interests but also by the continuing limited opportunities for blacks in politics generally and in presidential politics
in particular.

By 1983, however, things began to stir again. The debate over
whether or not there should be a black presidential candidate rekindled my memories and aspirations. My research interests had also
progressed and developed, and for a time, as indicated earlier, these
prevailed over my personal interests and aspirations. These personal-
professional cross pressures were highest on me during the Christmas
holidays of 1983, when I had the chance to think and the time and
opportunity to talk with colleagues and friends. And at some point
soon after this Christmas break, I began to lean more and more
toward active involvement and commitment to the Jackson campaign. The precise turning point was my decision to join a policy
committee to aid Jackson's campaign, a circumstance that never materialized. Nonetheless, in arriving at this decision, I reasoned that
I could still study and analyze the campaign but as participant-observer rather than as a detached, neutral scholar. Thus long before
April 18, 1984, the first step in the long process for the selection of
Missouri's 1984 Democratic national convention delegates, I had
become a strong and avid supporter of Jesse Jackson. And I thought
with great relief that I had resolved my role dilemma.

The Necessary First Step—
The April 18th Township Caucus

But my personal-professional dilemmas would recur time and
again. Indeed, even my actual presence at the April 18 township
caucus depended on whether or not I would attend a long-scheduled,
out-of-town professional meeting. I was at the time president of the
National Conference of Black Political Scientists; our national meetings were being held in Washington, D.C., in mid-April, and the pre-
conference meeting of the executive board was scheduled in Washington on Wednesday, April 18. Ordinarily, for a long-established
and fully developed organization, a president's attendance at a particular executive council meeting or any other meeting for that matter is relatively unimportant. At the time, I was also president of the
Midwest Political Science Association, and I fully understood the
nominal honor attached to presidents of professional organizations.

However, the NCOBPS was still a developing organization, and somehow I thought my presence could be important. Indeed, the potential contributions of NCOBPS to the training and development of future black scholars is for me a matter of very high priority. But I also considered my participation in my local township caucus as a Jackson supporter very important; Missouri's second congressional district, and particularly my home township, was anything but a hotbed of support for Jesse Jackson.

One telephone call to the president-elect of NCOBPS, Professor Huey Perry of Southern University–Baton Rouge, resolved my dilemma. Fortunately, Perry and I were not only close friends but, more important to me, also professional colleagues who attached great importance to the role of NCOBPS. And Perry also saw the Jackson campaign as a crucial development in black politics, one which we should in every way seek to promote and advance. So after discussing agendas and other matters, Perry assured me that I was doing the right thing and that both the executive board and NCOBPS membership generally would understand.

I was glad I could attend my township caucus with my wife and my daughter (a newly registered voter), but I remained somewhat apprehensive about the situation. I considered that the maximum we could do in my particular district was to see that Jackson's name was at least mentioned and placed in nomination; anything more would have been the height of wishful thinking. I knew of no concerted plans or efforts of the Jackson organization for our township, but I could understand why not much effort would be made. My township (Missouri River) is located in the Second Congressional District and includes one of St. Louis's most fashionable west-county suburban areas, Chesterfield. The few Democrats who live in my particular area are not likely to wear Jesse Jackson pins or sport his bumper stickers. Indeed, even though the congressional district was represented by a Democrat, Robert Young, I viewed Young as a conservative Democrat, far more congruent with the political climate in my district than a Jesse Jackson.[6] Jackson's organization understandably focused attention on those areas that looked more promising.

Nonetheless, as caucus meeting time drew near, I decided to call Charles Bussey and find out what, if anything, was being done in my area. Fortunately, despite his obviously heavy last-minute duties, I was able to reach Bussey, who expressed pleasure that I was actually planning to attend the caucus. And though he had had several calls such as mine, Bussey told me that he would really appreciate "all the help that you and anybody else can give us in Chesterfield." At this, both he and I laughed; the message was clear. When I indicated that I would be pleased to put Jackson's name in nomination if no one else had been designated, he again gave me the go-ahead, imploring me to arrive early and let my township chairman know what I planned to do. After a few more such instructions, I remember well telling Bussey that, after we had pulled some surprises in Chesterfield, I would call him later that evening. He told me how to reach him and wished us well.

After my conversation and at the last minute, my wife and I did make several phone calls to friends—a few blacks and whites—who we thought might be planning to go and might be disposed to support Jackson. We were able to reach only one or two persons who wanted to attend but were not quite certain. Frankly, these calls made me even more apprehensive that only my wife, daughter, and I and—stretching it—a very few others would be the only Jackson supporters among a crowd overwhemingly for Mondale and Hart, both of whom had made clear efforts to turn out supporters. Simultaneously, my wife and I became more determined than ever to represent Jesse, even if we were the only ones. Accordingly, I busied myself preparing about a three-minute nominating speech, one which I thought would reflect the important interests Jackson's candidacy represented.

Once at the caucus I was pleasantly surprised to find that some of my apprehensions about Jackson's chances in my township were more imagined than real. First, I was very much surprised at the unexpected sizeable support for Jackson's candidacy. Everything about past voting patterns and behavior in my township indicated that Jackson would have very few supporters, and even fewer who would turn out. But of the some 340 or so persons in attendance, some 46 persons came forward for Jackson on the initial call for division into individual candidate caucuses. The number of Jackson supporters came as a surprise not only to me but to several veteran observers of county politics as well. Of course, it was not at all surprising that, with the exception of one or two, blacks in the audience came forward en masse (some 34) to support Jackson.

I was surprised but delighted that this many blacks lived in the Chesterfield area. I soon discerned that a number of them were BUMPIES—Black Upwardly Mobile Professionals—well educated, highly skilled engineers, accountants, pharmacists, physicians. And it took Jesse Jackson to bring them out of the apartment and condominium complexes, the comfortable, middle-class homes hidden among the valleys, hills, and trees of suburban West County. But there were other blacks, not as upwardly mobile or as well educated, who had lived most of their lives in certain predominantly black enclaves which even today many do not know exist in Chesterfield. They too turned out for the township caucus. In the end, we all gathered this night to support a common cause, to support Jesse Jackson. And I was bursting with pride at this beautiful scene.

But equally as beautiful and surprising, to me and others, is that at least twelve to fourteen whites—young, middle aged, and older—also came forward to join the Jackson caucus. That Jackson could marshall this type of support in Chesterfield was indeed an unexpected but welcome development.

Another memorable aspect of my township caucus was the warm reception given to my nomination speech for Jackson. The nominations of Mondale and Hart met the expected enthusiastic support: they both were obviously well represented among the 340 or so persons in attendance. But it was far from clear how Jackson would be received. In the end, whether out of courtesy, the nature of my speech, or for other reasons, I was pleased that Jackson's nomination was received quite well. I was likewise pleased and surprised—so were others—when a middle-aged white woman came to the platform to second Jackson's nomination and made what I thought were some impressive remarks. To me just her appearance was important; at least, I thought, we had the makings of a "rainbow" even in Chesterfield. We did not think speeches would change anyone's position; we simply wanted to represent Jackson's cause in the dignified and forthright manner it deserved.

A third and most important aspect of the meeting was the coming together of the Nuclear Freeze and Jackson forces. To be sure, each group needed the other to become a viable caucus. Under state party rules, in order to be viable (to have the number necessary to be apportioned delegates to the congressional district caucus) a group must have at least 20 percent of the total number of persons in attendance at the caucus. In this instance, with approximately 340 persons present, some 68 persons were needed for a candidate caucus to be viable. Since we Jackson supporters had about two-thirds of that number (48), we needed an additional 20 or more persons to become viable, and as I surveyed the situation, the Nuclear Freeze group, which numbered about 27, was the logical and perhaps only possible group with which we could unite and simultaneously maintain our key positions.

What concerned me some, however, was the extent to which this union might be eroded by Freeze people who did not like Jackson's position on other matters or who might otherwise be influenced by the matter of race. Despite Jackson's repeated reference to women as a part of his Rainbow Coalition, for example, I have never been convinced that white women as a group wanted to be included. Fortunately, however, the leader of the Nuclear Freeze group, a white woman, Carole Hansen, and I, the temporary leader of the Jackson group, developed an immediate good rapport and working relationship. And though several Freeze persons, for whatever reasons, apparently opted to join other caucuses, in the end about twenty or so Freeze people joined our group to make the Jackson caucus viable. I shall never forget the loud cheers that erupted from all of us who now joined in this successful union. It was a beautiful, exciting scene.

Of course, the benefits and costs of union were clear to all: of the two delegates allotted to the now viable Jackson caucus, one would come from the original Jackson group and one from the Freeze group. And while our original Jackson group had about twice as many persons as those with Freeze, everyone understood that it was a good deal for both groups, neither of which would have any delegate representation at the congressional district caucus whatsoever except for merging our forces. I saw the merger as an especially good deal for us since many of the Nuclear Freeze people supported Jackson anyway. And what especially stands out in my mind is that while Carole Hansen and I were consulting with party leaders about formalities in selecting our two delegates, somehow an informal leadership emerged from our newly combined group, and when Carole and I returned to lay out procedures, an informal consensus over who our delegates to the congressional district should be was already jelling. And that consensus resulted in the selection of Carole Hansen and myself as the two delegates to the district caucus. The added plus, of course, was that Carole was a strong Jackson supporter.

Thus without doubt the story of the Missouri River Township caucus, as one veteran party leader told me, was "you Jackson people— whoever would have dreamed that Jackson would have two delegates (out of nine elected) coming from Chesterfield." I agreed that it was a wonderful and pleasant surprise. And with this a few of us were off to celebrate and to call Charles Bussey, who was surprised by the results from Chesterfield and obviously as thrilled as we were. Indeed, things were going very well for Jesse Jackson in the St. Louis area. It was a good night.

The next morning, I joined my professional colleagues at the NCOBPS meeting in Washington. Time and again I proudly recounted our unexpected success for Jesse Jackson. That evening, at a plenary session of the convention, I gave the annual presidential address: "Realism through Symbolism: Understanding Jesse Jackson's Campaign." And for this audience, appropriate academic jargon and standards were dutifully observed.

A Delegate Is Selected

On May 22, the next big day in the Missouri causus system for the selection of delegates to the Democratic National Convention, delegates selected in township and ward caucuses would convene in their respective congressional district conventions, where fifty-one of Missouri's eighty-six national convention delegates would be selected. Preparations for these conventions proceeded at an increasing pace. For some time the Jackson organization had conducted keep-up-the-spirit meetings every Monday evening at St. Paul's A.M.E. Church in St. Louis City. I attended several of these meetings, which focused primarily on problems and prospects of the First Congressional District. Most persons who attended were from that district—this was Congressman William "Bill" Clay's district—and Jackson forces seemed very much in control.

But the Second Congressional District was another matter. The congressman, Robert Young, staunchly supported Mondale, who also enjoyed strong support from organized labor leaders. Hart attracted strong support from the YUPPIE types in the district. Of course, Jackson too had pockets of strong support, mainly from black concentrations in certain suburban areas adjacent to or near St. Louis City. Even so, it was quite clear to me and others that Jackson's problems in the Second Congressional District were different from those in the first district.

Thus soon after our April 18 township caucus, I called Bussey to ask if he had any special plans for coordinating our district to prepare for the May 22 convention. I offered to convene a planning meeting for Jackson delegates from the second district, and Bussey immediately accepted my offer and agreed to attend. Accordingly, I invited our delegates to a meeting at my home in early May.

I must confess, however, that I was somewhat reluctant to call such a meeting: I certainly did not want to appear to be campaigning for the role of convention delegate. That's just not me. Rather, my main concern was that we Jackson delegates prepare for the upcoming congressional district caucus. I was so concerned that I called Bussey again and told him that unless he could assure me that he would attend I would not convene the meeting. I felt that if persons took the time to come to a meeting, on a Sunday afternoon yet, they should at least have someone who had much more information than I had, and that person, as I saw it, was Bussey. Bussey gave me his word that he would attend, and I am glad he did, and I am awfully glad we held the meeting.

For me it was one of the most memorable experiences of the campaign. All but one of the some seventeen Jackson delegates from the Second Congressional District attended, along with a few alternates and several other Jackson supporters—all together, about twenty-five persons, about four of whom were white, the rest black. To begin the meeting, each person was asked to say anything he or she wished, and not surprisingly the meeting soon took on the flavor of an old fashioned "testifying" meeting typically held in some black churches. One black woman delegate, for example, gave a particularly moving speech: "I sincerely believe," she said, "that God has really led Reverend Jackson to run in this campaign and to fill the void left by Dr. King." Delegate after delegate spoke of a strong principled commitment to Jesse Jackson, mentioning his strong positions on civil rights, on poverty, hunger, and unemployment, and his equally strong positions on foreign policy matters, on apartheid in South Africa, on nuclear testing, and generally his strong commitment to peace and justice.

One white delegate, also a Nuclear Freeze leader, spoke in glowing terms of Jackson's commitment to the freeze position and the excitement he brought to the overall campaign. Another white person—an alternate delegate from another district—spoke of the reactions to Jackson at her workplace. She told the group, "You might be surprised at what are still some of the views and perceptions about blacks among whites that are expressed over lunch and during breaks. . . . I think Jesse Jackson's candidacy is causing some of these people to rethink their views. . . . Some whites, I know, grudgingly admire Jackson's agressiveness and his articulation of issues." "I believe," she concluded, "that it cannot help but bring about gains." These were not just hollow comments; one could feel the depth of feeling and sincerity with which this young white woman spoke.

Still other delegates talked about how this was their initial venture into active party politics and how they had assumed or were thrust into leadership positions and were enjoying it. Without exception, all who spoke told of their deep and fundamental reasons for supporting Jackson and of their equally deep commitment to his cause. And some of those present openly expressed their interest in becoming national convention delegates. After this testifying session, Charles Bussey got down to the real nuts and bolts, the politics of national convention delegate selection in the Second Congressional District, which most of us definitely needed. While testifying bolstered our spirits, we needed concrete plans to bolster our chances in the upcoming congressional district convention. And Bussey laid it out, fielding questions and suggesting strategy options. It was a useful, beneficial exchange. There was an obvious general feeling that the meeting had been altogether worthwhile. This greatly pleased me.

If nothing else, this meeting convinced me that Jackson's support among blacks was very deep, more than just a matter of voting for him in a caucus or a presidential primary election. The attachment was much, much deeper, strikingly akin to that for Martin Luther King and the civil rights movement. The meeting also convinced me that some whites were also deeply committed to the causes represented by Jackson's candidacy. At least those whites who attended the meeting indicated clearly that what Jackson stood for transcended altogether racial divisions; in fact they saw, as I did, that Jackson was indeed trying to bring people of all classes, colors, and creeds together to work for their overall common good. It was overall a very good meeting. Not incidentally, the next day my two young daughters (one eighteen, the other fifteen) told me how engrossed they both had become in listening to one after another person testify about their commitment to Jackson and the causes he represented.

But testimony aside, we had to get down to the politics of the situation. Jackson forces had done exceptionally well in the First Congressional District and were now expected to win all of the national convention delegate seats at that district's May 22 caucus. Only two real problems faced the first district: (1) turning out their full delegate strength selected earlier in the city ward and township caucuses; and (2) slating nominees for national covention delegates. In the Second Congressional District we too had to turn out our delegates and to caucus, along with several Freeze delegates who were strongly pro-Jackson, and by secret ballot choose one male and one female candidate for delegate slots. I was designated as the male candidate; and Mickey Thomas was designated as the female candidate from our caucus. We were both flattered and honored, but we knew lots of work would be needed before either of us could actually become a national convention delegate. In the second district, unlike the strongly pro-Jackson first district, Mondale forces were clearly in control and were expected to win at least four, and conceivably all six, national convention delegate seats at stake. Specifically, Mondale had about 59 of the some 101 delegates elected to attend the Second Congressional District convention; Hart 18, Jackson 17, with some 7 delegates uncommitted. Under the 20 percent rule for a candidate caucus to be viable, Mondale's was at the time the only viable caucus in the second district; both Hart and Jackson had less than 20 percent of the total number of delegates, 101. Thus, the only thing that could prevent Mondale from a landslide was a coalition of Hart and Jackson forces. Of course, Jackson's man in Missouri (Bussey), Hart's man (Vincent Volpe), and Nuclear Freeze leaders all recognized that to survive and be most effective under the 20 percent rule, it would be necessary to pool delegate resources. And in the end, this happened in my district and in other congressional districts around the state.

However, at least in my district, this union of Hart and Jackson delegates was distasteful to a number of Jackson delegates; I have no idea how the Hart delegates felt, I did not want to know! To be sure, we all recognized, as Bussey so well put it, that this joining of forces was strictly a "marriage of convenience, not of philosophy."[7] But it was just this philosophical aspect on which we Jackson delegates were not willing to compromise. As a result Bussey had to remind us time and again that though it was "admirable and important to pursue lofty goals, we should constantly remember that we also still face a very practical political situation."

Consequently, Bussey warned us on many occasions that it might be necessary to make tradeoffs with the Hart people in certain districts in order to maximize Jackson's strength as well as Hart's. For example, Bussey indicated that Hart needed the three or four Jackson delegates in the Third Congressional District (which Congressman Richard Gephardt and other leaders controlled for Mondale) in order for Hart to have a viable caucus. On the other hand, in Kansas City, where Jackson had more delegates than Hart, the Hart people joined with Jackson to increase the strength of both. In short, in many districts Hart and Jackson, as well as the Nuclear Freeze people, profited from this pooling of resources—a necessary trade-off that, as a political scientist, I readily appreciated.

What really disturbed many of us, however, was the rumor (later confirmed) that a deal was in the works wherein all seventeen Jackson delegates in the second district were to become part of an expanded Hart caucus. To be sure, we recognized that, since neither Hart nor Jackson had enough delegates to be viable, something would have to give in our district. But we Jackson delegates hoped, with reason, that we could pick up enough Freeze and uncommitted delegates to become viable on our own without Hart. In any case, the situation became so embroiled that on May 21, just one day prior to the congressional district convention, we Jackson delegates held a showdown meeting with Bussey and Hart's state coordinator, Volpe.

This meeting became rather heated and tense as one Jackson delegate after another strongly denounced the impending merger and argued that Jackson delegates were not to be tossed around, that Jackson's campaign was very unlike Hart's, making it difficult for any Jackson delegate to operate under a Hart banner, no matter how perfunctorily or expediently. To be sure, Bussey and Volpe clearly explained how, though Jackson forces would join Hart, it would be for the sole purpose of becoming a viable caucus able to elect two delegates, rather than perhaps one, and that both Hart and Jackson would in fact have one delegate. Otherwise both sides could very well be shut out.

Nonetheless, this still did not set well with Jackson delegates. And I shared this discomfort even though, as I understood the proposed arrangement, Hart was to get the female delegate and I was to be the male delegate, technically elected under the Hart banner, but in reality a Jackson delegate. The problem was that many Jackson delegates, especially blacks, did not identify at all with Hart or his new ideas. Mondale was clearly far more preferable to Hart among blacks, but we had to hold Mondale in check if either Jackson or Hart were to win any national convention delegates at all from the second district.

Finally, after the emotions and heat of the meeting subsided, someone suggested what we should have done at the very beginning: add up the cold hard numbers in the second district, including late switches of Freeze delegates and uncommitteds, and look at state-wide support for Hart and Jackson to see who would be in the stronger position at the state convention, where other national convention delegates were to be selected. During a brief recess, Hart and Jackson leaders meticulously went over the numbers and, to our relief and surprise, did indeed find that Jackson was not only stronger in the second district but appeared also to have more support in the state overall. Only after such calculations did Hart's coordinator, Volpe, feel that it would probably be more expedient for Hart delegates to join Jackson delegates, although he would have to check before the deal was finalized. This calmed things considerably among Jackson delegates, although some were still not satisfied since Volpe, understandably I thought, left the door somewhat ajar pending appropriate checks. Because of this bit of uncertainty, Ed Harris, chairperson of Jackson's second district delegates, and I (as the prospective Jackson delegate) were asked to serve as liaisons with Volpe, who would call one of us should there have to be a change in our tentative agreement.

For the next twenty-four hours (from May 21 until meeting time, 7:30 P.M., May 22), I was really reluctant to answer my phone although I dutifully did so all day long. Fortunately, the one call I dreaded receiving did not come. Late that evening, however, I did receive a call from Bussey, who said that, insofar as he knew, the deal was still on and told me, as he had openly told all delegates that

Monday evening, that "Lucius Barker was in charge of Jackson delegates at the Second Congressional District convention" and that he
had confidence that I would do the right thing. I did not relish this
confidence, since the situation was not firmly settled as yet. Fortunately, upon our arrival at the convention, Volpe informed us that
the Hart delegates would join us once Hart's name was placed in
nomination, and the Hart and Freeze delegates did join the Jackson
caucus.

Our congressional district caucus, which met at the suburban Park-
way East Junior High School, was well attended. Mondale, Hart, and
Jackson organizations turned out in full strength with delegates or
their alternates all in place well in advance of the 7:30 show time.
Throughout Missouri, fifty-one national convention delegates were
being selected in such caucuses; six of these delegates were to be
selected from our congressional district in this meeting. But with the
last-minute merging of Hart and Jackson forces, the outcome was
indeed determined before the congressional district convention con-
vened: Jackson's caucus (which now included Hart's delegates) would
be able to select two delegates and two alternates, while Mondale
forces would be allocated four delegates and four alternates. The
real contests of slate-making for these positions had clearly taken
place prior to the meeting and formal ratification was all that was
left. Even so, all of this pre-planning did little to overcome the interest and excitement that pervaded the meeting hall. Television
crews, reporters from the local press, and visitors all turned out to
record and witness the proceedings.

With the crucial decisions on delegates basically in place, the nominating speeches became the focal points, and how the various organizations used this opportunity seems to have been very much
related to their relative power positions in the district and state party
organizations. Hence, Mondale's nomination was done in a rather
perfunctory manner; why put forth much effort in making speeches
when you have the votes. But Hart and Jackson forces obviously
chose to make the most of the opportunity to push their candidates
and their causes. As the de facto Jackson delegate, it was my lot to
place Jackson's name in nomination. And in my nominating speech,
I chose to discuss what I saw as the deeper meanings and implications
of Jackson's candidacy, emphasizing the basic themes of the campaign. The following are excerpts from that speech.

The issues and principles being articulated and represented by Jesse Jackson go beyond and transcend Jackson the person. He articulates and represents issues and principles of which we all as Democrats and as Americans can feel proud.

At this critical point in history, I believe Jackson's candidacy is abosolutely necessary for the future strength and vitality of the Democratic party and of our country. As a party, we need to reexamine our positions and policies; we need to reexamine our structure and operation, including the inclusiveness and fairness of the very rules under which we are conducting this presidential nomination contest. Moreover Jackson's candidacy is forcing each of us to re-examine our own consciences—our values, attitudes, and the very way we treat each other. For the first time since John F. Kennedy, you and I have an opportunity to help forge fundamental changes and new directions in our party that can materially alter the course of history and politics in our country and the entire world. Regardless of who our party nominates, our support of Jesse Jackson will indicate to all that we need more than a new president, which is obviously true, but we also need fundamental change and bold new directions to realize the full potential and great promise of this nation.

Hence, I trust that you will reflect deeply tonight about what kind of message we wish to send to San Francisco, to the American people, and to the entire world. More than any single act you can do, a vote for Jesse Jackson now, in this meeting, will indicate to all that we believe that new directions and fundamental changes are needed in this country and in the world. This would thus make it possible that, in our own lifetime, we can come to know how beautiful it feels to live in a country where the content and character of each of us, rather than our race, sex, color, or occupation, will be the sole determinants as to what we want to make of our lives. We can see how beautiful it feels to plan for a world of peace and understanding, rather than one of war, violence, and distrust. We can see how beautiful it is to enthusiastically support the nominee of our party, not because of our own understandable desire to retire the incumbent president, but because we support a person whose strong, positive programs and courageous leadership represent the hope and aspirations of so many.

Let me conclude in a very practical vein. Jesse Jackson's candidacy offers the Democratic party an unusual and golden opportunity to unearth and activate large numbers of voters who, as the 1980 election vividly demonstrates, will surely be needed to defeat Ronald Reagan. In short, Jackson's candidacy stands to advance both the material interests of those he represents as well as the interests of the Democratic party. I sincerely hope that leaders and officials of the party realize the very positive benefits of Jesse Jackson's campaign. A "politics as usual" campaign will not defeat Ronald Reagan. The Democratic party desperately needs the vision, the appeal, and the deep commitment of Jesse Jackson. His whole effort is altogether consistent with the highest principles and values of the American political tradition. The central thrusts of his candidacy go far beyond the Democratic nomination and the 1984 presidential election. This is a development that all Americans should fight for. I invite you to join us in the Jackson campaign, for it is a campaign, similar to that of John F. Kennedy, that will be recorded as one of the most important developments in American politics and history. I trust you will become a part of this exciting and history making venture. We welcome all of you.

The two seconding speeches for Jackson struck similar themes. Carol Hansen, a white Jackson delegate and a Nuclear Freeze leader whom I had come to know from our April 18 Missouri River Township Caucus, gave what I considered a most effective seconding speech. She told the hundred or so assembled delegates in bold yet eloquent terms that Jesse Jackson was "by far the most attractive candidate and that everyone knew it." "But for his color," she straightforwardly told the delegates, "he would probably be leading" the race for the nomination. The other seconding speaker, Ray Howard, a black attorney, was equally effective. Howard supplemented well earlier comments and emphasized the important symbolism of Jackson's candidacy, especially its providing an alternative and much needed role model for black and minority youths as well as a model for others.

Overall, I was most pleased with how we put forth our candidate, and our fellow Jackson delegates were obviously pleased too. And while others in the audience were less enthusiastic, several delegates pledged to Hart and Mondale told me how well they thought our nominations had gone. We thought they had too, for above all, to paraphrase Jackson himself, the most important thing for us was not whether we won or lost, but whether we raised the right questions and issues. And in our nomination speeches I felt that we did just that.

After the nomination speeches, as indicated earlier, the selection of delegates was rather pro forma, key decisions having been made prior to the meeting. In the end Mondale won four national convention delegates and the expanded Jackson caucus two, with one pledged to Hart and the other (myself) pledged to Jackson.

It is difficult to express the joyful, appreciative, yet awesome feeling that consumed me upon my formal election as a delegate to the San Francisco convention. What pleased me most was the obvious, openly expressed warmth and support I received from my fellow Jackson delegates. I felt a responsibility to them and to myself to do the best job possible to promote the interests of Reverend Jackson. However, one major contribution, about which I told my fellow delegates all along, would lie in my efforts to capture for the historical record the deeper meaning and implications of the Jackson campaign. This book is one effort in that direction.

Overall, May 22, 1984, was a day I will long remember. And Eddie Harris, chair of our district Jackson caucus and one of the many friends I gained through the Jackson campaign, wanted to do all he could to help me remember. He suggested that we should celebrate, and off we went. I thoroughly enjoyed the few moments of celebration, especially when Maude, my wife, joined us.

By and large the Jackson organization had done well in the congressional district caucuses, electing ten national convention delegates throughout the state. This was particularly gratifying since one early political analysis had given Jackson little chance of capturing any delegates outside of a few in the first district, the City of St. Louis, and perhaps one or two others in Kansas City's fifth district. But ten national convention delegates for Jackson was quite a feat. We were justifiably proud.

The next step in the delegate selection process, the state convention, was scheduled for June 2 in Columbia, Missouri. Seventeen more delegates were to be selected there. Our state coordinator, Charles Bussey, reminded all of us that each delegate to the congressional district caucus was also a delegate to the upcoming state convention and was expected to attend. Although Columbia was some two hours or more from St. Louis and getting people there could prove a problem, it was important to do so since the 20 percent rule held for the state convention also, and some of the deals worked out between Hart, Jackson, and Freeze people depended on commitments that had to be fulfilled at the state convention.

Fortunately, these commitments were honored. Nonetheless, a few Jackson delegates grumbled about the wheeling and dealing that took place before and at the state convention. In my presence, for example, one Jackson delegate from the Kansas City area complained about the undue influence of "Bussey and the St. Louis people" in slate making. Said he to a friend, but loud enough to be heard by others: "This is the same old smoke-filled-room politics. They're cramming things down our throats." This comment stayed with me, for indeed some slate making did take place in smoke-filled rooms; I witnessed some of this and was intrigued by it all. I did wonder whether I too might have felt the same way as the young delegate I heard, had I been in his apparent situation. But I also wondered whether there was any conceivable way for any fairly large political organization to overcome such criticism—i.e., to function effectively without advance planning. I just wondered.

The Interim Life of a Delegate

With state caucuses and convention over and delegates selected, attention now focused on the upcoming San Francisco convention. But in the interim, for me as a delegate, the pace began to quicken. For one thing, the national media, including major television networks and several big dailies (e.g., *Los Angeles Times, New York Times*) conducted telephone polls of convention delegates, and some were directed my way. At first, especially as a political scientist, I enjoyed the phone interviews, some of which could last the better part of an hour, depending on the chemistry developed between the interviewer and me. Questions covered subjects ranging from one's personal socioeconomic characteristics to views about abortion, school prayer, nuclear freeze, candidate preferences, etc. As such polling continued, however, the repetitive nature of the questions—which as a political scientist I well understood—plus the time-consuming nature of the interviews all began to take their toll.

Additionally, perhaps due both to my professional position as well as my newly elected status, I continued to receive interview requests from local media. On at least two occasions local television crews came to my home for interviews. Such media attention obviously evoked interest (and some confusion) in my household and among understandably curious neighbors who could not help but see TV crews invading an otherwise tranquil neighborhood. But again, regardless of personal inconvenience, I felt obliged to accommodate as many such requests as possible. One such request, which I honored and which proved intriguing to me and others, was to allow Karen Foss, a TV anchorperson from our local NBC affiliate and her crew to shadow me and my activities at the convention. This meant that during the convention Foss and her camera persons would follow me and zero in on my life as a delegate. It would also include some interviews.

Futhermore, once I became a national convention delegate, I began recieving all sorts of mail: official correspondence from state and national party officials; questionnaires, flyers, memos from various interests pushing their respective causes; notices about various convention caucuses; and invitations to attend receptions, parties, dinners, and all sorts of events. Obviously, of course, I received a number of memos and materials from the Jackson national organization. Overall, as a convention delegate, I could invariably count on having some sort of daily communication via television, print media, telephone, or mail.

Of all the interim activities, the National Rainbow Coalition Briefing Conference held in Chicago on June 29-30 proved by far my most memorable experience, due to both expected as well as unexpected occurrences. Leaders and delegates from each Jackson state organization were invited to attend. In my view the conference was sorely needed to revitalize our spirits and plans, and to once again remind Democratic party leaders that they could not ignore Jesse Jackson or take the black vote for granted. After the primaries, with a Mondale nomination seemingly assured, the party seemed ready to return to politics as usual. I thought the impending Rainbow Conference could help stem this view. In any case, I looked forward to the Chicago meeting and was not disappointed.

As Jackson supporters from across the nation gathered at the Chicago lakefront McCormick Inn Hotel, one could feel an air of excitement, accomplishment, and anticipation pervading the entire conference atmosphere. And Jesse Jackson's supporters had every reason to feel this way: he had done what few professional analysts thought could be done—capture almost 400 national convention delegates and, most important of all, remain an active force that had to be reckoned with at San Francisco. And Jackson did remain active, in more ways than one. Even as his supporters made their way to Chicago, Jackson was returning from a trip to Latin America and Cuba. He obviously was one who had not let up once the primaries and caucuses were over; he kept up the pace and kept both his own staff and the news media on the go.

I found it very heartwarming and reassuring to see and meet Jackson supporters from across the country. Though I knew that Jackson called us to Chicago to plan and prepare for San Francisco, just the sheer interaction with other Jackson supporters was altogether a wholesome, exciting experience. I found it gratifying to renew acquaintances, such as with my friend Bob Starks from Chicago, a professor at Northeastern University; and my colleague Barry Commoner, formerly of Washington University, now a professor at Queens College of New York. And it was refreshing and reassuring to meet still others I did not know, including persons of many races and colors whose occupations spanned the socioeconomic spectrum. To be sure, most of those in attendance were black, but a sufficient number of other groups were present to give more credence and hope to the Rainbow idea than many persons were wont to believe or to accept.

Of course, the real business of the conference was to get ready for San Francisco. But no matter how often conference organizers reminded us of the important work to be done, for me and many others the main attraction was Jesse Jackson. We waited most anxiously for his keynote address that Friday evening (June 29), and we were not disappointed. The address was billed as an after-dinner speech, but far more than just diners showed up. Some 500 or more persons, including hordes of news and television crews, jammed every nook and corner of the meeting room to hear Jackson.

Naturally, the audience had to be warmed up prior to the main event, and while it never seemed difficult to warm up Jackson's own people, the warm-up speakers left nothing to chance. Congressman

Gus Savage (D., Chicago), for example, really stirred the crowd, bringing many to their feet. The Democratic party had better realize, said Savage, that they "have to talk to Jesse Jackson and no one else, not Bradley [Tom Bradley, mayor of Los Angeles and a Mondale supporter], not Goode [Wilson Goode, mayor of Philadelphia and also a Mondale supporter], but they have to talk to Jesse." In a more professorial yet similarly effective fashion Barry Commoner reminded us all of the enormous debt we owed to Jesse Jackson for his tremendous contributions. Commoner's comment immediately brought to mind a law review article I had read sometime ago describing "The Debt of Constitutional Law to Jehovah Witnesses."[8] This was an idea that I later developed in a brief paper I wrote on the Jackson campaign.

But it was left to Maxine Waters, colorful California state assemblywoman, to finally introduce Jackson. She did so with enviable style and substance. Calling Jackson's campaign thus far a miracle, she recounted his many feats and accomplishments—the Goodman release, his performance in the debates, his raising of issues, and his obvious success in increasing voter registration and turnout and the political consciousness among the locked out, especially blacks. I found it sheer delight to hear Maxine Waters; only a Jesse Jackson could afford to follow an introduction such as she gave and not be viewed by his listeners as anticlimatic. As one of my friends put it, "The sister can speak."

But the brother she introduced could also speak, and speak he did, after receiving a stomping, cheering ovation from his people. There could be little doubt that we were his people, and the feeling was obviously mutual. What I especially liked about this particular Jackson speech was that it was very well crafted for the occasion—an excellent contextual review (and overview) of his campaign. "Without vision," Jackson reminded us, "a people perish." But this campaign, he said, "has a vision." Slowly but carefully setting the framework for what was yet to come, Jackson continued. "This is the beginning of a new movement, and it will not go away. . . . We are here to stay. Ours is a moral cause, not just a political campaign. Politics must be an instrument of social change not just social service. The Rainbow shall be known by its destination."

Then Jackson stated that "we hope to speak at the national convention," a remark which brought thunderous applause. I interpreted the remark as a measured and not so subtle response to party leaders and others who were questioning whether or not Jackson should be allowed to address the convention, since allowing Jackson to speak could imply party acquiescence in his reluctance to separate himself from Minister Farrakhan and some Democratic leaders did not wish to risk any such implication. But in speaking to the Rainbow Conference, Jackson served notice that he would not give in one inch to those who would deny him his day at the convention. "We have our self-respect," he intoned sharply, "and we will not sell it." This, as expected, turned the crowd on: we were listening to Jesse Jackson at his best and we loved every word.

Jackson then discussed his positions on ten major issues raised in his campaign, including the issue of fairness, enforcement of the Voting Rights Act, affirmative action, jobs development, peace and foreign policy, justice and equal protection, leadership, unity, voter registration, and continuation of the Rainbow movement beyond San Francisco. Jackson's comments on affirmative action were especially straightforward. Outlining the background that gave rise to affirmative action, Jackson said: "Don't apologize for quotas. We can afford to lose votes, but we can't afford losing chances to raise the right issues." Overall, Jackson's speech was a holistic treatment and review of his campaign. And without question it set the stage for the workshop and business session that were to follow the next day at the conference.

But the next day (Saturday, June 30) began for me with sadness. About 7:30, while I was eating breakfast, my brother Twiley called to tell me that he had received word that our mother had just passed. While this news was not totally unexpected, I was obviously temporarily stunned by mother's death. I began to reorient myself from presidential politicking to the sobering development that now faced me. Immediately, I contacted my family in St. Louis and made plans to leave Chicago about noon that day.

In the interim, however, I did decide to sit in on the beginning of our conference workshops and I am glad I did. During a time like this it helped me just to be with others; plus I very much enjoyed listening to well-known black leaders such as Richard Hatcher, Percy Sutton, C. Delores Tucker, and others. It helped me to forget, even for a little while, my personal situation. I particularly appreciated Hatcher's business-like review of what was involved in putting Jackson's national organization together. He noted the obvious sparsity of blacks and minorities who had had prior experience working in a presidential campaign. "Persons who were ostensibly in top leadership in previous presidential campaigns," he said, "were not really on the inside of those campaigns." Thus, said Hatcher, "we had to build a complete new cadre of people and on-the-job training was required. But as a result," he concluded, "never again will we have to go searching for people to run a national presidential campaign." Then I listened to Percy Sutton and others, including Jackson's national campaign chairman, Arnold Pinckney, who outlined what was in store for the remainder of the conference. At mid-morning I had to leave and make my way to St. Louis and from there to my hometown of Franklinton, Louisiana. Only at this point did I tell my two delegate friends from Missouri and my state coordinator, Charles Bussey, about my mother's death and my early departure from the conference.

A Time for Homage and Reflection

As my family assembled for my mother's funeral in my small hometown in Washington Parish, I reflected over how proud my mother and my father, who passed some years earlier, would have been to know that I was a national convention delegate. Though my mother had just passed, for some years she had not been able to talk or to recognize anyone. Nonetheless, I thought about how my family had long been active in my home community, particularly in education. My mother and father had both been public school teachers, and my father had also been a high school principal and parish supervisor of what were then called "colored" or "Negro" schools.

More recently—since 1974—my younger brother, Bringier, has also been active in local politics. He was the first black person to contest and win public office in Washington Parish, having won a seat on the Parish School Board in 1974. In 1987 he was elected president of the school board. Our family is very proud of this younger brother. Whereas the rest of the six children left Franklinton for larger, and perhaps greener, environs, my brother stayed home and became a community leader in his own right. Following the lead of my mother and father, he too was a public school teacher. And he had the courage and stamina to weather through and help to desegregate public schools in my home parish—a parish that certainly could not be charged with a high degree of racial justice!

Soon afterwards, however, my brother left the public school system and took a job in the corporate sector. From this position he ran for the school board and won. Thus he has had the opportunity to help fashion the overall destiny of public education in the parish. Those of us who left home were indeed very proud of my brother, his wife Juanita (a public school librarian), and family for their courage throughout and, of course, for their being with Dad and now Mom until the very end.

On occasions like this, when family members gather from across the country, everybody tries to catch up on what everyone has been up to. Naturally, members of the family wanted to know about my being elected a national convention delegate. Of course, they did not have to ask but one question: I both anticipated and answered the others. My sisters and their families from San Francisco were especially interested and excited, as they told me of the feverish preparations being made for us delegates in their hometown. I was pleased with the universally strong support Jackson commanded throughout my family and among my many friends in Franklinton.

I was also pleased with certain signs of racial progress that were evident in my hometown. Rayfus Martin, a good friend of the family and a strong political ally of my younger brother, had now been elected to the town council from basically the same predominantly black area from which my brother had won his school board seat. And before I left town, Rayfus was kind enough to take me on a tour of city hall. Though the building was closed for the July 4th holiday, Rayfus had a key and we went through the *front* door. Obviously, some things had changed for the better since my day. For one thing, blacks are apparently now registering and voting without difficulty. This is a far cry from the discriminatory yet interesting experience I myself had when registering to vote in the early 1950s. That experience is worth a brief recounting.

At the time Louisiana required applicants for voter registration to pass what was called an "understanding" test, which was particularly imposed on blacks who wished to register as Democrats. The state operated under a closed primary system wherein only registered voters of a particular party could vote in that party's primary. And since at that time, in Louisiana and the South generally, elections were actually decided in the primary of the dominant Democratic party, I therefore wanted to register as a Democrat. I thus was subjected to Louisiana's test, which required me as an applicant for voter registration to understand and interpret the Constitution of the United States or of the state of Louisiana to the satisfaction of the registrar of voters. I shall never forget that for my test I was asked to identify and explain such matters in the U.S. Constitution as letters of marque and reprisal, ex post facto law, bill of attainder, and due process of law. Though racially discriminatory and offensive, in a sense the experience was rather intriguing. At the time I had recently received an M.A. degree from the University of Illinois–Urbana and had developed a strong interest in the study of constitutional law. Thus, I entered the voter registration office with a reassuring confidence that my educational background would allow me to pass rather perfunctorily an understanding test that even today many educated persons might find difficult. Though I passed the test with ease, the idea that it was imposed especially on blacks and not on whites was insulting and demeaning. Fortunately, however, such obstacles have been overcome largely through the Voting Rights Act of 1965, a major legislative response to the civil rights movement.

But some other things that I observed in my hometown, such as a still-thriving private academy that thwarts public school integration efforts, indicated to me that serious problems still remain. Thus, as my family and I gathered to pay homage and celebrate the life of my mother, we also shared a strong though unarticulated resolve to carry on the work that remains to be done.

Overall, none of us had much reason to grieve, for my mother had had a long and beautiful life. Indeed, I certainly had little time to grieve even if I wished to, which I did not. Upon returning to St. Louis on July 5, I found that I had only a few days to prepare for San Francisco. By this time my Democratic National Convention calendar was quite full—caucuses of all types, invitations to dinners, parties, you name it. In fact, my calendar showed that every day and evening in San Francisco were so full that my wife, who relishes any opportunity to go to San Francisco, decided not to go this time. "You're too busy," she said. And she was right.

7

The 1984 Democratic National Convention:
A Delegate's Diary

Friday, the 13th was anything but a bad omen. July 13, 1984, was an exciting day, a day to which I had long looked forward, the day I was to leave for the San Francisco convention. And my journey could not have started better, for it was on this day at the St. Louis Airport that the diary idea really blossomed and I sharpened my observing eyes and note taking to capture what was to come. By the time I landed in San Francisco some three hours later, my convention diary was well underway. It became an integral, intimate part of my convention luggage.[1] It was with me whenever and wherever I went and proved a great way to record my views and impressions of a convention that was tightly organized, fast paced, and subject to sudden, rapid changes in mood and tone.

Friday the 13th: Off To San Francisco

This time the ordinarily long flight from St. Louis to San Francisco seemed much shorter. I was consumed with anticipation and excitement and fully engrossed in the convention. For one thing, I tried to sort out (rather unsuccessfully I might add) the inevitable conflicts that occur in a delegate's convention schedule—the caucuses, meetings, receptions, dinners, parties—all of which I was going to try to attend somehow. In addition I had opportunity to talk more with my friend and professional colleague who was enroute to the convention as an observer.

While enroute I also had a chance to chat briefly with a fellow Jackson delegate from Massachusetts, Bruce Bolling, whom I had met earlier at the Jackson Rainbow Conference in Chicago. At the time Bolling was a member of the Boston City Council; in 1986 he was elected its president. Meeting Bolling was not surprising: since St. Louis is a major air hub, I expected other Jackson delegates to be on my flight. What I did not expect, however, was to be ferreted off to a corner of the plane for a radio interview. But an enterprising reporter did just that. Somehow I expected to be away from such things while in the air, but obviously I was mistaken. All this, however, was only a preview of what was to come.

The San Francisco branch of the Barker family met me at the airport, where I was greeted both by them and by an unusual San Francisco heat wave. But my family also brought me some news: representatives from NBC's "Today Show" had called my home in St. Louis and would be in touch with me the next day (Saturday) at my hotel. This lent an added air of anticipation to the already exciting convention atmosphere. But absolutely nothing could overcome the appetite I had developed for the meal that I knew awaited me at my sister's home that evening—seafood gumbo, Creole style. Louisianans always find time to relax over a steaming bowl of gumbo, no matter what the situation, and all who were at dinner could testify that I was a *real* Louisianan that evening!

After dinner, however, I did find time to focus more directly on the convention and to review a stack of local newspaper clippings and materials that my family—repeatedly warned by me and my wife that I wanted to see and read everything I could about the convention—had saved. I could not have asked for a better clipping service. I felt fully briefed on the local goings-on and plans for the convention.

Setting The Stage: A Cast of Thousands

At this point, let me give several summary statements describing the delegates who attended the convention. These descriptions, for the most part, are based on data taken from poll of delegates by the *Los Angeles Times*, which received detailed responses from 3,607 of the some 3,947 delegates who attended the convention.[2]

Seventy-three percent of the delegates had never before participated in a convention, and 75 percent were selected by primary, caucus, or convention. The delegates came from fairly homogeneous socioeconomic backgrounds. Over 70 percent had household incomes of over $30,000, and 60 percent were between thirty and fifty years old, with only 9 percent under thirty. Also, over 70 percent of the delegates had completed at least four years of college, with 17 percent holding law degrees. Nearly 75 percent of the delegates worked in business, government, law, or some other profession, and 63 percent had no labor union or teachers organization ties. Prior party involvement was high, with nearly 60 percent having held some party office. Split evenly between men and women, the delegates were 76 percent white, 18 percent black, with only 6 percent Latino.

Two-thirds of the delegates described themselves as either very liberal or somewhat liberal. Only 4 percent would refuse to support any form of affirmative action. Nearly 90 percent expressed disfavor with the Moral Majority, and 84 percent felt favorably toward organized labor. Ninety-three percent of the delegates felt defense spending was too high, and the delegates lent strong support for increases in education, social security, health care, public service employment for the unemployed, and general welfare. Finally, on the issue of reforms in the nomination process, 51 percent of the delegates felt that not enough had been done, and only 15 percent said that reforms had gone too far. Although 44 percent of the delegates disagreed with Jackson's criticisms of the delegate selection rules, 80 percent would support a commission to revise the rules for the nominating process. Overall, this is what the delegates looked like as a group.

In addition to the delegates, there were scores, even hundreds, of media people of every type and description: the print media (the big, not-so-big, and small dailies; the weeklies, monthlys, newspapers, magazines, etc.) and the broadcast media (television and radio—the big three commercial networks, the independents, cable television, public broadcasting, etc.). Few delegates or others could escape the hordes of media people who thronged Convention Hall or were ever present at various hotels and in and around San Francisco generally. They were all interviewing, reporting stories, or looking for stories to report. They were indeed an integral part of the convention: convention facilities, even convention programming, were geared to aid them in their jobs and to maximize media coverage. Their presence and jobs (of reporting, interviewing, etc.) only added

to what I viewed as mass organized confusion, and sometimes confusion that seemed not at all organized. But the media were part of
the excitement and interest, part of the cast of thousands that somehow managed to survive on the convention floor.[3]

Throughout it all, however, the focus remained on the delegates—
people like me. What follows, then, is how I as one of the thousands
of delegates viewed what happened. Essentially it is the diary of my
experiences at the convention, starting with the time I checked in
at the Sir Francis Drake Hotel. Where profitable and pertinent, some
entries have been amplified to convey more fully the substance and
tone of the moment.

SATURDAY, JULY 14, 1984.
The Preliminaries: Adjusting to the Environment

**Major Scenes: A "Today Show" message; Mayor Schoemel's
reception; Mondale rumors; and a Jackson rally.**

3:00 P.M.—Arrived and checked into the Sir Francis Drake Hotel.
—Received message to call NBC's "Today Show." Message labeled
"important." Did make call and finally reached contact person. Was
told that I was one of several first-time delegates being interviewed
by phone for an appearance on the "Today Show." Asked if I were
interested and I indicated that I was. Then interviewer asked several
questions about occupation, etc., and previous convention experience. I indicated my attendance at 1960 convention as an observer.
(Actually I received a special fellowhip, along with other political
scientists from the Eagleton Institute of Rutgers State University, to
study and report on various aspects of the national convention process. Similar fellowships were awarded for study of the Republican
National Convention.) After two or three other questions, interviewer told me that if I were selected someone would call. But I did
not receive call and somehow I did not expect to receive one. Had
feeling during interview that they were interested in a real, new,
altogether-first-time delegate—one who had not been exposed to the
convention in any fashion. Whether this was the factor or not, I of
course do not know since no explanation was expected or given. Was
somewhat disappointed. Must confess that I had thought of appearing
on the "Today Show," on what could prove an exciting, challenging
interview, especially if done by Bryant Gumbel. He comes across as

a sharp, alert, resourceful, combative type, the kind I like to duel. But so much was going on in and around my convention hotel that I had no time to feel disappointed—too much was happening!

5:00 P.M.—Heard news via TV of Mondale's appointment of Burt Lance to direct National Campaign Committee and of Party Chairman Manatt's removal. Was literally shocked by both events. Surprised that Mondale would take on Lance after his well-publicized problems, some of which were continuing even at the time. Really surprised that he would try to remove Manatt in his home state and particularly before he (Mondale) formally won the nomination. Listened to TV coverage and heard reactions of California delegates and others.

—Had hopes that Mondale's actions might be the break needed to prevent his first ballot nomination. Thought both Hart and Jackson could profit from this obvious gaffe. But high hopes dashed when Mondale relented on removing Manatt. Still thought Lance would cause problems but not enough to really hurt in nomination battle, at least not as directly as would have been the case had Mondale's California delegates deserted him over Manatt's removal.

6:00 P.M.—Attended St. Louis Mayor Vincent Schoemehl's reception for Missouri delegation at top of the Sir Francis Drake. Lots of Missouri state officials and party elites were there, so were city officials. And lots of good food of all types, so much so that attending the reception meant that no dinner was needed.

7:00 P.M.—Went to Jesse Jackson's Union Square Rally, a huge Peace rally, with crowds spilling over in the streets. Bands, singing groups, and speakers warmed up the crowd and kept them entertained while awaiting Jackson. Excitement and expectancy of Jackson's arrival was pervasive. One had to really jockey to get good position. This was the first real feel of convention excitement—TV cameras and newspeople everywhere.

—Jackson's appearance drew an explosive cheer and applause from the crowd. And Jackson knows how to work a crowd. He told them what they wanted to hear—which was after all what he had campaigned on. While these were his people, there were many others too. It soon became clear to me that where Jackson was, that is where the real action was. Neither Mondale nor Hart could generate the excitement that Jackson could.

—After speech, Jackson decided to walk to his hotel (Hyatt on the Square) rather than ride in sleek black Cadillac limousine. Jackson shook hands and was mobbed by crowd. Secret Service was obviously concerned but attended to their duties as best they could.

—I followed Jackson to hotel, where he was ushered apparently to his private quarters. But though Jackson was no longer physically present, a festive air and huge crowds nonetheless converged on his headquarters. The hotel (at least Jackson's headquarters) was jumping with operatives—men, women with attache cases and business looks—going about the business of taking care of business. Met and chatted with several fellow black political scientists from Ohio State, Howard University, University of Massachusetts–Amherst, Northeastern University of Chicago, and Jackson (Mississippi) State University. In fact, so many black political scientists were in attendance—mostly as Jackson delegates—that it reminded me of the convention of the National Conference of Black Political Scientists. Lots of Ph.D.s, I thought. Also met Barry Commoner again.

10:30 P.M. The Making of a Delegate—Bussey (Missouri state chair) came out of meeting of Jackson state coordinators and reported that NOW (National Organization for Women) had reneged on pledge to support minority planks. At that point one delegate remarked, "Now that NOW has what they want (Ferraro), they forget you!"

SUNDAY, JULY 15, 1986.
The Day Before: The Pace Quickens

Major Scenes: A church service; Mayor Feinstein's reception; Congressman Clay's buffet; and Jesse Jackson's initial delegate caucus.

9:00 A.M.—Checked with Charles Bussey, my state coordinator. Free to go to church services at St. Cyprian's Episcopal, my family's church in San Francisco (mostly a black congregation).

10:00 A.M.—Went to church. Near end of service, priest asked for visitors to stand and introduce themselves. This done, he then asked if any of us were here for the Democratic National Convention. I told him that I was attending as a Jackson delegate. Congregation broke out in spontaneous applause. Felt really good. Priest then wished me well and services concluded. During reception after service, a number of persons came up to me and indicated how proud they were of Jackson and me, and how it meant so much to everyone. This really made me feel good. These people confirmed what I had really felt all along; rank and file blacks overwhelmingly supported Jackson.

1:00 P.M.—Returned to hotel. Found message indicating that Ron Walters—Jackson's deputy issues director, fellow political scientist, and personal friend—wanted to see me.

—Went to Jackson's headquarters hotel. Picked up Jackson delegate credentials, almost as important as convention credentials (everyone wanted to somehow get access to Jackson's delegate caucuses since one was almost certain to see and hear Jackson himself, so accredited delegates had to have Jackson, not convention, credentials.

—Finally got beyond security types and found Ron Walters, who asked me if I could help out by serving as an issues surrogate for Reverend Jackson to brief state delegations on Jackson's minority planks. After brief chat, Walters and I looked over assignment sheet and discovered, happily, that only a few delegations were not covered. My assignment: Samoa and Guam. My job: to contact chairpersons of these delegations and ask to speak to delegations.

3:00 P.M.—Went back to my hotel room to try and work through my scheduling dilemma. So many events coming up: Mayor Feinstein's reception at City Hall for all delegates; Teamster's party and buffet honoring Congressman Bill Clay; Missouri state delegation party in town honoring Senator Eagleton; and Jackson's delegate caucus. All overlapping and wanted to attend all. But Jackson's delegate caucus is Top Priority.

4:00 P.M.—My constant delegate friend throughout the convention (Joy Johnson) and I decided to make everything except state delegation party for Eagleton. Decision made easier since we had reliable information that the senator himself would be unable to attend.

—First went to Mayor Feinstein's party. Arrived late, official ceremonies were over: San Francisco Symphony had finished, but Gay-Lesbian Band was in fine tune in front of City Hall performing for a rather curious group of onlookers including a number of delegates who peered to get a glimpse of what was going on. Crowd in City Hall was still quite large. Still a large assortment of foods and drinks.

6:00 P.M.—Went to Teamster's party and buffet for Clay at Marriott. Impressive, well planned, receiving line with Clay and others. Lots of people—delegates, Missouri state and local officials, several other members of Congress, etc. Lots of food—no need to go out for dinner. Wonderful souvenirs from Teamster's party—paper weights with appropriate inscriptions, etc. Having good time but kept eye on watch. Could not afford to be late for Jackson's initial delegate caucus scheduled for 8:00 P.M. In fact, decided to leave about 7:15 in order to avoid expected crush of delegates, press. So did other Jackson delegates attending Clay's party. Mad rush for cabs, cars, anything to get to Hyatt on the Square.

7:45 P.M.—Arrived at Hyatt on the Square and, as expected, hotel corridors jam packed, literally a mob of delegates, press, and others trying to get into the tightly secured Jackson caucus room. A penetrating, contagious air of excitement. Jackson credentials paid off—could not get in without them. Room would only hold about 500 at most.

—Finally got into caucus room and sat near front. Electricity in air as we awaited to get our first collective glimpse of each other (all Jackson's delegates) and, of course, our first close-up meeting with Jackson at the convention.

—Start of caucus delayed by size of crowd. Soon meeting room packed. Only Jackson delegates and alternates allowed in. News media, TV cameras everywhere. Thought that if Jackson had as many delegates as people who were in and outside meeting room, he would have easily won nomination.

—Meeting called to order by Mayor Richard Hatcher of Gary (Jackson's national campaign committee chair). Hatcher at his finest. His words will always stay with me: said he was so "happy tonight . . . (for one day) I will be proud to tell my children and grandchildren that their grandaddy was on the right side of history" [in supporting Jesse Jackson]. And I know all of you will be able to do the same." Hatcher's comments greeted with wildly, cheering, standing applause.

—Hatcher introduced several Jackson staff people to discuss several business items.

9:00 P.M.—Stage now set for Jackson to receive a hero's welcome, and he did. Delegates, newspeople, everyone present struggled to get good positions. Again, Secret Service had its hands full. The crush of people was overwhelming, the roar and applause of delegates was even more so. (With such attention and support, I wondered how could Jackson lose. He might, but I believe he will do much better than expected. This kind of atmosphere makes it easy to lose sight of reality—to obscure one's cold rational analysis of things.)

—As Jackson finally mounted the platform and waved his arms, the cheers and roar became even more deafening.

—Finally, Hatcher able to quiet the crowd and introduce Jackson. As Jackson took his seat on platform, he began to nod his head and point toward certain persons in the audience whom he recognized. And sure enough, he nodded and pointed toward me as if to recognize mutual acquaintance. (I had met Jackson and served as his official faculty host when he recieved an honorary doctor's degree from Washington University in 1972). Whether he was indeed pointing toward me I do not know, but I thought so and that is all that mattered.

—Jackson gave stirring speech. Repeatedly interrupted by applause and standing ovations. Told delegates that we all have come a very long way, from November 3, 1983, to San Francisco Democratic National Convention in July 1984. Emphasized the business nature of this venture, the importance of raising the right issues, indicated the openness and candor with which he would act toward his delegates. About thirty-minute speech. Left to standing ovation and crush of newspeople. Delegates asked to remain to take care of more business.

—Pennsylvania delegation read resolution that would warn "Democratic party that rejection of Jackson's minority planks would in effect be rejection of blacks." Received with empathy but held over. (Believe resolution would have passed overwhelmingly but clear that most delegates, including me, wanted some cue from Jackson or his people. Do not know what eventually happened to resolution per se, but it did capture spirit and thinking of a number of Jackson's delegates.)

10.00 p.m.—Meeting ended.

—Made initial contacts with Guam and Samoa caucuses. Appointments confirmed for me to appear at caucuses on behalf of Jackson's minority planks.

MONDAY, JULY 16. Governor Cuomo's Day

Major Scenes: Jackson delegate breakfast caucus; speech to the Guam caucus; Governor Cuomo's keynote speech; and Speaker Willie Brown's "Oh, What A Night!" party.

7:30 A.M.—Visited Stewart Hotel and talked by phone to chairperson of Samoa delegation. Could not confer then, he had another meeting. Arranged to talk later.

8:00 A.M.—Went to Jackson delegate breakfast caucus at Jackson's headquarters hotel. Jackson gave stirring speech as usual. Main message to us was to be alert to rumors of all sorts of deal. Emphasized to delegates that he personally and no one else would give the signal. Enthusiastic response to this (rumors were rampant that deals were in the making.) No one would ever tell us (or at least me) what the deals involved. I suspect no one knew. Rumors perpetuate themselves.

—Crush of press and media at breakfast caucus overwhelming and frustrating. Cameras and crews made it difficult for some delegates to have good view, or any view, of Jackson. When one Jackson delegate complained—somewhat loudly—about the frustrations, a Missouri delegate (Margaret Bush Wilson, former national president of NAACP) responded in her always soft but straightforward tone: "Sure, they (the press) might be an inconvenience for us right now, but it's very important for them to be here—they get our message all across the nation."

10:00 A.M.—Spoke to Guam caucus on Jackson minority planks. Karen Foss, co-anchor for St. Louis NBC local affiliate, followed me there as planned. That media was with me lent an air of importance to both me and the message. Representative from Guam caucus escorted me to the meeting room to meet the governor, had to repeat this for television.

—Reviewed each of Jackson's minority planks. Reception was quite cordial but few questions; even less indication of what effect my presentation might make. Planned to look at vote tonight. That is the concrete index.

—Left Guam caucus to have formal interview with Foss and St. Louis NBC alliliate.

10:45 A.M.—Went to Missouri delegation caucus (held each morning) to get convention credentials for the day (credentials were given on daily basis, security apparently enhanced by this procedure).

12:30 P.M.—Left for convention at Moscone Center. Very tight security on boarding buses—(special buses for delegates only and credentials were checked before boarding). Security even tighter at Moscone Center. Huge concrete barriers—similar to expressway dividers—all around. Police in evidence, so were huge crowds of onlookers, sightseers, tourists. Areas roped off and only delegates could get near convention center. In fact, the massive show of police force—motorcycles galore, patrolmen, concrete barriers, etc., did cause me to wonder, but not for long.

1:00 P.M.—Additional checks (at least two or three more) before one could get to floor: check to enter lobby of convention hall, check to enter main corridors, and check to enter onto convention floor itself. Felt great just to survive all these checks. But these were not most difficult problems I was to face.

—Most difficult problem was maneuvering (just sheer walking) once on the floor. Arrived early enough to man telephone designated for Jackson Missouri delegates. As hall filled, the crush of people, of humanity, was simply unbelievable. How did all these people get through those checkpoints? What are they all doing here? News and TV media of all types from all over the world were obviously present, so were staffers of all types, so were delegates. Alternates were seated far from convention floor and could only come to floor if delegate left and transferred credentials. This is organized (more unorganized) chaos. Makes one concentrate on sheer survival from the mob on floor. Going to restrooms was battle you tried to fight only when absolutely necessary. Even then, experience shows to face the direction you want to go, and the mass of humanity will push you there. Free escalator service.

—Hart and Mondale supporters had lots of signs; Jackson signs were not to be seen until two of our delegates fashioned our own sign out of two Hart signs, turning them inward and putting Jackson buttons on either side. Soon, however, Jackson floor people distributed a few big pictures of Jackson. Allowed us to put these on our newly created poster. Something had to be done for tomorrow—we must have more signs, etc.

2:00 P.M.—At last convention formally opened amidst all this—what could now be called organized chaos.

—Felt sorry for various and sundry speakers who spoke on and on. Even Julian Bond, Georgia state senator and normally a fairly attractive draw, made little dent on crowd. Now and then, a speaker would elicit a round of applause from the few who were attentive. I wondered, however, how they knew when to applaud. How could they even follow in this confusion? Somehow, things seem to work out; speakers appeared happy to speak, and most delegates appeared happy to speak while speakers were speaking. All got along well. Most applause came when speaker finished.

6:30 P.M.—President Carter's speech. Carter received polite, warm reception. By now rather tired of speeches, but really awaiting Cuomo's speech. Wondered how Cuomo would compare with Jackson, who was to speak tomorrow night (Tuesday). Buildup for Cuomo was great.

7:30 P.M.—Main event of the first day was Governor Cuomo's keynote speech. Cuomo had been widely advertised as a good speaker. And he was. Being the keynote speaker allowed him to get initial attention—but after that he was on his own to maintain the attention of this mob. He did! Cuomo was able to capture and hold attention of delegates and various others and this in itself was quite impressive. Silence and order temporarily invaded the convention, and I found it a welcome respite from the noise and activity. Cuomo's speech was good, well balanced, and appealed to all segments of party, well delivered and obviously well crafted. Good response from audience. Cuomo talked about how his parents came over as poor immigrants, worked hard, and now, "look at me—I'm governor!" Talk like this dramatized work ethic, openness of America as land of opportunity, etc. Delivered with passion, emotion—good appeal. But as I listened, I could not help but wonder how long would it be before blacks—as opposed to poor immigrants—could say, "Look at me, I'm governor."

Cuomo pulled out all strings, hit all bases. He talked about how Democratic party was a caring party and pointed to how problems of various types of people in all parts of the country were our problems and how party cared about each and every one, etc. Party cares about the poor, blacks, women, school children, welfare mothers, middle class, everybody—you name it, I thought, as I heard Cuomo—we care. I had no doubt, however, that as a caring party the party perhaps cared more for some than others. Overall, speech was very effective, spiced with enough partisanship to elicit spirit and applause and with enough compassion and facts to be listened to seriously. Received thunderous applause and standing ovation. All expected after keynote speech anyway, but there was obviously something special about Cuomo's speech. The response seemed genuine, not perfunctory.

11:00 P.M.—Went to Willie Brown's "Oh, What A Night!" party down at San Francisco's famous Fisherman's Wharf, given by Brown (speaker of California State Assembly) for about 10,000 of his closest friends. Talk was that this was the hardest and hottest ticket in town. Local newspapers speculated about how Brown was trying to outdo Mayor Feinstein's party, held the day before. Brown, just as Feinstein, apparently invited all delegates and some others.

—Crush of people at party was unbelievable, and from my perspective party itself was unbelievable. Simply too many people. Lots of live entertainment and foods exemplifying San Francisco's finest, but just too crowded for me. My friends who were early arrivals thought party was great. But for me, it was a bust. Ended up at Holiday Inn (across from Sir Francis Drake) trying to get anything to eat. By 1:00 A.M. and after fighting crowds at Brown's party, I was terribly hungry. "Oh, What A Night!" turned out to be just that. (Parenthetically, reviews I heard of the party the next day were quite good and upbeat. In keeping with his reputation, Willie Brown had thrown another great party! Obviously, I missed it!)

TUESDAY, JULY 17, Jesse Jackson's Day.

Major Scenes: General black delegate caucus; convention consideration of Jackson's minority platform planks; Jesse Jackson's convention speech: and Mayor Barry's party.

10:00 A.M.—Spoke briefly to Samoa caucus as issue surrogate on minority planks. Most polite and attentive.

—Talked to several reporters on phone and in hotel lobbies. Had to get used to giving reaction on the spot to anything.

10:30 A.M.—Went to Missouri caucus and heard Professor Leslie McLemore of Jackson State University (Mississippi) speak to Missouri caucus on enforcement of Voting Rights Act and runoff primary. Barry Commoner had spoken to caucus earlier on foreign policy issues—defence, freeze. Did not hear him; I was at Somoa caucus.

—Got credentials for day.

11:15 A.M.—Went to general black delegate caucus. Mickey Leland of Texas presided; Jackson was expected. Special press gallery constructed and media was literally everywhere.

—Jackson entered a jam-packed room—about 600 people. Started speaking and thanking God. Spoke very passionately and response was great. This was expected: these were his people, but Jackson has way of stirring anybody's people.

—Spoke of minority planks and ridiculed Hart's new ideas for not turning up in minority reports. "Where are they?" Said he might lose, but important to raise the right issues. Spoke of historic importance of his candidacy and asked for support of black delegates: "Vote 'conscience,' 'conviction,' and 'candidate,' " he thundered. Asked audience to repeat. Analogized his campaign to civil rights movement and historic struggle to liberate blacks and minorities. He said: "For those who did not have opportunity to participate in 'March on Washington,' or in Selma, God has provided you another opportunity." Jackson said his campaign provided that other opportunity. I happened to be standing in right place and as he left room was able to shake his hand.

1:00 P.M.—Went to Moscone Center. This time we had lots of signs. After all, this is Jackson's night. He is to address convention in prime time. Lots of speculation even among Jackson delegates as to what tone speech would take. Personally, as I write this, I wonder how I would respond if I were Jackson to what seems to be an obvious defeat of his planks. Hopeful about some sort of deal and believe it necessary if Mondale is to hold not only Jackson but, more importantly, Jackson's delegates. Convinced that delegates, except me, are leaders in their home communities, at least among those voters who do not ordinarily vote and certainly would be needed in November. Deep down I expected to lose on minority planks but was forever hopeful that Mondale and his people would respond to Jackson as they had to California delegation that demanded Manatt's reinstatement as party chairman. But we kept watching our telephone light, it did not blink. We received no word before voting. Then I hoped for a miracle.

—As expected Mondale flexed his muscle to summarily defeat three of the four Jackson minority planks and reached some sort of compromise on affirmative action by calling for verifiable measures rather than quotas.

—The Enforcement of Voting Rights Act and runoff primary minority
plank was of course Jackson's litmus test. Impressive array of speakers in favor: Tony Bonilla, chairman of National Hispanic Leadership
Conference; Albert Vann, assemblyman from New York; Mickey Mi-
cheaux of North Carolina, whose case Jackson cites as classic example
of evils of second primary; and Victor McTeer. McTeer has com-
manding presence, a lawyer with booming voice. Has filed suit in
federal court in Mississippi challenging runoff primary. McTeer's
speech brought Jackson delegates to their feet. McTeer was powerful, so was Michaeux. I thought to myself, "These people are living
through what they're talking about!"
—Mayor Arrington, presiding over platform committee report since
Ferraro was selected for vice president, then announced speakers in
opposition. They too were an impressive list, including Andrew Young
of Atlanta and Bob Slagle, chairman of Texas state Democratic party.
Was surprised and shocked that Andrew Young would choose to
oppose Jackson's key plank openly on national TV.
—When Arrington introduced Young, all hell broke loose. Mondale
delegates began to wave their banners and shout for Young. The next
thing I knew was that Jackson delegates were responding to Young
with boos. Reaction from both sides seemed spontaneous. After all,
runoff primary symbolized Jackson's campaign for inclusion. The
convention floor was bedlam. Young tried to continue speaking but
no one paid him any attention. The matter was far beyond him: it
was Jackson delegates and new black politics versus Mondale and
old traditional politics. Emotions were very high, very, very high.
—At this point, or perhaps a little earlier, we received word, pre-
sumably from Jackson headquarters, that if this plank was defeated
we were to stage some sort of demonstration to show our disgust.
However, we were to remain at convention. At one point, rumor
was that we were to stage a symbolic walkout of convention hall. I
never knew whether this was true. Final word—which was official
through our state coordinator—was that when vote was announced
we were to all go to Mississippi delegation, since Mississippi symbolized oppressive nature of runoff primaries. Vote was announced
and minority plank lost 2,591.6 to 1,127.6. At this point, all Missouri
Jackson delegates left the state delegation to join with Mississippi.
Just before we started, however, someone said that word had just
come to cancel any kind of demonstration lest it be misinterpreted

that Jackson delegates were walking out. But this was too late; we went, and probably just as well. Some Jackson delegates were really upset and at Mondale. Something had to be done to vent feelings!

—Believe that Mondale had made critical misjudgment as to impact of defeat of Jackson's minority planks—not necessarily in defeat of specific planks but in the way in which Mondale people wanted to show their control of the convention, particularly to show how badly he could beat Jackson and generally how he could show other interests that he was not giving in to yet another interest. Along with many other Jackson delegates, I personally resented deeply this kind of treatment. Wounds deep and won't heal easily.

—At this point, I had to calm down and become more of a professional analyst. I really began to wonder how Jackson, who was scheduled to speak in about an hour, would handle the situation. Rumor had it that his speech would be conciliatory, but I wondered how it could be so and maintain his credibility among his own delegates.

—Soon after things somewhat quieted down, word was passed among Missouri's Mondale delegates that their headquarters had indicated that Mondale supporters were to show Jackson utmost respect, they were not to wave their signs, etc. Similar word apparently came from Hart people. In any case, I found this of little consolation.

8:00 P.M.—On came Jackson. The air of expectancy was great. At that point, I thought, Jackson literally held a tremendous amount of power; no one knew how he would use it, but everyone knew he had it. For example, if Jackson had told for his delegates to leave, my own belief is that most would have done so gladly. I cannot overemphasize the deep feelings of hurt and disappointment felt by many Jackson delegates. However, I also remembered that during the campaign Jackson had renounced any intention of walking out of the convention. [1]

I empathized with Jackson's dilemma. How could he satisfy his angry and disappointed delegates, preserve the more fundamental needs of his party for unity, and maintain his own credibility with his delegates and the many people who had voted for him in the primaries? Jesse Jackson's speech was, realistically, the high point for blacks at the convention. At no other time were they to hold such spotlight.

I was pleased that the nation could hear Jackson, but I was uncertain as to how he would handle a tough, tough defeat—one that appeared calculated to embarrass him. Thought it was most insensitive of Mondale to not try to make more accommodation for Jackson's cause. If Mondale was in control of the convention, he was in control, but maybe he could only be certain that his forces would stick together to control Jackson and blacks, the same old story.

But as Jackson's speech developed, for the first time I sensed the drama of the occasion, of the moment. The huge, pushing, milling throng of humanity stopped as one in hushed silence, captivated by Jackson. I began to fill with emotion, my eyes watered, especially when Jackson intoned, "If I have made a mistake, charge it to my head, not my heart." As he went on, tears rolled down my face, and I sneaked my handkerchief to wipe my face and as if to blow my nose. (Real men don't eat quiche—real men don't cry!) But when I looked around, other's eyes were also flowing with tears. (For complete text of Jackson's speech, see Appendix.)

After Jackson's speech (about fifty minutes long), crowd rose as one. Singing of "Ordinary People" topped off Jackson's speech. Good therapy, at least for the moment, for everyone. We needed it. As singing was going on, I thought of what might have been had such black leaders as Andy Young, Richard Arrington, Coretta King, Julian Bond, and Coleman Young supported Jackson. I wondered what would have been had Milton Coleman treated Jackson's Hymie remark as off the record and not reported it. But I also thought of a colleague of mine here who said, "Off the record or private conversation or not, Jackson was wrong." Certainly he was, but I still wondered what might have been if. . . .

I also thought of how to state my reactions to Jackson's speech using his own rhythmic tones. My diary thus states that Jackson's speech "demonstrated to all the rich, tremendous talent and resources that America still tries to conceal and frustrate rather than reveal and motivate." I also penned that "Jackson is the first black person to really become a *national political* leader in terms of national *presidential* politics." Here was a man who had been beaten by the sheer power of Mondale—and, I thought, Hart—forces but whose support all knew would be needed in November. Jackson's head was not bowed, as I suspected some would like to have seen. His speech that night was a masterpiece. It will forever give him a medal of honor in my book. I don't know whether any other person would have been big enough to handle the situation as he did. In my view,

Jackson's behavior put to rest altogether those who said that Jackson was driven by a super ego. If he was, I believe it would have easily taken over, and it did not. But he was obviously in excellent control of his own deep feelings.

—But this control of emotions did not characterize some of his delegates. In general, black delegates reacted to the Jackson speech with happiness and anger, with frustration and despair. Feelings in the Missouri delegation ran very high, and Jackson delegation leaders openly expressed their deep resentment of the treatment Jackson had received from Mondale and his supporters. The situation was tense and would have been worse but for Jackson's speech, which undoubtedly defused an otherwise damaging, deep split in the party.

What made the situation even more tense, after Jackson had defused it, was the manner in which the media and some Mondale supporters played up the Jackson apology and forgot the other parts of the speech. A fairly prominent black Missouri delegate provides a good example of the anger and frustration that followed later that evening. "I don't like what happened one damn bit," this delegate said. "They screwed us." When I asked what that meant—I was constantly probing—the delegate complained that "Jesse Jackson had given his all, and Mondale and his delegates in the Missouri caucus had not done one damn thing, showed no respect and appreciation for all the help that blacks had given in the past, and unless they do something fast, they can write off the governor and all others, for they damn sure can't win without the black vote." This black delegate insisted to me and several others that we had to let the entire Missouri delegation know our feelings, how they offered little or no support for Jackson's minority planks, and to have done so at least on one or two would not have hurt them one bit, and would have shown concern and appreciation and empathy for Jackson's position. All of us agreed that this would have been a relatively small price to pay in exchange for the loyal support that blacks have always given the Democratic party. Many black delegates, at least Jackson delegates in Missouri, wanted to bring the issue to the floor of our state caucus to be held the next day.

10.00 P.M.—Mayor Barry of Washington, D.C., hosted a party for Jackson delegates at the Sheraton Palace, and several of us decided to go. As usual, lots of good food and drinks. Met some of my friends from my graduate days at University of Illinois–Urbana. Usual ca-

maraderie, except for one important bit of news: in informal remarks
to the gathering, Barry indicated that he was to formally place Jesse
Jackson's name in nomination at the convention tomorrow night
(Wednesday). Was somewhat surprised by this, as well as a bit disappointed. In my own scenario, I wanted Maxine Waters, state senator from California to do the job. Heard her introduce Jesse before,
and the sister did a job! She's terrific. But really have not heard or
seen Barry in similar role. Hope he's good! For his speech is all we
really have left in the convention. He needs to do one helluva job!

WEDNESDAY, JULY 18.
The Day After: Nomination Day

**Major Scenes: Missouri delegation caucus; the black
delegate caucus I missed; a caucus in Jackson's presidential
trailer; Mayor Barry nominates Jackson; the Mondale-
Ferraro ticket and the first woman major party nominee;
Jackson's final delegate reception.**

7:30 A.M.—Not much enthusiasm left after last night. Drained by
defeat of minority planks as well as by Jackson's engrossing speech.
Wanted the moment of Jackson's speech to last. But reality was taking
over. Disappointed, angry, and hurt by lack of concern shown by
Mondale to Jackson and to us! Comments from news reports and
from fellow delegates did not soothe my feelings. Began anew to
rehash pros and cons of Jackson's speech. Why was the speech so
conciliatory, or conciliatory at all? Why did Jackson feel compelled
to apologize for the Hymie remark for the umpteenth time? Hadn't
he already apologized for the remark? Would it make any difference?
Why did he try to be so much of a party man? Did he try too hard
to convince Mondale's black supporters that they could trust him,
that he knew how to handle the situation? Did all this overshadow
his strong stands on policy issues? Did it compromise his credibility
with his own delegates and the many blacks who supported him
during the primaries? Did it tarnish the forthrightness and freshness
of his candidacy, of his campaign, of the causes he represented? Why
didn't he walk out and leave the convention?
—But, as I pondered the whole matter, I concluded that there was
so much more to Jackson's speech. Sure, the speech had its conciliatory aspects; he did offer an apology, and the media and others did

focus on this. But Jackson's speech held fast to his positions and views—all of them. He really did raise the right tough issues, and many people simply didn't like that. Somehow they prefer to finesse such issues. Jackson stayed in the party to fight at least another day. Some would have preferred him to walk out.

—Overall, I still thought Jackson handled situation courageously and showed himself much bigger than Mondale and the party. Was proud of the substance and tone of his speech. Was angered and hurt that party officials and rank and file members generally did not appreciate what Jackson had done and how much he could mean in the future. Shortsighted, I thought.

10:15 A.M.—Missouri State Caucus. As expected, a number of us Jackson delegates expressed our deep concern about the lack of support, or at least appreciation, Jackson's overall effort had received and our specific disappointment about how Missouri delegates hewed the party line instead of supporting any of Jackson's minority planks. Ensuing discussion evoked sharp words and exchanges. State senator J. B. "Jet" Banks took the lead and was especially vocal, reminding Missouri white delegates that blacks were needed by the state Democratic party to win in Missouri state-wide elections and that they had better not forget it.

—Other blacks told the caucus that the press and many other whites had purposefully misinterpreted Jackson's speech, playing up only the apologetic aspects, not other parts. State Delegation Chairman Daniel McVey (also president of the Missouri State Labor Council) attempted to defend the position of those who voted as they wished last evening. Caucus was extremely quiet—not from tenseness, it seemed, but from lack of concern. Many of the state's delegates were either not from or enamored with St. Louis anyway, and most of the complaints were coming from St. Louis. In any case state party leaders realized that St. Louis Jackson delegates were clearly unhappy over the outcome and how, as one black delegate put it, "we have been royally shafted." More, these white party leaders clearly recognized that the St. Louis black vote was essential to the party in statewide and city elections. The matter ended when it was suggested that McVey and State Party Chairman Pat Lea meet with Missouri's Jackson delegates immediately after the state delegation caucus.

11:00 A.M.—After open state delegation caucus, McVey and Lea met with us Jackson delegates to try to iron out differences. State and local press (especially St. Louis media) wanted to attend, but we decided that, initially at least, the meeting would be closed, with comments promised to the press afterwards. Again, delegates expressed deep concern that Jackson's speech was being misinterpreted in such a way as to suggest almost complete abandonment of Jackson's mission. All of us (Jackson delegates) told state party leaders that Jackson's speech had transcended ordinary convention and Democratic party politics, that it was really an appeal to the nation, and that the party had better listen. I expressed the view that Jackson had skillfully and masterfully used opportunity to snatch victory from defeat. (I thought to myself, however, what a Pyrrhic victory, at least in the short run.) The only real agreement reached in the meeting was to try to work out a structure that would allow Mondale, Hart, and Jackson delegates to work together in Missouri. Our Jackson delegation leaders and party leaders were to get together on this. As I saw it, the meeting was a good venting of feelings on the part of us Jackson delegates, but not much more. Party leaders dutifully and properly expressed concern but also not much more. Meeting broke up when TV and newspeople were allowed to enter. Several people were interviewed by media. Overall, Missouri Jackson delegates believed that the ball was in Mondale's court. He must proceed with caution, sophistication, and action.

11:30 A.M.—Word came to us (from somewhere) that an all-black delegate caucus, scheduled for 11:00, had been cancelled. Just as well, we were woefully late anyway. To my disgust, found out later that caucus had indeed been held and was very spirited. Should have known better and not paid attention to rumors. In any case, I was able to briefly catch my breath and grab a sandwich.

12:30 P.M.—Boarded bus for convention hall. Arrived much too early but at least beat the big rush. As several of us Jackson delegates made our way from buses through maze of security and onto convention floor, several ushers put thumbs up, indicating that they liked our huge pictures of Jackson and, indeed, that they liked Jackson. Jackson signs, pictures, buttons, remained hot items throughout the convention. Jackson's speech was still the talk of many delegates who were ambling into the hall. The speech certainly could be interpreted in so many ways, and was! This was its genius and weakness. But to me that's what made Jackson's speech stand out. Cleverly crafted and exceptionally well delivered.

—Several reporters also stopped us to ask if blacks were dissatisfied with what happened last evening to the minority planks. The answer given was a strong "Hell, yes! How do you expect us to feel?" By now most Jackson delegates who were coming on the floor were in anything but an upbeat mood. We thought Jackson's speech was great for the future, but we had taken a bitter defeat in the present and this did not look good for whatever the future might hold, particularly the election. But back to reality. As I saw it, nominating our presidential candidate—the highlight of this Wednesday session—was somewhat anticlimatic.

1:00 P.M.—Convention session opened with that inevitable parade of speakers who fill up the program and platform while delegates gathered for the main event, which today was nomination of presidential candidates. But I recognized this was important aspect of convention—these fillers were local, state, and national dignitaries who now had the chance to speak and to be seen from the convention.

—While speeches were going on, I was brought up to date by another black delegate on what transpired at the black caucus that I missed— "a really good one. You should have seen how Coretta [Scott King] was booed and shouted down. She had the nerve to try and chide us for booing Andy [Young] last evening. . . . Of course, Jesse quieted things down and talked of Coretta's great contribution. Still, she should have known better. . . . Jesse gave a good speech. You have heard most of it, but he said it quite well, summed up everything." (Press reports I later read indicated that Vice President Mondale— soon to be the party's candidate—also received rough treatment from the black caucus.[5] What did Mondale and his supporters expect, given the roughshod manner in which they treated Jackson and us delegates the day before in summarily brushing aside our minority platform planks? People don't forget *that* soon!) Missing this caucus reminds me anew that a delegate should never pay attention to rumors—find out first hand for yourself. Every chance I got, I tried to get other versions of what happened at the caucus, and they pretty much corroborated what was said above.

5:00 P.M.—Was told by Jackson floor coordinator that Rev. Jackson wanted an immediate meeting of all of his state chairs in his trailer, just off convention floor. At that time our state chair, Bussey, was not on floor, and floor coordinator suggested that I represent Missouri delegation until Bussey could come. Reluctant to do so at first, but decided that I would go. Why not? As I made way to trailer area through cluster of humanity on convention floor, I found that I was really thrilled to be going to a presidential trailer at a national convention. Had long seen trailers on TV but never seen one first hand and certainly had not been in one. Thought again of how this was an opportunity I probably would not have had but for Jesse Jackson. Passed other trailers and finally reached Jackson's trailer. After some staff people identified me to security I was admitted to trailer. Was good to see up close all state chairs and Jackson's top staff people. Was a beautiful sight. Jackson's top staff and supporters certainly had a Rainbow coloration, more than many think. To be sure, blacks predominated among those in the trailer but there was a distinct Rainbow flavor. Really beautiful.

Trailer was jam-packed with Jackson people awaiting, as I was, the latest word. While waiting, I again sought and got reports about what happened at the black caucus earlier in the day. Soon Arnold Pinckney, Jackson's national campaign chair, called meeting to order and asked for questions, information, or reactions on almost anything from state chairs. Lots of comments. Staff briefed us again on what to expect once nomination and balloting began. But these discussions quickly subsided as Jackson himself entered the trailer.

—Was awed by the obvious respect and admiration that all had for Jackson. What had previously been a sort of teeming, free-for-all discussion turned into a hushed, expectant, respectful silence. All stood. Immediately, Jackson mounted a chair so as to be seen and heard by all in these crowded quarters. Never shall forget how the first thing he did was to look around the room as if to note who was present. He then put everyone at ease just through sheer personality. Jackson began by reviewing major points he had made at black caucus earlier in the day (again I kicked myself for being absent). Was excellent way for Jackson to underscore one of the major tenets of his campaign: that it would be open and that there would be no secret deals. (At this point I spotted Bussey, my state chair, who had entered the room apparently somewhat earlier. But I was not about to leave now. This was too good, being in on history. And I'm glad no one told me that my state chair had come and I could leave.)

Jackson again emphasized that up to that point no deals had been reached although some things were on the table, such as a fairness commission, key Rainbow representation in the campaign and any

ensuing presidential administration, meeting with ten southern state
chairs as basis for supporting state tickets and discussing integrated
slate-making, funds and resources needed to mount extensive registration campaign, etc. He also mentioned why he had so much
wanted and had openly appealed for blacks to unite and others to
vote for him on the first ballot: to show unity and solidarity and
broad support for these broad concerns.

Jackson then began to put campaign and convention into broad
perspective. He sought to interpret his speech of last evening. Jackson indicated that he used the occasion to speak to and beyond the
convention and the Democratic party, and to speak directly to the
nation. "Real change for blacks and the people I represent," said
Jackson, "has historically come from outside the party, and the party
catches up." But he said we must "get all from the party that we
can. . . . The party can be useful. . . . Don't get caught up in convention hoopla, which will be over in a couple of days. Our mission,"
he said, "is to change, not to carry on politics as usual. Creative
tension may be necessary." Jackson indicated that the Rainbow Coalition would become a national political organization that would
continue and grow long after the convention and would become a
force to be reckoned with. The meeting in the trailer ended by
Jackson noting that if more than one ballot were needed, he would
reconvene chairs to discuss strategy.

—As trailer cleared I had chance to say hello to Jackson and asked
how things were going. Later I reflected on how stupid this could
have sounded to Jackson who certainly had many other things to
think about rather than returning perfunctory greetings, which he
of course did quite graciously. But this was my way of saying to
Jackson how proud I was for all he had gone through and done.

—As I made my way back to the floor, I was enveloped with all sorts
of thoughts, about the private meeting in Jackson's trailer, about the
convention, about the nomination speeches about to take place.

—Delegates were anxiously awaiting my return to report on what
happened. But deference suggested that I should wait for Bussey,
who was on his way, and to allow him as state chair to report. He
did, and asked me if I wanted to add anything. I indicated to several
delegates that the biggest thing, as I saw it, was to see and hear
Jackson at close quarters.

Interestingly enough, even after our little delegate huddle on the floor, one or two of my close friends still pressed me for what really went on in the trailer. I knew their feeling, for one invariably believes that more takes place in such private meetings than actually transpires. I assured them I told them all, and after several times, I believe they finally believed me.

—We all hoped that many black delegates and others would vote for Jackson on first ballot as symbolic gesture of unity for the important things he stood for. Even though realism told me that Mondale had nomination locked up, nevertheless an air of uncertainty and hope remained until the very end—"you never know." Still I thought that Jackson deserved more recognition and appreciation from party than he had been given. Felt Geraldine Ferraro profited from Jackson's campaign. I thought Jackson's running himself (a black—minority—person) and making a good showing, plus his unequivocal and early advocacy of putting a woman on the ticket—helped to plant the idea in people's mind and keep it alive. This allowed women's groups and others to follow through. Selecting Ferraro was great boost for Mondale, the convention, and, I suppose, generally: Mondale really needed it! But what about Jackson or another black for vice president? Perish the thought! The matter of race is still a major concern of party leaders. They wanted Jackson's help and the black vote but not too much of a black presence. White middle America would not like too much of a black presence. So much for reminiscing.

5:45 P.M.°—Time for Gary Hart's speech. Convention hall is aglow with signs and colors of all sorts. Beautiful scene. Signs all around for Hart and Mondale. Lots of signs, but not much enthusiasm, at least among Jackson people.

Gary Hart's speech was well received but no match for Jesse Jackson's. Mondale's lucky he comes tomorrow and not so soon after Jackson. Mondale comes across as sincere, nice guy, but dull. Not even Mondale people impressed me as being that enthusiastic about their man. Wide agreement that Mondale was a good, honest person. But there lurked that uncertainty as to whether he was the best candidate, or more important, that he could actually beat Reagan. It was just that Mondale was destined to be the nominee, no matter

°Diary shows time of trailer meeting (5:00 P.M.) but records show no time entries after that until balloting is over for presidential candidate—about 9:00 P.M. Accordingly time entries are approximate.

what. My assessment could be wrong, but this was the feeling I sensed in convention hall.

6:30 P.M.—Time had now come for nominations. McGovern's name was put in nomination, allowing him to withdraw and make a speech in which he would endorse Mondale, which he did. This was not unexpected but supporting a front-runner doesn't take much courage.

7:30 P.M.—Now "OUR TIME HAD COME." Marion Barry, mayor of Washington, D.C., came to the podium to nominate Jesse Jackson. This was obviously an historic occasion—the first full nomination of a black person for the presidency of the United States. As Barry spoke, I found him to be a good, forceful speaker but one who seemingly tries too hard. Maybe it was the occasion. Barry was not as captivating as some others that I had wished to nominate Jackson (e.g., Maxine Waters), but then, I thought, Jackson selected Barry for many reasons, and it was after all his choice, so that's that! I had been quite pleased that Barry was a highly placed, well-known, black public official who had stood with Jackson *throughout* from the very beginning. That's worth a lot! Amidst continued but somewhat subdued crowd noise, Barry's forceful delivery continued and the serious nature and tone of his message were plainly evident. Overall, Barry captured well the sense of this historic moment.

> I stand before this Convention tonight to place in nomination the name of the person who has energized this presidential campaign, a person who has given full meaning to the democratic process, and a person who has changed the course of American politics.
>
> I stand before you with a great sense of personal pride, for never did I think and imagine that one day I would be standing here to nominate the President of the United States of America. This pride is not simply my own pride. This pride is shared by Blacks, by Hispanics, by Asians and women. This pride is shared by small farmers, unemployed workers, senior citizens, environmentalists, peace-seekers, and by those who are gays and lesbians. It is a pride shared by the Ph.D.'s, and the no-Ds, by handicapped persons, the mentally retarded and the poor. Now is our time. Now is our time because we are the Rainbow Coalition. (Applause)

The man I nominate tonight has brought us all together and for that the Nation owes him a debt of gratitude. Twenty years ago many of us were outside of the Convention Hall in Atlantic City demanding that members of the Mississippi Freedom Democratic Party be seated. Twenty years ago, Fannie Lou Hamer, Julian Bond, Henry Kurtze and Dan Henry were on our side fighting to help us get on the inside. Because of their struggles, because of their jailings and even killings, we are on the inside tonight. Twenty years later, things are different.

Tonight I am speaking from the same podium from which this Party nominated Franklin Delano Roosevelt, John Fitzgerald Kennedy and Hubert H. Humphrey, and tonight I am speaking to many of you who in the past have been taken for granted, left out, put out, left out and kept out. Tonight we are on the inside, together, participating, negotiating and nominating. (Applause)

Tonight we are all part of the Rainbow Coalition that makes us the Democratic Party. The man I am nominating tonight has shown compassion for the young, compassion for the old, compassion for the ill and infirm. He has reached out to those whom our society has cast aside and locked out.

He has met the challenge and the controversies of his time with boldness, honesty and tenacity. He has pursued aggressive, creative and visionary diplomacy. The fruits of his labor reach far beyond the borders of the United States into Central America and to the Middle East, and to Europe, and into Africa.
....

The person I'm nominating tonight believes that everybody counts, that everybody is somebody, that everybody has a place in the sun, everybody has a place in the rainbow. (Applause)
....

The man I am nominating tonight was the first presidential candidate during this campaign to firmly commit to having a woman on his ticket. And because my nominee's strong commitment created an environment which would ensure that Geraldine Ferraro will be the vice presidential nominee of this Party (Applause) the man I'm nominating tonight has earned a place in our world, has made an everlasting impression on the political landscape of our country. Like Shirley Chisholm, he is a role model for America's children. He is a catalyst for a political revolution.

His candidacy is not simply the candidacy of a man but is a candidacy of a movement. A vote for this man is a vote for the struggles of Sojourner Truth, Nat Turner, John Brown, Adam Clayton Powell, Martin Luther King, Jr., Michael Swerner, Andrew Goodman, James Chaney and Cesar Chavez.

Let us take the encouragement from the words of Martin Luther King, Jr., who said of my people, "My people, listen. The battle is in our hands."

I know you are asking today how long would it take. I come to say to you that however difficult the moment, however frustrating the hour, it would not be long, because troops [sic] crushed to earth will rise again.

Therefore, I urge you to vote your conscience, vote your conviction. A vote for your conscience and a vote for your conviction would allow you to go home to face your children, to face your grandchildren and not be ashamed. A vote for conviction and a vote for conscience will allow you to go home to face your children, to face your grandchildren and tell them that you are on the right side of history. (Applause)

Now is our time. Now is our time. Therefore, vote for the nominee for the Rainbow Coalition.

My friends, I am honored to take part in history tonight. I am honored that I am going to place in nomination for President of the United States of America, the name of my friend, the name of my brother, the name of the peacemaker, the name of the advocate of people, the name of Jesse Louis Jackson.[6]

At the conclusion of Barry's nomination speech, we carried on the usual expected demonstration for our candidate. But in reality "Our Time Had Come" the night before. Even though we lost on our minority planks, Jackson's speech had lifted us, igniting and captivating all and leading to an outpouring of good will, good feelings, and really spontaneous demonstrations. This was a different setting, a different time, a different occasion. Barry's speech could not rank with Jackson's; no one could have been at that level, even if circumstances had been the same.

—Jackson stayed with his Rainbow Coalition to the very end. His nomination was seconded by Shirley Chisholm and a Nebraska farmer,

Merle Hansen. I was pleased to see Shirley Chisholm second Jackson's nomination, for not only had she been an original black pioneer in presidential politics, she had also been one of few well-known black leaders who were with Jackson from the very beginning, from the time he announced his candidacy in Washington on November 3, 1983.

—Nominations of Hart and Mondale proceeded as usual and evoked the usual demonstrations. I thought that for any candidate to literally lock up the nomination before balloting takes too much steam and interest out of the convention. Demonstrations and balloting become too perfunctory; they lose interest for the public and even for the delegates. Something must be done to keep future conventions from being showcases, where no really important decisions are made.

—The roll call of states proceeded, but this too was of little more than nostalgic interest for those who wanted to make believe that the outcome was in doubt. Strangely enough, however, one still never loses hope until the very end. And the end came out as expected. Apparently, few if any blacks pledged to Mondale or Hart, or few other delegates heeded Jackson's call to join with his own delegates in what would have been an uncommon show of unity for the causes he espoused. On the first ballot Jackson received 465 votes—certainly more than many thought he would receive when he first announced his candidacy but far less than those who supported him thought he should have received. On the first ballot, Mondale had 2191 and Hart 1200.

9:00 P.M.—Balloting was now over and perfunctory "unanimous" motions were made for Mondale's nomination.

—Geraldine Ferraro's nomination for vice president, even though expected, held a great deal of interest, for nominating a woman on the ticket of one of the two major parties was indeed a breakthrough, a milestone. Still, I could not help but think, why not a black? Sure, I recognize the politics of it all, but why are blacks invariably passed over—even those with more obvious qualifications? Once again, I thought, even in affirmative action, white women still come first!

—After the party ticket had been set, we hurriedly made our way back to our hotel to get ready for Jackson's reception for his delegates, scheduled for 9:00 P.M. but obviously already late.

10:30 P.M.—Arrived at Jackson's reception for his delegates. Banquet hall literally jammed, standing-room-only crowd. Food and drinks

were available but everyone was waiting for the MAIN COURSE—Jesse
Jackson himself. While reception was billed as Jackson's reception
for his delegates and supporters, I thought this was the perfect occasion to show our reception for him, and we did!

—Jackson entered the hall to a hero's welcome. The affection, respect, and admiration were pervasive. The platform was jammed with
leaders, some of whom spoke and all of whom Jackson dutifully and
enthusiastically acknowledged. Here was Jackson's last real opportunity to speak to his people, and he said almost literally the same
thing, in almost identical language, publicly that he had said in the
privacy of his trailer meeting. While I was impressed with Jackson's
speech in the trailer, I was even more impressed with the man Jackson this evening. He told cheering supporters how far they had come
and, more importantly, where they were going. He reminded us
anew that "real change for blacks and the locked out had historically
come from outside the party; and the party catches up." But he
cautioned delegates and supporters not to desert the party; we must
"get all from the party that we can. The party," he intoned, "can
be useful." And just as he told his state chairpersons earlier, he once
again warned delegates and his supporters "not to get caught up in
convention hoopla, it will be over in a couple of days." "Our mission," he said, "is to change, not to carry on politics as usual," and
"creative tension may be necessary." (At this point, it was clear that
Jackson had not ruled out peaceful demonstrations to accomplish
political objectives, although he did not say so directly. But this
implication pleased me and others.) Finally, Jackson told the huge
gathering of his hopes for the Rainbow Coalition, which he said
"would become a *national* political organization that would continue
and grow long after San Francisco and would become a force to be
reckoned with."

—Throughout his remarks Jackson was applauded and cheered re-
peatedly. An obvious warmth and chemistry was at work between
Jackson and his supporters—the kind of warmth and chemistry that
I truly believed would not be left in San Francisco.

THURSDAY, JULY 19, 1984.
The Party's Over: The Convention Ends

Major Scenes: Private reminiscing at a state delegation caucus; lunch at the Top of the Fairmount; a final visit to Jackson's campaign headquarters; and a family dinner.

7:30 A.M.—Not much enthusiasm left. My convention ended last evening at Jackson's reception. That was my farewell. Began packing to leave hotel and spend night with family in San Francisco.

10:30 A.M.—Joined delegate friends at our state caucus room to pick up credentials for the day. My Jackson delegate friends feel as I do—not much enthusiasm. Real question in my mind is whether to attend closing session this evening to hear Mondale's and Ferraro's acceptance speeches. Really torn. Certainly I had lost some enthusiasm and held some disappointment and a little anger, not because Jackson lost on his key issues or did not do better in the final nomination battle—certainly these outcomes were not unexpected—but because of the manner in which party leaders summarily defeated his minority planks. These were not only Jesse Jackson's ideas; they were ideas and concerns of many blacks and others, and very strongly mine. Consequently, I deeply resented the roughshod manner in which party leaders treated us. It will not be soon forgotten! Why should I go to see the final coronation of all of this? Why should I attend the final session?

On the other hand, as a professional political scientist and as a person keeping a diary of the convention, I was greatly tempted to see Ferraro become the first woman to officially accept a major party nomination. This too was history, I thought, and I should see it! Then, too, I did not want to appear a sore loser, although at times I think one has to demonstrate displeasure with things. But overall I did not think that this was such a time or occasion. If a number of Jackson delegates, particularly in the Missouri delegation, did not show up, there would be little "color" left in that delegation. We would be missed. Several of my friends expressed similar concerns.

Simultaneously, however, my alternate delegate from Missouri, a white woman, had indicated to me her fervent desire to see Ferraro, the first woman, accept her nomination and had asked me to let her have my credentials for the evening if I did not plan to go. I thought of how I would have felt if I had been in her position and a black person was on a major party ticket for the first time. Wouldn't I too like to see it? I wondered. . . . Oh well, I thought, any decision of whether or not to go to the final session could be made later. It was only 11:00 o'clock and acceptance speeches would not come until later that afternoon.

11:00 A.M.—Several of us were ready for brunch or something. Rarely did I take the time to eat breakfast, and I did not this morning either. To my delight, Pearlie Evans, Congressman Clay's assistant for his home district office in St. Louis, invited two or three of us to join her for brunch at the Top of the Fairmont. Apparently this is where the VIPs dined, and I was anxious to see as much as I could, particularly Nob Hill, where the Fairmont was located. Everything was as elegant as I had imagined—delightful atmosphere and food, very relaxing, sufficiently removed from convention-like things. I had time to unwind, to chat intimately and casually with a few friends, and to reflect over experiences of the past few days.

1:00 P.M.—As my friends and I rode a cable car back to our hotel, I thought to myself that this was a wonderful way to end my convention experience. I would not have to fight the crowds at the convention and could relax at my sister's home and watch the proceedings on TV. After all, I had had enough of the flavor of the actual convention. But perhaps most of all, my not attending the final session would give my alternate delegate that opportunity that she fervently wanted—to see Geraldine Ferraro become the first woman on a major party ticket. Thus, my decision was made; I would forgo the final session.

As I entered the hotel, I immediately called my sister, telling her when and where to pick me up. And I left my delegate credentials for the final session, carefully sealed and marked *important* at the hotel desk for my alternate. However, to make things all the better, as I was about to board the elevator to go back to my room, my alternate delegate spotted me and called out, "What have you decided to do?" When I told her I had just left my credentials in her mailbox at hotel desk, she was aglow and obviously delighted. We both went over to the mail clerk, got the credentials, and that was that. I did not feel guilty for leaving; in fact, I felt good I could make my alternate really happy, and she was just delighted!

2:30 P.M.—My final act before meeting my sister at 3:30 was to go back to the Hyatt on the Square for a final glimpse of Jackson's campaign headquarters. And to my surprise and delight there was still a good amount of activity; it was still an exciting place to be. People were wandering around, still sensing the history of it all. A number were still searching for Jackson pictures, for souvenirs, for almost any memento of what had happened here. Some of my Missouri friends back home and my sisters and their families in San Francisco had implored me to bring a souvenir. The women especially wanted that "attractive color photo of Jesse, any size." I complied with their requests as best I could.

3:30 P.M.—As I waited for my sister to pick me up from the lobby of Sir Francis Drake, I said goodbyes to my friends and other acquaintances gained during the convention.

—Soon I became comfortably ensconced in my sister's home. I have two sisters in San Francisco: before the convention I stayed with one, and tonight after the convention I must stay with the other. We Barkers believe in equal time and equal opportunity—that way we keep family harmony. We watched some of the proceedings on TV, especially Ferraro's speech—obviously an exciting occasion. But I was more exhausted than I realized. Bed and TV proved an excellent combination. I could nap, watch a while, and nap again.

8:00 P.M.—My extended family and I gathered for dinner on my final night in town and for our final chat and analysis of the convention. All, of course, had been and were still strongly supportive of Jackson and all did express views! I certainly expressed mine. I explained to them why for me the convention really ended last evening at Jackson's reception for his delegates. Then I quoted almost verbatim from my diary entry for Wednesday evening. "To me," I told my family, "this (Jackson's reception) was really the *end* of my convention. I was ready to leave. Had little interest in coronation of Mondale. Thought Jackson and blacks generally had really been shafted! Really wondered how blacks who supported Mondale were feeling, they seemed to have been shafted too! At least we Jackson delegates were up front and took risks that I believe will pay off and not in the too distant future."

But how Jackson and blacks generally fared at the convention convinced me that party leaders have not as yet found it necessary to view black concerns as quid pro quos for black support and black votes in elections or in party conventions! Why should they? They apparently get black support without quid pro quos such as would

be forthcoming for support or expected support from other groups—
e.g., the obvious appeal to women made through Ferraro's nomination. What kind of appeal was made to blacks? Only a straightforward challenge such as that posed by Jackson could lay bare the
real relationship and importance of blacks to the party, and to me
the San Francisco Democratic Convention failed this test miserably.
But so did black leaders! They were divided.

Our dinner conversation and my stay in San Francisco ended with
the usual refrain, "Wait 'til next time!" Largely due to Jesse Jackson's
1984 campaign, however, this usual refrain could now be said with
unusual conviction and hope. Indeed, "wait 'til next time" could
well carry a lot of punch, particularly as it relates to the future of
black politics and American politics generally.

8

Our Time Has Come
Lessons for the Future

As I reflect over my experiences with the Jackson campaign, one thought stands out: Jackson provided for many an opportunity to participate in politics in a manner that would not have been possible but for his candidacy. Jackson put the matter much more dramatically when he told a caucus of black convention delegates that through his campaign God had now given those unable to participate in the civil rights movement—in Selma, the march on Washington, etc.—another opportunity to work for the objectives for which Martin Luther King and others fought and died. Despite differences between King's movement and Jackson's campaign, the similarities in goals and challenges both offered account for much of the driving force behind Jackson's remarkable successes and unusual staying power which have kept him going while others with considerably more resources have fallen by the wayside.

Jackson's 1984 effort was the most broadly based campaign ever undertaken by a Black American to win a major party presidential nomination. The campaign not only met with some notable successes and achievements but also concretized a number of challenges that many of us faced for the very first time. The Jackson experience allows us to comment more informatively on a number of important, continuing concerns: the nature and problems of black politics; the character and operation of our two-party system; the role of the "rules of the game" in shaping politics and public policies; and the nature, functions, and dynamics of presidential nominating cam-

paigns. The Jackson campaign also sheds light on the capacity and
limits of party, electoral, and coalition politics to achieve fundamental changes in public policy, especially in attempts to fully include the locked out in the political-social order. This chapter focuses
on some of these concerns in terms of lessons from the 1984 Jackson
campaign that might prove instructive as we look to the 1988 elections and beyond.

   1. *Black Americans must develop a common unifying strategy to
maximize their influence and standing in the Democratic party and
capitalize more effectively on the strength and strategic importance of
their support for that party's success in presidential elections.* Jesse
Jackson's candidacy demonstrated the black community's potential
for mobilizing strong support for black leaders—the kind of unprecedented, direct, popularly based support that could be skillfully used
for timely intervention in Democratic nomination politics in order
to more effectively protect and promote the interests of blacks and
their supporters. Yet the Jackson candidacy was not so utilized, or
if utilized it was not successful. Why?
   Clearly, the division among black leaders over Jackson's candidacy
contributed to this failure. Jackson's success in amassing convention
delegates far surpassed the expectations of many, especially since
he achieved such success despite open opposition from some important, highly visible black leaders who supported Mondale. However, in one sense, it mattered little that these leaders were at odds
with the consistent and overwhelming support Jackson enjoyed among
blacks across the country. To the outside world (white), this black
leadership support for Mondale indicated strong enough splits among
blacks that party leaders, and white Americans generally, could minimize the messages and meaning of Jackson's unprecedented huge
black vote. And nothing, such as a highly visible common agreement
among Jackson and Mondale's black supporters on bottom-line concerns, dispelled this impression. This contrasted sharply with the
bottom-line agreement among women to put a woman on the party
ticket as vice presidential candidate, or the bottom line reportedly
reached by the California delegation, which demanded that Mondale
retain their fellow Californian, Charles Manatt, as national party
chairman. Both groups achieved their objectives. Of course whether
blacks would have been similarly successful in achieving their bot-

Table 8.1 Jackson's Strength among Black Voters

State Primary	Size of Black Electorate	Black Support for Jackson
AL	30%	60%
FL	13	62
GA	24	70
IL	28	74
NY	20	70
PA	11	75
IN	13	70
MD	26	76
NC	22	84
OH	14	76
CA	14	83
NJ	18	80

Source: NBC News, 1984.

tom-line objectives is another question, but these kinds of strategies and calculated risks can produce important benefits.

The bottom line in this discussion is that, no matter how much party leaders (black or white) deny it or how much we wish the situation were different, in many ways Black Americans are still treated in group, not individual, terms.[1] Certainly the actions and policies of the Reagan administration have impacted negatively and disproportionately on blacks and minorities as groups, and these actions and policies are tolerated by an increasingly sympathetic public, including Republicans and Democrats alike. Necessarily then, blacks tend to act and respond on the basis of group concerns.

This black group activity affects the political arena in various ways—in the support Jackson received from the black community and in the strong and loyal group support blacks have consistently given over time to the Democratic presidential candidates. And this importance cannot be minimized. The very rules of the game in presidential election politics—i.e., the structure and operation of the electoral college—are fashioned so that under particular circumstances groups might wield an influence in such elections which they might not be able to exercise in other contexts. For example, the winner-take-all allocation of electoral votes in presidential elections puts a premium on group influence and solidarity in key states. And

Table 8.2 Black and White Voting Patterns in Presidential Elections
1952-84

Year	Race	Democratic	Republican	Other
1952	Black	80%	20%	—
	White	40	60	—
1956	Black	64	36	—
	White	39	61	—
1960	Black	71	29	—
	White	48	52	—
1964	Black	100°	0	—
	White	65	35	—
1968	Black	97	3	—
	White	36	52	12%
1972	Black	87	13	—
	White	30	70	—
1976	Black	94	5	—
	White	50	48	—
1980	Black	85	11	3
	White	36	55	7
1984	Black	90	9	—
	White	34	66	—

Source: Survey Research Center, University of Michigan (Presidential Elections
from 1952-1976). Data for 1980 and 1984 from the *New York Times*/CBS News
Poll from the *New York Times*, November 8, 1984.

°The 100% voting of blacks for the Democratic party probably results from the
small size of the sample. Certainly a few blacks voted for Goldwater, as probably a
very few voted for Wallace in 1968. Furthermore, the reported 100% Democratic
support is consistent with a bias to report having supported the winner—a well-
known artifact in re-call data.

the distribution of the black population in these states, plus their
strong inclination to vote as a bloc (usually for the Democratic candidate), could make the black vote crucial, even determinative, in
close elections. Yet in the past blacks clearly have not capitalized on
this advantage, and this strategic importance of the black vote in
presidential elections has been minimized in Democratic nomination
politics by party rules that promote and protect established, entrenched interests and dilute and restrict the influence of aspiring
and developing groups such as blacks.

Thus, blacks do not exercise the influence in party politics—in
nominating a candidate, in shaping the campaign, and in forming the

eventual national leadership coalition of the party or the presidency—which their strength and support in presidential elections would seem to warrant. The intimate link between these various stages is clear: the measure of influence and access exercised in the *nomination* stage is vitally related to such influence and access in the subsequent *election* and *governing* stages. But a long tradition of strong support at the election stage is obviously no guarantee of support or access in either the earlier nomination stage or the subsequent governing stage.

Nonetheless, black political leaders have not been able to capitalize on this structural advantage accorded them by electoral college politics, one of the few instances in which blacks at present stand to profit from the rules of the game. Blacks, just as others, have to play different games in different contexts, and how these games are played depends very much on the rules. Groups must fashion their strategies and utilize their resources accordingly. Clearly, the rules, requirements, and stakes involved in games played at state and local levels may vary from those of games played at the level of national presidential politics.

Obviously, there is an intimate relation between one's role as leader in a given community, e.g., the black community, and one's role as mayor or member of Congress. And the delicate balancing of these roles under particular circumstances might prove advantageous. Thus, for example, an individual black mayor might find that, in his role as leader in the black community rather than in his role as mayor of the city, he might be in the stronger position to deliver dividends to both the black community and to the city. In Democratic presidential politics the strategic importance of the black vote to that party's success in elections, and the apparent influence of particular black leaders in delivering that vote, make the support of these leaders crucial to presidential candidates.

In 1984, just at the point when the group influence of blacks in presidential politics was perhaps at its highest point, primarily as a result of Jackson's campaign, not whites but blacks themselves impaired the group's bargaining leverage. Simply put, the failure of the black leadership family to reach accord on some unifying strategy in advance of the convention, or even at the convention itself, severely limited the role and influence of blacks in the convention, the election campaign, and the subsequent governing coalition in the party. Therefore, white party leaders were not concerned about any threats that Jackson might raise with respect to key issues or concerns. Indeed, the status of some of Mondale's key black supporters in itself took much of the potential sting out of any hard-nosed bargaining about the platform and any talk of a convention walkout. Similarly, it could be argued that Jackson weakened his own bargaining leverage by renouncing in advance both the convention walkout or independent movement options.

In any event, the importance of group unity cannot be overemphasized: groups in democratic politics must bargain from strength in both symbolic as well as substantive terms. With outspoken support from highly visible black leaders, Mondale could summarily defeat Jackson's minority planks with little regard for possible consequences, which he could not have done if black leaders had closed ranks on specific issues of concern to both Jackson and Mondale supporters. In view of Jackson's persistently strong support among blacks in the presidential primaries, this consolidation would have conveyed strong symbolic and substantive threats to Mondale and to party leaders.

The tradition of the Democratic party as champion of the poor and downtrodden would have been threatened by having blacks—its major symbol of the poor and downtrodden—turn against it. Of course, some might suggest that the party would profit from more visible "whitening" of its membership and policies. That the party would so act, however, would serve to underscore dramatically the strength of racism and the shallowness of the party's attachment to such constitutional and democratic principles as equality, liberty, and justice. In substantive terms, by running roughshod over key demands of blacks, the party could stand to lose the votes of one of its largest and most loyal constituencies. Since 1964 blacks have voted consistently and overwhelmingly for the Democratic candidate, approximating almost 25 percent of the total Democratic vote.[2] But in the 1984 Democratic national convention, these symbolic and substantive threats were effectively negated by the open split in black leadership ranks. Mondale and Democratic leaders undoubtedly breathed a sigh of relief that they did not have to deal with these symbolic and substantive threats posed by Jackson's success among black voters.

However, Mondale and party leaders did accord Jackson an opportunity to address the convention during prime-time national television. The move was of obvious potential benefit to the party:
apparently, party leaders saw the need to do something to close ranks
and promote unity and in the process assuage Jackson and the unexpectedly large following he amassed during the primaries. Although this healing process, as I saw it, came much too little and too
late, it did provide Jackson with certain potential benefits.

Jackson used his speech as a dramatic, highly visible opportunity
to lay bare his soul and political objectives, forcefully projecting
himself as a reasonable, caring, knowledgeable, and experienced
professional leader and in the process countering critics who saw
him as an unreasonable, insensitive, inexperienced, and self-centered
individual. He thus used the opportunity to reassure long-time supporters, to win new ones, to answer critics, and to quiet concerns of
those who might not know him. Moreover, through his speech Jackson tried (some think too hard) to reach out to others in the party.
And, very importantly, he indicated clearly that, despite past errors
or his own human frailities, he was not about to abandon the dynamic
world of electoral politics. "As I develop and serve," he implored,
"be patient. God is not finished with me yet."[3]

But the 1984 Democratic National Convention seemed to have
been finished not only with Jackson and his delegates but with Mondale's black supporters as well. As the convention moved toward an
end, it became increasingly and painfully clear—at least to me—that,
for whatever reason, Mondale and party leaders were not disposed
to reach out to Jackson or to blacks generally. Without the kind of
essential unity and solidarity which could have forced party leaders
to respond, other than his one-hour, prime-time, nationally televised
speech, Jackson had little to show from the convention for the overwhelming record black vote he received during the primaries. Black
leaders who supported Mondale also had little to show.

However, to be more fully understood, Jackson's historic speech,
as well as his overall 1984 campaign, must be placed in broader
perspective. The Jackson campaign was an educational experience
for many blacks (and minorities) in the practice of politics, especially
presidential politics; and many will practice that education in varied
contexts, even as active candidates for political office. Further, as
black voters and the locked out become more active and knowl-

edgeable in the ways of politics and increase their political participation, they will increasingly hold black leaders, white leaders, party
leaders—all leaders—accountable for their actions.[4] The stakes involved are too great and affect far too many people for the black
leadership family, Democratic party leaders, or any other group of
elites not to be more sensitive and responsive to the kind of tremendous vote that Jackson amassed during the 1984 primary campaign, especially from among those who are least likely to participate
in electoral politics at all.

However, on a second time around, Jackson could face certain
credibility problems: some who supported him in 1984 might wish
to know why they should support him again when they see very little
or nothing in return. Jackson faces similar problems in convincing
blacks who voted for Mondale to now support him rather than someone else. On the other hand, black leaders who supported Mondale
might encounter credibility problems of their own. They certainly
have little evidence to support their determined assessment of Mondale as the candidate who could beat Ronald Reagan. In short, the
effect of the division among black leaders during the 1984 nomination battle on convention outcomes and subsequent developments
is bound to engender dialogue and decisions that could affect black
politics, party politics, and American politics generally in 1988 and
for some time to come.

The lesson to be learned from this discussion is that in pluralist
democracy *individual* influence is calculated in terms of *group* support and influence. Because of the split in black leadership ranks,
the full impact of Jackson's presidential candidacy as a viable political
strategy could not receive a full and fair testing. By contrast, however, the traditional patron-client strategy followed by Mondale's
black supporters has been frequently tried, fully tested, and generally found wanting, and nothing in the Mondale campaign altered
this assessment; if anything it would strongly attest to the bankruptcy
and stagnation of traditional clientage politics, i.e., white patron–
black client. Indeed, after the San Francisco convention, Mayor Andrew Young of Atlanta, one of Mondale's most loyal black supporters,
publicly characterized Mondale's campaign advisers as "smart-assed
white boys" who refuse "to take advice" and accord blacks more of
a role in the campaign. "But I can't let them lose this election," said
Young, because if Mondale is defeated by President Reagan, "black

people 'are the only ones that will suffer.' "[5] Young's remarks reflect all too well how in presidential politics blacks are central to the party in voting and elections but are left on the periphery in developing campaign strategies and policies or in running the government, should the party win.

Jackson's attempt to move minorities from a passive role to a more active role in the Democratic party represented an important milestone in black political development. He hoped to forge a new pattern of relations (a "new covenant," as he put it) between blacks and the Democratic party. Although the attempt did not meet with much success at the convention, the campaign did draw attention to problems and concerns of the locked out, enhance black political consciousness and voter education, and increase black voter registration and turnout.

But though of immeasurable importance, these more generalized long-term benefits do not overcome the need to deliver more specific, tangible, immediate short-term benefits. Thus, any black presidential candidate in the future will have to convince black voters that the next time will be different. And much of that difference will depend on forging a greater unity among black leaders. This could prove formidable but the lack of an obvious sympathetic front runner might make the overall situation more amenable for blacks to achieve a greater unity of position and strategy in 1988 than in 1984. Also, since Jackson's candidacy proved far more successful than expected, more black leaders may be disposed to support Jackson next time because they might not wish to risk once again their ability (inability?) to deliver the black vote.

Overall, the 1984 experience suggests the need to formulate both a set of pro-active bottom-line concerns and an active strategy to promote them. As a strategy, for example, a presidential candidacy can actively develop and marshall resources and thereby focus attention and give clout to bottom-line concerns. In turn, these concerns give meaning, substance, and direction to the strategy, providing a more unified base of support that allows the strategy to more fully develop. It is the interactive force of the two and the actual presence of "clout," rather than its potential, that captures the attention of party leaders and spurs them to work to accommodate the group's bottom-line concerns. In the 1984 experience, Jackson went out, developed and marshalled resources, and won unexpected support—the kind of voter support and delegate strength that portended to give him clout in the convention. As suggested earlier, however, this never materialized. Indeed, the failure of black leaders to reach accord, even during the convention, on a common set of bottom-line concerns precluded the effective use of Jackson's clout and negated the leverage of both Jackson as well as Mondale's black supporters. But most important of all, it precluded blacks generally from having the kind of influence at the convention and in the party that they would otherwise command.

In general, however, the advantages in presidential elections accruing to blacks due to their strategic population distribution and unified voting patterns must be tempered by reality. Since 1968, with the exception of Carter's 1976 victory, the overwhelming black support for the Democratic candidate has been offset by a strong conservative trend among white voters. This has resulted in the election of Republican candidates, despite the fact that they have received less than 10 percent of the black vote (see Table 8.2). If continued, this trend could clearly minimize the strategic advantages that the rules afford to a group such as blacks in presidential elections. It could also lessen meaningful coalition politics between blacks and whites to pursue mutually beneficial ends and increasingly isolate blacks from majority coalitions in presidential elections. Clearly this holds serious implications, not only for blacks, but for the Democratic party, the two-party system, and for American politics generally. The counsel that blacks could end this political isolation by following white voters to the right (including their increased participation in the Republican party) does not, as things now stand, seem to hold much appeal; blacks, not unlike others, should not be expected to support parties, candidates, or programs adverse to their interests.[6]

2. *Party leaders must use the convention to unify party factions and to agree upon the terms on which they will work together in the presidential campaign.* The party convention has traditionally served as a forum in which party leaders could reach accord after the divisiveness of the pre-convention campaign. However, at San Francisco Walter Mondale and party leaders failed to use the convention as a vital integrative force to bring together the various interests in the party.[7] To be sure, reconciling contending candidates, factions, and

interests is a major task, especially when they are as widely divergent as those in the Democratic party. Normally, however, success in reaching such accord can prove vital to success in the campaign and election.

Essentially, this traditional function of national party conventions views the convention as an emotionally binding experience that brings together the people who will have to wage the campaign and gets them in a mood to do so. But as I left San Francisco, I was certainly not in any mood to wage the campaign. I felt that the party had reached little more than surface unity—if even this—with one of its largest and most loyal constituent groups—Black Americans. To me this lack of real, meaningful, and highly visible accord with "contending candidates, factions, and interests" in the party was the single most important failure of Mondale at the convention and one from which I do not believe he ever fully recovered. Specifically, that such an accord was not reached with Jackson and blacks generally was the single most disappointing and disturbing aspect of my convention experience as a Jackson delegate.

What Mondale, party leaders, and many others failed to see, or chose to overlook, was that Jackson's effort and its tremendous appeal to blacks was and is based on very fundamental principles which Jackson simply called "dignity" and "respect." And by not working out some meaningful accommodation at the convention, especially in view of Jackson's powerful and moderately toned speech, Mondale and party leaders managed to transgress the self-esteem, dignity, and respect not only of Jesse Jackson but many of his supporters as well.

As a result, I and undoubtedly a number of other Jackson delegates as well, did not approach the elections with a high level of enthusiasm for the party ticket. Rather, what incentive I had remaining after San Francisco was generated more by my high level of enthusiasm against the incumbent administration, which spurred me to support my party ticket in November but not much more. Such negative reasons for voting cannot be sustained for long: as Jackson's campaign shows vividly, blacks and similar groups need someone and something thay can vote *for*, not *against*.

3. *The Jackson campaign reminds us that in American politics the rules of the political game itself do much to shape both how the game is played as well as its outcome.* Minority groups must be constantly

mindful of the importance of these rules and whenever possible use
them, or when necessary seek to change them, to their advantage.
The importance of rules in determining "who gets what, when and
how" cannot be overlooked by those who wish to succeed in American politics.[8] This, of course, is hardly surprising to scholars, analysts, and experienced politicians who have long since recognized
this basic fact of political life. However, it is not that obvious to rank-
and-file Americans. In fact, many of the rules are so deeply ingrained
in our political culture and value system that they are widely accepted and supported as givens in our politics. And those who attack
such rules are viewed variously as unpatriotic, radical, or at least as
poor sports who do not abide by the rules; and this applies with
special force to those who wish to change the rules once the game
has started.

However, close analysis of American politics shows that at one
time or another particular interests have found themselves unable
to live under the constraints or restraints imposed by the rules. For
example, blacks conceivably could still be living under the original
Constitution, a set of rules that considered them less than persons.
So would women and others whose life chances and rights have been
significantly affected by changes in the rules. Likewise changes have
occurred in the rules governing basic political arrangements and
structures—e. g., the manner of electing our president and U.S. senators—all of which came after the original rules were established.
To be sure, while relevant to the overall role and influence of rules,
this general argument does not directly address rules changes raised
by Jesse Jackson. A closer analysis, however, reveals that Jackson's
efforts are more relevant than might first appear.

For example, consider the runoff primary, which Jackson and many
others consider an unfair barrier to black political development. The
runoff primary may have been originally conceived to safeguard the
democratic principle of majority rule, but, as Jackson suggests, it is
also used to promote and safeguard prevailing, established political
interests. Similar arguments and counterarguments, of course, may
be made with respect to other structures and arrangements (at-large
elections, the open primary). No matter how much merit there is to
Jackson's arguments, and there appears to be a great deal, such arguments are often discredited, minimized, overcome, or overlooked
altogether through the sheer protection afforded to the runoff struc-

ture by our deep attachment to the rules of the game, and to traditional democratic principles (e.g.; majority rule).[9]

Jackson's attack on Democratic party rules was similarly met by disdain and criticism from entrenched political interests. Jackson vigorously attacked certain party rules relating to delegate selection and apportionment. He labelled as unfair, for example, the fact that entrenched established interests would profit greatly from super delegate rules wherein party leaders and elective officials (e.g., members of Congress, who are mostly white and male) could automatically become national convention delegates. Similarly, he objected to winner-take-all primaries and the 20 percent threshold rule, which required that presidential candidates receive at least 20 percent of the popular vote before being allotted any delegates. Clearly, such rules advantaged front-runners and centrist candidates and disadvantaged minority or insurgent candidacies such as Jackson's. At a meeting with Jackson in late April 1984, national party chairman Charles Manatt apparently agreed that the system had disadvantaged Jackson and indicated that he would urge state party leaders to give Jackson more delegates "because of the way the system had worked."[10] News reports I read, however, were unclear about whether or to what extent Manatt's position was an effort to be as responsive as possible to Jackson's assurance, made at the start of the meeting, that neither he nor his supporters had any intention of walking out of the convention.

In any event I certainly understood Jackson's complaints about the rules; he and those he represented were hurt by them! Overall, for example, Jackson received about 18 percent of the popular vote, but only 10 percent of the national convention delegates. In contrast, Mondale received 39 percent of the popular vote but garnered about 52 percent of the delegates, primarily due to the various devices and add ons (the *rules*) that favored front runner Mondale disproportionately. Had the party used the one-person, one-vote formula (proportional representation) favored by Jackson, however, Mondale's actual delegate total of 2,045 would have dwindled dramatically to about 1,591, and Jackson's actual count of about 388 delegates would have jumped to about 645! Hart's total of 1,249 would have increased marginally to about 1,307. This would have thrown the nomination battle wide open, a position obviously not favored by Mondale and party leaders. Thus Jackson used his campaign to

Table 8.3 Democratic Delegate Disparity

One of Jesse Jackson's main complaints with the Democratic
Party's nominating system is that, as a result of the rules, he
was awarded only slightly more than half the delegates than
his proportional share of the popular vote in primaries would
entitle him to. The following chart shows how the voting in
primary states translated into delegates.

	Primary vote %	Delegate %
Walter Mondale	39	49
Gary Hart	36	36
Jesse Jackson	18	10

Source: Congressional Quarterly *Guide to the 1984 Democratic
National Convention*, (San Francisco, July 16-19) 1984, p. 17.

show how rules for delegate selection and runoff primaries invariably
promote certain interests and retard or inhibit others.

That Jackson's attack on the rules should come after the game had
begun is not at all surprising. Though Democratic party rules are
subject to revision, say every four years, rules can be most vigorously
and effectively challenged only after real experiences in campaigns
or elections provide sufficient grounds and candidates to challenge
them—in short, only after those who mount the challenge have standing to do so.

Of course Mondale and established party leaders opposed such
changes and loudly complained that Jackson was trying to change
the rules after the game had begun. Such opposition was not only
good politics, it was also very clever. Mondale and established party
leaders understood clearly that they had more to lose than to gain
through such rule changes as proposed by Jackson. But more than
this, the argument that Jackson was trying to change the rules after
the game had started appealed to the strong penchant Americans
have to abide by the rules of the game, especially once the game
has started.

So deep is this attachment that we sometimes forget (and leaders
conveniently overlook) the fact that changing the rules is at the very
heart of our politics and on-going political battles. This is evident in
the invariable inclusion of procedures (themselves often biased to
protect the then prevailing interests) by which such changes may be

made. But unless supported by substantial and determined interests, proposals for change are unlikely to overcome the symbolic and substantive strength of our own current structures and rules, including the Constitution. Nonetheless, Jackson's campaign demonstrates anew and dramatically that rules and structures are and have always been at the very heart of American politics, and in large measure they determine who the players are, how the game is played, and thus shape the kinds of issues raised and the manner in which they are resolved.[11]

4. *An attractive candidate with an attractive message can mount an effective campaign and achieve notable accomplishments with a minimum of resources, but to attain even more success, Jackson must build upon the accomplishments and work to overcome flaws and obstacles evident in his 1984 campaign.* An attractive, charismatic leader, Jackson mounted an effective campaign with almost none of the requirements normally expected of political candidates running for a major party presidential nomination. But important as attractiveness and charisma are, Jackson had more going for him. His message was coherent and powerful—a holistic attempt to rally diverse groups, through strong appeals to human rights and economic justice, into a Rainbow Coalition and move all Americans from divisive battlegrounds (e.g., race, class, color) to economic common ground and moral higher ground that would fundamentally change the tone and nature of both our individual relations with each other and our overall domestic and foreign policies.

Jackson's message struck responsive chords among blacks and others, rekindling hopes of achieving the objectives of generations of blacks highlighted by Martin Luther King and the civil rights movement. His task was to re-energize and nourish past and present relationships and win support. Winning the support of the black church was vital. As in the civil rights movement, the black church played a crucial role in Jackson's campaign, giving him access throughout the black community—ready-made, well-established "campaign" offices, and help in fund-raising.

The four C's—charisma, courage, cause, and church—enabled Jackson to conduct a nationwide campaign with seriously limited funds and staff. Charisma and courage, for example, allowed him to take unusual risks which paid unusual dividends, such as his successful effort to win release of Lt. Robert Goodman from a Syrian prison camp. This unpredictability distinguished Jackson's campaign from others and kept him in the spotlight. He also gained immense publicity from the fact that he was the first black person whose candidacy for a major party nomination had to be taken seriously by all concerned.

However, these same factors which allowed Jackson to mount an effective campaign were also detrimental to his candidacy. For example, the same charisma and courage that allowed him to take unusual risks and kept him in the spotlight also caused him to be viewed as much too unpredictable. Some thought that the only thing Jackson had going for him was charisma. The causes he pushed (in both racial and nonracial contexts) undoubtedly cost him support, and the nature and scope of his agenda made it difficult to achieve such objectives through traditional major party structures and electoral politics. More immediately, the lack of money and of a more effective campaign organization forced him to rely greatly on the black church for organizational structure and funding, and his identification with the church undoubtedly stirred qualms, especially among those not familiar with the traditional role of the black church in the black community and in black politics. Although this support from the black church enhanced Jackson's campaign and allowed him to survive, it led him to spend more time campaigning in the black community and to focus on issues of especial interest to blacks, even though the overall concerns of his campaign were much more broadly based and potentially held wider appeal. This perhaps reinforced the tendency of some to view Jackson as an outsider and refer to him as a "black presidential candidate." In the context of American politics, this created an image problem that tended to limit the scope of Jackson's effort and hurt his broader presidential ambitions. And, of course, the Hymie and Farrakhan episodes also created an image problem for Jackson and frustrated his campaign.

Lack of a competitive campaign organization and shortage of campaign funds put Jackson "at the mercy of the news coverage in the 'free media' to get his message across." And though he was obviously successful at "generating visibility and coverage," he had "no control," as one study put it, "over the *content* (emphasis theirs) of this coverage, which restricted his ability to craft a public image through the use of broadcast advertising."[12] And Jackson certainly needed more control over the image he wished to project.

Additionally, the fact that Jackson is black also hurt him. Jackson himself noted the possible influence of race on his campaign: "Race may be a barrier, but, you know, all of us are growing up. At one time, we took the position on black athletes that, excellence be damned, America won't accept them. But then America made an amazing adjustment. America at first wouldn't accept desegregation. But America has adjusted."[13] Nonetheless, race remains a divisive, disadvantaging force in American politics. Public opinion polls continue to ask whether or not Americans would vote for a qualified black person to be president, or if the nation is ready for a black president. And, unfortunately, respondents' answers to these questions indicate clearly that Jackson or any other black candidate would be hurt simply because of his race. To be sure, other factors were involved. White voters did find Jackson, compared to Mondale, "less knowledgeable," "less fair," less likely to "care about people like me," and "far more prejudiced." However, some of these same polls show that "Jackson's profile among whites was surprisingly positive, and comparable to Mondale's in most respects." In fact, white voters "gave Jackson the edge in being exciting, getting things done, owing fewer favors, representing a new way of thinking, and being a strong leader." But most white voters still believed that the nation is not ready for a black president.[11]

How Jackson was able to withstand the effects of these kinds of attitudes on his campaign was summarized well by two scholars who wrote: "Skepticism about Jackson's candidacy was not limited to white voters, the press, and Democratic party leaders. Black leaders, as well, did much to reinforce the preconceived notion that Jackson could not win. That so many voters would cast their votes for a candidate with no chance to win shows both the extraordinary vote-getting ability of Jackson and the still more extraordianary reorientation of many Americans toward the voting alternatives."[15] That Jackson was able to do so well under such circumstances certainly attests to his extraordinary vote-getting ability and underscores the many positive achievements of his campaign.

Notwithstanding these and other problems, an important lesson from the Jackson campaign still remains that an attractive candidate with an attractive message can mount an effective campaign and win notable accomplishments with a minimum of resources. The effectiveness and accomplishments of Jackson's campaign, of course, cannot be assessed solely by traditional criteria in terms of winning primaries, delegates, or even the nomination. Attempts to evaluate Jackson's campaign by such criteria can prove erroneous, even obscuring the overall meaning and significance of Jackson's campaign.

As suggested throughout this volume, the real accomplishments of Jackson's campaign were achieved through what that campaign represented and what it stood for. The infusion of this high measure of symbolism with an increasing and potentially much larger measure of substance gave Jackson's candidacy a potency far beyond what traditional assessments would suggest—a potency grounded in the current and potential strength of black voters and black elected officials and in the untold possibilities of adding to this strong and developing black base through a Rainbow Coalition.

It provided a focused, highly visible opportunity for blacks and minorities to pool and further develop their increasing political resources and promote their interests directly in American politics at its highest level: the nomination and selection of a major presidential candidate. And in doing so, Jackson's candidacy fulfilled one of the chief functions of political campaigns—political education. It provided incentives for many to learn, through active participation, the workings of party structures and rules at local, state, and national levels. Many people from minority groups became more directly involved in the everyday operation of a national presidential campaign, developing skills, knowledge, and experience which could prove useful both in future presidential campaigns and in state and local politics.

Even more concretely, the Jackson campaign stimulated highly notable increases in black voter registration and turnout, leading some scholars to re-examine conventional theories about voter turnout and political behavior among blacks and similar groups.[16] It elected some 400 delegates to the national convention—more than double what some had thought initially possible. Still further, Jackson influenced the nature of the campaign debate, raising issues and bringing perspectives and insights which otherwise might have been overlooked or downplayed—e.g., South Africa, the Middle East, budgetary priorites and allocations, affirmative action, and enforcement of the Voting Rights Act and civil rights laws generally.

The extraordinary nature of Jackson's campaign in some ways resulted from its character as a "campaign-movement." Jackson adapted movement-like objectives and methods to traditional campaign structures and strategies, especially protesting and promoting long-held deep concerns of particular groups, e.g., blacks. To be sure, this effort met with problems but it also yielded important benefits. Consider the following comment from a black parent about Jackson's participation in the primary debates: "When my eight-year-old son saw the . . . debates on television, his reaction was one of surprise. He had not known before seeing these debates that a black person could sit down and debate a former vice president and a U.S. Senator as they all sought the Presidency. . . . That may be the most important lesson of Rev. Jackson's candidacy."[17]

Such generalized and relatively intangible wins—Jackson's growing effect as a role model—posed special problems for the media. One study suggests that "the 'symbolic' nature of the campaign has proven to be a major source of difficulty to the media. While it is undoubtedly true that Jackson's chances of nomination were virtually nil, the frequent repetition of this assertion (no matter how accurate) risked taking on the quality of a self-fulfilling prophecy. The ordinary criteria of electing delegates and winning primaries were largely irrelevant to the true meaning of Jackson's effort. The media were therefore shorn of their normal methods of evaluating the success of a presidential campaign."[18] One might well quibble with the view that the "ordinary criteria of electing delegates and winning primaries were *largely irrelevant* (emphasis mine) to the true meaning of Jackson's effort." Clearly they were relevant, but they constituted only part of the much larger meaning of Jackson's campaign. Nonetheless, Jackson's candidacy was evaluated—as were others—mainly in conventional terms of winning or losing.

The media and others, including some highly visible black leaders, simply did not think that Jackson could win the nomination or the presidency, and this perception carried certain consequences. As one study put it: "This perception that Jackson did not have a chance to become president, more than any other single factor, explains the type of news coverage that Jackson received. Presidential candidates who cannot win the presidency are like horses that can not win a horse-race. They are not newsworthy—or at best their story is a different story than the main racing feature of the day." In addition, the study goes on to suggest that, though their incentives and rewards are somewhat different, party convention delegates as well as the media have an interest in focusing on candidates who can win. For example, reporters who cover successful presidential candidates are usually rewarded by advancements in their profession, and journalists who are the "earliest to discern a political trend" come to be known as the "best analysts."[19]

Our major point here is that chief reliance on conventional norms of winning and losing to assess and report elections hurts a candidate like Jackson. The prevalent use of such norms, plus the sheer study and reflection time needed to assess Jackson's more complex and rather unconventional campaign-movement, made media coverage more difficult, especially given the work habits and requirements of the job. Jackson and similar candidates must take this problem into account and attempt to overcome it, and the media must assess its own effectiveness in reporting such campaigns. Of course, experience can help overcome such problems. The Jackson campaign provided a very practical national education seminar from which the media and all of us, including Jackson, might well learn, hastening the day when problems like these can be attacked from a broader understanding, leading to more positive results.

For such results to be forthcoming in more concrete form, Jackson clearly must build upon the accomplishments and overcome obstacles and flaws of his 1984 campaign. He *must* develop a greater measure of unified support among black leaders for his candidacy. He *must* hold on to his core black constituency and at the same time systematically expand his Rainbow Coalition. He *must* make amends to those whom he might have alienated in the past, especially in the last election (e.g., Jews). He *must* make potential coalition members realize that their successes in the primary campaign will determine their influence in shaping the party ticket, platform, and election campaign and—if the party's candidate wins—in running the government itself. He *must* recruit a more competitive campaign staff and provide it with the management and resources necessary to plan and implement an overall campaign strategy. He *must* expand greatly his fund-raising. He *must* convince both the media and the voters that he is a *serious* contender for the nomination. To accomplish all this and to have maximum impact in 1988, Jackson *must* above all start his "pre-campaign" acitivities much *earlier* than he did in 1984.

And there are some indications that he might be doing just this. In a speech to the April 1986 annual meeting of the National Conference of Black Political Scientists (NCOBPS) held in Chicago, Jackson openly and repeatedly indicated his desire to have criticisms and comments—certainly from a group of political scientists—about his last campaign. It struck me that Jackson expressed a rather balanced view of his campaign: it made progress, but it also made mistakes, and he had a real desire to look back critically in order to prepare for a better day.

In the discussion period following his speech, I asked Jackson directly whether we should consider his comments an open invitation to meet with him at a later date to rehash the campaign and offer advice and criticisms. He assured me and the some 100 other political scientists assembled for the meeting that he was indeed extending such an invitation. Though I have not had a chance to participate personally, I understand that meetings along this line have taken place.

Some may view Jackson's open invitation as good public relations, even good politics, and it is both. But I view it also as a very healthy and reassuring willingness to grow and profit from the lessons of his campaign. Persons whom I respect have told me that Jackson has indeed already begun interacting more frequently with black leaders and leaders from other groups; actively seeking experienced and knowledgeable campaign staff, especially to develop the Rainbow Coalition; and soliciting advice from a wide variety of individuals and groups.

Working to achieve these various "musts" constitutes a formidable undertaking, but the important objectives envisioned appear well worth the effort. Neither major party seems disposed to systematically address the needs and concerns of the locked out, as Jackson is wont to do. As the 1988 Democratic race unfolds, a closer look at support for Jackson's 1984 campaign proves instructive. Though his strongest support came from black voters, Jackson's base of support also included a sizeable proportion of nonblack voters as well. One study, for example, suggests that the fact that Jackson received only 5 percent of the white vote led most analysts to make the rather surface—albeit reasonable—conclusion that "no interracial hue was added to the basic black of Jackson's Rainbow."[20] However, closer analysis indicates that though Jackson received only 5 percent of the

Table 8.4 Jackson's Support from Nonblacks: Selected States

State	Total Vote Received by Jackson in State	Number of Jackson's Total Votes Received from Nonblacks	Percent of Jackson's Total Votes Received from Nonblacks
Alabama	83,943	1,624	1.9%
California	544,953	266,777	50.0
Georgia	143,754	6,655	4.6
Illinois	348,479	62,726	18.0
Indiana	98,223	27,777	28.3
Maryland	129,256	31,484	24.4
Massachusetts	31,548	22,031	69.8
New York	355,315	115,426	32.5
Ohio	236,947	45,240	19.1
Pennsylvania	265,007	64,344	24.3

Sources: *Congressional Quarterly Weekly Report*, June 16, 1984, p. 1443, and U.S. Census Bureau, *Current Population Reports*, Series P-20. Reprinted with permission from Linda Williams and Lorenzo Morris, *Jackson and the Rainbow in Primary and General Election* (University of Illinois Press, forthcoming).

white vote that 5 percent accounted for some 22 percent, or approximately 788,000, of Jackson's total 3.4 million votes nationwide. In fact, votes from nonblacks accounted for a substantial proportion of Jackson's total vote in every nonsouthern state, ranging from 18 or 19 percent in Illinois and Ohio respectively to a high of 33 percent, 50 percent, and 70 percent of Jackson's total vote in New York, California, and Massachusetts respectively. These data suggest that there are at least the makings of a rainbow out there, and the challenge for Jackson is to both broaden his support among nonblack voters generally and increase his already strong and wide support among blacks. Clearly this is an awesome challenge, but it is also an exciting opportunity.

5. *Jackson's campaign illuminates the capacity and limits of party and electoral politics as a way to achieve fundamental policy change.* The nature of electoral politics suggests the need to form coalitions that can win popular majority support. Although these coalitions are difficult to achieve when a candidate is attempting to bring about fundamental, and therefore controversial, policy change, it does not

mean that such efforts should not be attempted. What it does suggest is the difficulty of achieving them through electoral politics.

The price of winning electoral majorities is usually a toning down of one's policy objectives. This applies to electoral arenas as well as to more formal policy-making forums, e.g., Congress. If, as Jackson suggested, some of these objectives are non-negotiable, this effectively narrows the base of popular support. Matters of what Jackson referred to as "self respect" (e.g., eradication of individual and institutional racism) are matters that many consider nonnegotiable. The basic reason for this narrowing of support for strong, unambiguous positions on particular causes is that such issues—i.e., the role of government in social welfare, in affirmative action, in school integration, and in protecting civil rights generally—cause strong disagreement. Moreover, some of the very objectives sought—attempts to overcome institutional and structural bias (runoff primary, at-large elections, delegate selection process)—themselves protect and are protected by structures that perpetuate the status quo—federalism, separation of powers, etc.

More than this, these very changes necessitate the support of those who stand to be hurt by such changes. Even such basic matters as making voter registration easier encounter opposition from those whose interests might be adversely affected by increased voter registration, particularly among certain groups. Obviously then, Jackson's call for stronger enforcement of the 1965 Voting Rights Act is not likely to meet with approval from some established and entrenched political interests.

Moreover, as Jackson found, garnering support, even from those who ostensibly stand to profit from such changes, is difficult, for complex and varied reasons. For example, Jackson projected his Rainbow Coalition on the quite plausible assumption that groups that he would bring into that coalition had such strong common economic, social, and political interests that they could override whatever differences might be involved. This assumption seems well-grounded, but its implementation has incurred major difficulties, ranging from the internal politics and cultural differences to the nature of intergroup relations, perceptions, and contacts. Among blacks, for example, Jackson's problems were apparent from the outset: he was unable to draw certain well-known black leaders into his coalition because some perceived that he had little if anything to offer in return for their support.

Politicians, of whatever color, have concrete reasons to develop and nourish ties and access to people in power, which they are reluctant to forego when they have little reason to expect anything comparable in return. However, aware of the black community's feelings, black leaders were careful not to disparage the causes Jackson represented; they suggested that they could better achieve these causes through Mondale, an established party leader who could win. Similar forces were apparently at work among, as well as between, other groups: some leaders thought they already had access or could work out better deals within existing arrangements.

Moreover, Jackson's problems in forging the Rainbow Coalition illuminate the problems of trying to bring the locked out into the active political arena. Overcoming systemic barriers to such participation requires the support of those whose very power and influence might be diminished or certainly minimized by such increased participation. Hence, entrenched politicians of whatever color are reluctant to do any more than necessary to satisfy the requirements of our democratic symbolic value system—e.g., giving general support for registration and get-out-the-voter drives in keeping with the ever-abiding democratic faith in the people. Also, the deprived and locked out are reluctant to forego present benefits—admittedly few and inequitable but at least there to be utilized in the present—on the basis of promises that even the most ardent Jackson supporter would have to concede are highly problematical and distant. Thus any coalition faces the basic problem of meshing short-term needs and realities with long-term hopes and objectives.

Additionally, the *costs* of increased political involvement and participation account for a tragic chapter in the history of Black Americans.[21] Many in the South, for example, remember that the costs of getting involved in politics ranged from loss of jobs and other benefits to loss of life itself. And while many of the more obvious and brutal barriers to participation have been overcome, Justice Department prosecutions of certain black activists in Alabama in 1985 and 1986 serve as reminders that even formal, much less informal, barriers and methods of discouragement still exist for those to whom Jackson would appeal.[22] Just as obviously, of course, Jackson's call for vigorous enforcement of the Voting Right Act and civil rights laws generally is limited by the politics of implementation, vividly exemplified during the Reagan administration by the policies and practices of those very departments and agencies (Justice, EEOC) charged with the enforcement and implementation of such laws.

Jackson's candidacy further illuminates the kinds of resources and resource mobilization and management needed to succeed in politics. The key concern, of course, is to win more votes than anyone else on election day. And here Jackson could draw upon resources— in symbolic and substantive terms—offered by such legal supports as important court decisions (e.g., *Brown*) and civil rights legislation (e.g., the Voting Rights Act of 1965) which had been spurred by blacks and their allies through the NAACP and the civil rights movement. Jackson also profited from resources offered by the black church. But though votes are the key resource, maximizing that resource requires other resources—money, expertise of various sorts, organization, etc. And Jackson's campaign faced enormous resource problems from the outset, especially in getting people registered and then getting them out to vote, and otherwise informing them about the different rules and requirements for participation in presidential primary and caucus systems.

These difficulties were *real* among the groups to whom Jackson was appealing. He and his organization had to fight long-established traditions of nonregistration, nonvoting, and nonparticipation created and perpetuated by law and practice. Fortunately, Jackson provided the kind of charismatic symbolism and articulated the kind of message that stirred an unprecedented number of blacks to register and to vote. From 1980 to 1984, for example, black voter registration in eleven southern states increased by almost 700,000, from 4,254,000 to 4,949,000.[23] This unprecedented interest and activity was undoubtedly also spurred by reactions against the blatantly negative policies and actions of the Reagan administration. The important challenge for Jackson and black leaders in the 1988 campaign and in the long run, however, is how to nurture and maintain this unprecedented political interest.

The business of campaigning, of overcoming formal and informal barriers to political participation, also requires financial resources. However, the same socioeconomic variables that militate against political participation also militate against raising money from those to whom Jackson appealed. Hence, Jackson's campaign funds were limited—a fact well publicized by his repeated boast of how little money he spent to get such great returns in contrast to the vast sums spent by Mondale and Hart.

Similarly, among these groups relatively fewer persons possess the kind of expertise, not to mention the experience, needed to run a major party presidential nomination campaign. Lawyers, policy analysts, economists, journalists, and computer specialists are relatively few in number, and even fewer of these can afford the time to give to such endeavors. In short, volunteer help—so essential to campaigns—is sparse among the groups to whom Jackson appealed, and limited funds could support only a limited staff. Numerous stories focus on the organization and staff problems—scheduling, planning, publicity, advertising—of the Jackson campaign; most in one way or another related to lack of funds and suggest how Jackson's efforts were limited in these respects.[21] And, given the relatively limited political experience of his targeted groups, the Jackson organization would have to do much more than the usual amount of education and encouragement usually associated with political campaigning.

At best a campaign like Jackson's illuminates the nature and vagaries of our political system. Given the kind of strong supports needed to surmount various structural and ideological barriers, electoral politics is unlikely to process definitive, non-negotiable demands but may be able to process the kind of broad parameters in which such demands can be more favorably negotiated. These broad parameters, in the main, result from the kind of coalition politics that our system fosters. But even the enactment of such broad parameters, those that envision fundamental social-political change, requires an enormous and unusual combination of resources. Consider, for example, the kind of resources needed to enact the 1964 and 1965 Civil Rights Acts: revolutionary court decisions; massive protests and demonstrations by racial, religious, labor, and civil groups; and key bipartisan support in the Congress. Obviously, the 1964 and 1965 legislation enacted the kind of broad parameters within which fundamental political-social change could, and in many ways has, come about.

Jackson's campaign may also be viewed both as a response to the incremental pace by which these important policies (including civil rights and antipoverty legislation) have been implemented and as an example of the difficulty of maintaining the kind of support that was

originally needed to get these measures enacted. The politics of enactment can be quite different from the politics of implementation.
Those who stand to be primary beneficiaries of such policies must
follow through; they cannot relax once policies are enacted. Moreover, what groups saw as common interests at the enactment stage
they might well view as conflicting interests at the implementation
stage. The affirmative action controversy provides a good example
of how those who were once supporters have now become open
adversaries: whereas past administrations generally supported affirmative action, the Reagan administration openly opposes such policies.

The broad scope and nature of Jackson's campaign really envisioned fundamental changes in both party politics and American politics generally. But such fundamental changes go far beyond what
has been traditionally and currently viewed as politically acceptable
and in the mainstream of American electoral politics. Consequently,
such changes are highly unlikely to gain approval from either major
party. Yet Jackson chose to raise these issues and conduct his campaign-movement through the Democratic party. And most blacks
supported Jackson and continue to support the Democratic party.

Why did Jackson decide to launch his effort within the Democratic
party rather than to form a third party or a movement outside both
major parties? A primary reason, as I see it, has to do with the stark
history of limited successes and failures of such third-party ventures
in American politics, including the dismal experience of blacks in
the early 1970s.[25] To be sure, the nature and structure of American
politics—with its premium on building majority coalitions—provide
powerful incentives for working through the major parties. Further,
it makes sense for blacks, as one of the Democratic party's largest
and most loyal constituent groups, to attempt to seek rewards more
commensurate with their past and continuing support and to build
on their positions of influence gained in local mayoral and congressional elections. Still further, unlike special-issue or limited-agenda
third parties of the past, Jackson's campaign was holistic in nature,
covering the range of domestic and foreign policy concerns. And
such a broad agenda would need a broad coalition, such as generally
can only be mustered by the major parties.

On the other hand, it also makes sense for blacks to re-evaluate
their political strategies and options in view of the Jackson experi-

ence and the indifferent, even negative, postures of both major parties. The goal of Jackson's Rainbow Coalition—to gain for the locked out a continuing presence and influence in the political process—clearly cannot be achieved through a continuous "politics of crisis." But given the nature of our political system, unconventional methods (marches, demonstrations, protests), including those that engender crisis politics, cannot be eschewed altogether. Nor, of course, can such groups overlook the importance of legal strategies in their efforts, even though judicial decisions are, in the long run, also subject to changes in the overall political-social climate. Consider, for example, adverse policy changes portended for blacks and minorities as a result of appointments of the Reagan administration to the federal judiciary.[26]

In general, given the present structure and operation of our political system, electoral as well as less conventional methods may be necessary in order for the locked out to gain and maintain influence and access. Jackson's 1984 campaign was directed at gaining influence and access through conventional methods. Given its lofty goals and limited resources, that proved a most difficult task. But it is a campaign that must be won if such groups are to be fully included and exercise continuous influence and access in the political system.

6. *The strength of Jackson's candidacy, in combination with other factors such as the party's attempt to develop a more centrist image, might well spur blacks and other disadvantaged minorites to take much more aggressive stances within the Democratic party and to embrace a more independent style of politics that could well go beyond that party.* This is an important lesson for both major political parties and for others as well. Despite many signs that Jackson could not possibly win the nomination, including opposition from certain key black leaders, black voters still voted for Jesse Jackson in record numbers, clearly suggesting that blacks and others want candidates for whom they can vote with their hearts as well as with their heads.[27] And the fact that blacks voted for Jackson in unprecedented numbers suggests that they viewed Jackson's candidacy with sophistication and understanding, perceiving it in context of long-term, rather than merely short-term, benefits. The strength of Jackson's support, especially among blacks, suggests a large measure of dissatisfaction

with status quo politics and status quo politicians, whatever their race or color.

These factors could well provide the incentives for blacks and others to take more aggressive stances within the Democratic party and even move toward a more independent "movement" style of politics that could go beyond the party. Some evidence already indicates a slight but discernible softening in black allegiance to the Democratic party. Moreover, a kind of independent politics, with independent candidacies, has been going on in Mississippi for some time, mainly in reaction against runoff primaries—an issue that Jackson raised to a litmus-test level during his campaign. This does not necessarily mean breaking ties with the Democratic party. Rather, it could allow those who pursue such strategies to gain more leverage in bargaining within the party or, if necessary, in other arenas—e.g., the Republican party.

Obviously, of course, there are drawbacks and impediments to independent, third-party politics in a two-party system. But a combination of factors could strengthen the appeal of some type of independent strategy, at least in selected arenas. For example, third-party black candidates could circumvent runoff primaries. Another incentive for an independent movement at the national level is the obviously poor treatment Jackson and blacks generally received at the 1984 Democratic National Convention, a situation further exacerbated by apparent efforts of white party leaders to recapture white middle America in the wake of Mondale's devastating defeat at the hands of Reagan.

Specifically the open, bold attempts by Democratic party leaders to reshape the party image to placate the white South and conservatives generally send rather definite cues to Black Americans. These attempts, viewed in context of the continuing basic policy differences between blacks and whites, could pose serious problems for the Democratic party. To be sure, a 1986 poll taken by the Joint Center for Political Studies and the Gallup organization suggests an increasing policy convergence between whites and blacks on what they consider the most important problems facing the nation. Indeed, though their ordering of issues somewhat differed, both whites and blacks named unemployment, drug abuse, and the high cost of living as the top three issues. In a similar 1984 poll blacks named unemployment, government programs to help the poor, and civil rights as the most important problems. Whites too named unemployment but then listed the federal deficit and inflation as the most important. Thus, the 1986 poll indicated some convergence between whites and blacks on what they consider the nation's top priorities.

On the other hand, blacks and whites continue to differ sharply on the role of government in solving these problems. They also continue to differ sharply on issue priorites that disproportionately affect blacks. For example, blacks ranked government programs to help the poor as the fifth most important problem, but it ranked fifteenth among whites. Similarly, blacks ranked civil rights sixth, but whites ranked it near the bottom of their list of priorities, nineteenth. Overall then, these continuing sharp policy differences between blacks and whites portend problems enough for party leaders without open attempts to court whites and effectively ignore blacks, a strategy guaranteed to increase rather than lessen divisions within the party. Nonetheless, in their apparent attempt to develop a new centrist image, party leaders seem to be following just such a strategy both in their 1986 Democratic Policy Commission Statement of Principles as well as through the Democratic Leadership Council, an independent policy group established in 1985 "to give elected officials a greater voice in party affairs."[28]

Everything about the 1984 campaign and elections indicates that blacks have more than paid their dues to the Democratic party, and they have every right to expect, even demand, more in return. Jackson's nomination campaign activated precisely those voters (e.g., blacks) whom evidence suggests are likely to support Democrats. His actions at the national convention, highlighted by his speech, showed clearly Jackson's fervent attempt to work *within* the Democratic party despite the poor treatment accorded him and his delegates by party leaders. And subsequent developments, such as the criticisms leveled by Mayor Andrew Young against Mondale's campaign staff, suggest rather forcefully that, in exchange for their support, black leaders want to be fully included in party deliberations. But they were not. Despite it all, however, Jackson and blacks did indeed support Mondale and Democrats in the November elections, giving him some 90 percent of their vote, far more than any other group. That blacks supported Democratic candidates in the 1986 elections at the state and local levels is clearly reflected by the crucial role black voters played in certain key successful senate races, e.g., Alabama, North Carolina, Georgia, and Louisiana.[29]

In any case, I myself, and I suspect many other blacks as well, did not approach the 1984 elections with a high level of enthusiasm for the party ticket; my high-level enthusiasm against the incumbent administration gave me the incentive to turn out on election day. But such negative reasons for voting cannot be sustained for long, for, as stated earlier, blacks and similar groups need someone and something they can vote *for*, not *against*. The plain truth, however, is that neither party seems disposed to systematically and satisfactorily address the major concerns of these groups.

Should circumstances like this persist, it could indeed become increasingly difficult to answer the question put by Georgia Democratic state representative Tyrone Brooks, who headed Jesse Jackson's 1984 campaign in that state: "If the two-party system works well for business men, for teachers, for labor, for Jews, for Catholics, for everyone else," asked Brooks, "why shouldn't blacks make it work for us?"[30] Certainly it should work for blacks too, and for blacks to act on this basis would undoubtedly tell us a lot about the nature of our two-party system and about American politics generally. On the other hand, it could also tell us about how that system has *not* worked to overcome particular problems facing blacks and minorities as it does for others.

The success of Jackson's 1984 campaign indicates that black voters and other minorities, no longer satisfied to remain clients whose benefits would still determined largely by white patrons, may be on the verge of participating more directly in American pluralist politics. The success of black candidates at state and local levels plus the highly visible and vigorous campaign waged by Jackson provide incentives, experience, and encouragement for increased black participation. Again, however, the problem for Jackson and other black leaders will be how to maintain and nurture such mass interest long enough to provide more tangible benefits and incentives to those most in need but who, for a host of reasons, are least likely to participate in politics. Essentially, it remains a problem of achieving *short-term* benefits while simultaneously pursuing *long-term* goals.

The 1988 elections offer various interests, including blacks and minorities, a wonderful opportunity to assess and re-evaluate their national political strategy and options. The presidential nominations of both parties appear wide open: there is no incumbent running for re-election nor does there appear to be an heir apparent in either party, especially among the Democrats. All of this, of course, must be kept in mind as we look toward the 1988 elections and beyond.

7. *The nature, tone, and substance of Jackson's campaign and his success among blacks suggest strongly that Black Americans are not satisfied with their current conditions and remain firmly committed to the principles and goals of the civil rights movement.* Though obvious progress has been made, there is no stopping at some inclusion until there is full inclusion of blacks and minorities in every sector of the American political-social order. Only in this way will we reach our full potential as a nation and as a free people. This is an important lesson from the Jackson experience that all Americans would do well to study. Jackson struck a responsive chord in the black community. From the outset he repeatedly emphasized that the central thrust of his effort was to bring about the full inclusion of blacks and similar locked-out groups into every sector of American politics and society. That this met with wide approval is clear from Jackson's strong and deep support among blacks regardless of socioeconomic status and class.

But while Jackson straightforwardly emphasized the unfulfilled goals and objectives of the civil rights movement, his campaign went much farther. It encompassed the full spectrum of issues, proving that blacks can no longer be assuaged by attention to civil rights issues only: they are concerned about the whole range of domestic and foreign affairs. Jackson continuously stressed how such issues as the military-defense budget influence directly issues such as social welfare that are of vital concern to those whom he would represent. By reminding us of such relationships, Jackson's campaign served important educational functions.

Thus Jackson's campaign dramatized the problems and divisions that we face as a nation and as a people, such persistent conditions as hunger, poverty, and unemployment that continue to plague significant portions of our population despite important and meaningful progress engendered by court decisions and legislative actions. To be sure, such progress indicates to some that the political process is now sufficiently open so that any person who wishes to can overcome his or her individual circumstances. This view seems represented especially in the Reagan administration and increasingly in Democratic party thinking and planning.

However, if there is any one lesson to be learned from the Jackson campaign, it is that a very large number of persons, particularly blacks, do not share this view. Structural, institutional, and systemic barriers continue to hurt and discriminate against blacks and minorities disproportionately. Moreover, the genius of Jackson's Rainbow Coalition is that he rightly conceives that there are many other persons—especially minorities and many poor whites as well—who, like blacks, share more of the hardships and pains of exclusion than they realize or care to admit. The guiding objective of the Rainbow Coalition, as I understand it, is to make these diverse groups more aware of the commonality of interests that they all share.

Forming such a coalition faces difficult, perhaps intractable, obstacles. But regardless of its eventual shape or success, no matter how hard we try, we cannot ignore the substance of the issues raised by Jackson. Matters such as providing adequate food, decent shelter, meaningful jobs, quality education, and fair and equal treatment for all persons are too important, too central and intimate to the full development and recognition of individual human potential and worth, to be brushed aside. Campaigns like Jackson's will either successfully overcome such problems, making for a peaceful, prosperous society, or such problems will remain and become a persistent, perhaps increasing threat to the peaceful and prosperous society that we all desire. If the latter situation should prevail, more campaigns like Jackson's will occur, though the form and methods may vary.

Essentially, Jesse Jackson's campaign engaged him in a basic struggle of definition. It was an attempt to redefine the basic symbols of American experience: What is the meaning of "flag," "country," and "patriotism," of "freedom," "justice," "liberty," "equality," and of the "American Dream?" It was a struggle for identity: How are we to define ourselves and others? Who are we? Who counts and who doesn't, or doesn't everybody count? It was an attempt to redefine some basic sociopolitical roles and relationships: How does government relate to individuals and groups, such as blacks and the Democratic party? What are to be their rights, their opportunities, and their futures?

Jackson attempted to reverse much of the harmful symbolism that has long plagued American politics and society. He argued that social outcasts are victims who deserve and should demand justice, that what is "black" or "outcast" is of positive value and not a source of contamination, a threat to be ostracized, repressed, or denied. This refers not only to black people, who obviously are of value, but of what "black" has for too long symbolized to many whites. Much of what has kept people excluded from full participation in American society is the meaning many whites attach to color, and gaining full inclusion requires that the meaning of color and all that it implies must be addressed more holistically. He extended this argument to other groups to whom similar negative connotations have attached, such as the poor or the underclass.

At a more substantive level, Jackson's campaign attempted to redefine the nation's policy agenda, to reorder and redefine old, recurring issues and to identify new emerging ones. It also attempted to redefine resource allocation, to distribute benefits and costs more equitably among individuals, groups, and classes. At base, Jackson's campaign may be viewed as an attempt to restructure government and recast society itself so as to bring about the full inclusion of all peoples and groups.

Jackson, like Martin Luther King and the civil rights movement, called for a rebirth of America by appealing to the basic goodness and morality of all Americans, to the ringing symbols and glowing objectives embodied in the Declaration of Independence and the Constitution. He urged Americans to turn against ideas, structures, and institutions that serve as bastions for protecting the established, the haves against the have-nots. Jackson's effort clearly was not a short-term endeavor that could be accomplished in a single presidential campaign. Therefore Jackson's campaign threatened the status quo and those who would prefer that only marginal changes be made as needed to maintain normalcy.

The slogan "Our Time Has Come" conveys a number of messages. One message that came through clearly in Jackson's 1984 campaign is that the time has come when the locked out must be fully included throughout the entire socioeconomic and political spectrum, having full and equal opportunity to enjoy its benefits as well as share in its responsibilities. But another interpretation of "Our Time Has Come," one that did not come through as definitively in Jackson's campaign (and certainly in no other campaign), is that the time has now come when the entire country must come to grips with the serious problems and divisions that continue to plague us and proceed with carefully planned programs and unrelenting resolve to overcome them. Only then will all Americans—regardless of race, sex, nationality, religion, sexual preference, age, and economic status—achieve their full potential individually as free people and collectively as a nation.

The basic challenge of Jackson's campaign cannot be minimized or ignored. It seeks to clarify and stress the importance of fully including the locked out so we can more readily understand how full inclusion will redound to *all* of our collective and individual benefit. The serious problems and divisions we face affect *all* Americans: they stunt our growth and development, limit our potential, restrict our enjoyment, hem us in, and in general restrict and narrow our freedom at home and abroad. "OUR TIME HAS COME" to do something about this. "OUR TIME HAS COME" to realize America's potential.

Appendix

Address by the Reverend Jesse Jackson to the Democratic National Convention, July 17, 1984*

Tonight we come together bound by our faith in a mighty God, with genuine respect and love for our country and inheriting the legacy of a great Party—the Democratic Party—which is the best hope for redirecting our Nation on a more humane, just and peaceful course.

This is not a perfect Party. We are not a perfect people. Yet, we are called to a perfect mission: our mission to feed the hungry; to clothe the naked; to house the homeless; to teach the illiterate; to provide jobs for the jobless; and to choose the human race over the nuclear race. (Applause)

We are gathered here this week to nominate a candidate and adopt a Platform which will expand, unify, direct and inspire our Party and the Nation to fulfill this mission.

My constituency is the desperate, the damned, the disinherited, the disrespected and the despised. They are restless and seek relief. They have voted in record numbers. They have invested the faith, hope and trust that they have in us. The Democratic Party must send them a signal that we care. I pledge my best not to let them down.

There is the call of conscience, redemption, expansion, healing and unity. Leadership must heed the call of conscience, redemption, expansion, healing and unity, for they are the key to achieving our

*Source: *Democratic National Committee, Official Proceedings of the 1984 Democratic National Convention* (Washington, D.C., 1984), p. 301.

mission. Time is neutral and does not change things. With courage and initiative, leaders change things.

No generation can choose the age or circumstance in which it is born, but through leadership it can choose to make the age in which it is born, an age of enlightenment, an age of jobs, and peace and justice. (Applause)

Only leadership—that intangible combination of gifts, discipline, information, circumstance, courage, timing, will and divine inspiration—can lead us out of the crisis in which we find ourselves. The leadership can mitigate the misery of our Nation. Leadership can part the waters and lead our Nation in the direction of the Promised Land. Leadership can lift the boats stuck at the bottom.

I have had the rare opportunity to watch seven men, and then two, pour out their souls, offer their service and heed the call of duty to direct the course of our Nation. There is a proper season for everything. There is a time to sew, a time to reap. There is a time to compete, and a time to cooperate.

I ask for your vote on the first ballot as a vote for a new direction with this Party and this Nation. (Applause) A vote of conviction, a vote of conscience. (Applause)

But I will be proud to support the nominee of this Convention for the presidency of the United States of America. (Applause) Thank you.

I have watched the leadership of our Party develop and grow. My respect for both Mr. Mondale and Mr. Hart is great. I have watched them struggle with the crosswinds and crossfires of being public servants, and I believe they will both continue to try to serve us faithfully.

I am elated by the knowledge that for the first time in our history, a woman, Geraldine Ferraro, will be recommended to share our ticket. (Applause)

Throughout this campaign, I have tried to offer leadership to the Democratic Party and the Nation. If in my high moments, I have done some good, offered some service, shed some light, healed some wounds, rekindled some hope, stirred someone from apathy and indifference, or in any way along the way helped somebody, then this campaign has not been in vain. (Applause)

For friends who loved and cared for me, for a God who spared me and for a family who understood, I am eternally grateful.

If, in my low moments, in word, deed or attitude, through some error of temper, taste or tone, I have caused anyone discomfort, created pain, or revived someone's fears, that was not my truest self. If there were occasions when my grape turned into a raisin, and my job-bell lost its resonance, please forgive me. Charge it to my head, and not my heart. My head—so limited in its finitude; my heart which is boundless in its love for the human family. I am not a perfect servant. I am a public servant, doing my best against the odds. As I develop and serve, be patient. God is not finished with me yet. (Applause)

This campaign has taught me much; that leaders must be tough enough to fight, tender enough to cry, human enough to make mistakes, humble enough to admit them, strong enough to absorb the pain and resilient enough to bounce back and keep on moving. (Applause)

For leaders, the pain is often intense. But you must smile through your tears and keep moving with the faith that there is a brighter side somewhere.

I went to see Hubert Humphrey three days before he died. He had just called Richard Nixon from his dying bed, and many people wondered why. I asked him. He said, "Jesse, from this vantage point, with the sun setting in my life, all of the speeches, the political conventions, the crowds and the great fights are behind me now. At a time like this you are forced to deal with your irreducible essence, forced to grapple with that which is really important to you. And what I have concluded about life," Hubert Humphrey said, "When all is said and done, we must forgive each other, and redeem each other, and move on."

Our Party is emerging from one of its most hard fought battles for the Democratic Party's presidential nomination in our history. But our healthy competition should make us better, not bitter. (Applause)

We must use the insight, wisdom and experience of the late Hubert Humphrey as a balm for the wounds in our Party, this Nation and the world. We must forgive each other, redeem each other, regroup and move on.

Our flag is red, white and blue, but our Nation is a rainbow—Red, Yellow, Brown, Black and White—we're all precious in God's sight. (Applause)

America is not like a blanket—one piece of unbroken cloth, the same color, the same texture, the same size. America is more like a quilt—many patches, many pieces, many colors, many sizes, all woven and held together by a common thread. The White, the Hispanic, the Black, the Arab, the Jew, the woman, the Native American, the small farmer, the businessperson, the environmentalist, the peace activist, the young, the old, the lesbian, the gay and the disabled make up the American quilt. (Applause)

Even in our fractured state, all of us count and fit somewhere. We have proven that we can survive without each other. But we have not proven that we can win and make progress without each other. We must come together. (Applause)

From Fannie Lou Hamer in Atlantic City in 1964 to the Rainbow Coalition in San Francisco today; from the Atlantic to the Pacific, we have experienced pain but progress as we ended America's apartheid laws, we got public accommodations, we secured voting rights, we obtained open housing, as young people got the right to vote. We lost Malcolm, Martin, Medgar, Bobby and John and Viola. The team that got us here must be expanded, not abandoned. (Applause)

Twenty years ago, tears welled up in our eyes as the bodies of Schwerner, Goodman and Chaney were dredged from the depths of a river in Mississippi. Twenty years later, our communities, Black and Jewish, are in anguish, anger and in pain. Feelings have been hurt on both sides.

There is a crisis in communications. Confusion is in the air. But we cannot afford to lose our way. We may agree to agree; or agree to disagree on issues; we must bring back civility to the tensions.

We are co-partners in a long and rich religious history—the Judeo-Christian traditions. Many Blacks and Jews have a shared passion for social justice at home and peace abroad. We must seek a revival of the spirit, inspired by a new vision and new possibilities. We must return to higher ground. (Applause)

We are bound by Moses and Jesus, but also connected with Islam and Mohammed. These three great religions—Judaism, Christianity and Islam—were all born in the revered and Holy City of Jerusalem.

We are bound by Dr. Martin Luther King, Jr., and Rabbi Abraham Heschel, crying out from their graves for us to reach common ground. We are bound by shared blood and shared sacrifices. We are much too intelligent; much too bound by our Judeo-Christian heritage;

much too victimized by racism, sexism, militarism and anti-Semitism; much too threatened as historical scapegoats to go on divided one from another. We must turn from fingerpointing to clasped hands. We must share our burdens and our joys with each other once again. We must turn to each other and not on each other, and choose higher ground. (Applause)

Twenty years later, we cannot be satisfied by just restoring the old coalition. Old wine skins must make room for new wine. We must heal and expand. The Rainbow Coalition is making room for Arab Americans. They, too, know the pain and hurt of racial and religious rejection. They must not continue to be made pariahs. The Rainbow Coalition is making room for Hispanic Americans who this very night are living under the threat of the Simpson-Mazzoli bill. (Applause) And farm workers from Ohio who are fighting the Campbell Soup Company with a boycott to achieve legitimate workers' rights. (Applause)

The Rainbow is making room for the Native American, the most exploited people of all, a people with the greatest moral claim amongst us. We support them as they seek the restoration of their ancient land and claim amongst us. We support them as they seek the restoration of land and water rights, as they seek to preserve their ancestral homelands and the beauty of a land that was once all theirs. They can never receive a fair share for all they have given us. They must finally have a fair chance to develop their great resources and to preserve their people and their culture.

The Rainbow Coalition includes Asian Americans, now being killed in our streets, scapegoats for the failures of corporate, industrial and economic policies.

The Rainbow is making room for the young Americans. Twenty years ago, our young people were dying in a war for which they could not even vote. Twenty years later, young America has the power to stop a war in Central America and the responsibility to vote in great numbers. (Applause) Young America must be politically active in 1984. The choice is war or peace. We must make room for young America.

The Rainbow includes disabled veterans. The color scheme fits in the Rainbow. The disabled have their handicap revealed and their genius concealed; while the able-bodied have their genius revealed and their disability concealed. But ultimately, we must judge people by their values and their contribution. Don't leave anybody out. I would rather have Roosevelt in a wheelchair than Reagan on a horse. (Applause)

The Rainbow is making room for small farmers. They have suffered tremendously under the Reagan regime. They will either receive 90 percent parity or 100 percent charity. We must address their concerns and make room for them.

The Rainbow includes lesbians and gays. No American citizen ought to be denied equal protection under the law.

We must be unusually committed and caring as we expand our family to include new members. All of us must be tolerant and understanding as the fears and anxieties of the rejected and the Party leadership express themselves in many different ways. Too often, what we call hate, as if it were some deeply rooted philosophy or strategy, is simply ignorance, anxiety, paranoia, fear and insecurity. (Applause)

To be strong leaders, we must be long suffering as we seek to right the wrongs of our Party and our Nation. We must expand our Party, heal our Party and unify our Party. That is our mission in 1984. (Applause)

We are often reminded that we live in a great Nation, and we do, but it can be greater still. The Rainbow is mandating a new definition of greatness. We must not measure greatness from the mansion down, but the manger up.

Jesus said that we should not be judged by the bark we wear but by the fruit that we bear. Jesus said that we must measure greatness by how we treat the least of these.

President Reagan says the Nation is in recovery. Those 90,000 corporations that made a profit last year but paid no Federal taxes are recovering. The 37,000 military contractors who have benefitted from Reagan's more than doubling of the military budget in peacetime, surely they are recovering.

The big corporations and rich individuals who received the bulk of the three-year multi-billion tax cut from Mr. Reagan are recovering. But no such recovery is under way for the least of these. Rising tides don't lift all boats, particularly those stuck at the bottom.

For the boats stuck at the bottom, there is a misery index. This Administration has made life more miserable for the poor. Its attitude has been contemptuous. Its policies and programs have been cruel and unfair to the working people. They must be held accountable in November for increasing infant mortality among the poor. In Detroit (Applause)—in Detroit, one of the great cities of the western world, babies are dying at the same rate as Honduras, the most underdeveloped Nation in our hemisphere. This Administration must be held accountable for policies that have contributed to the growing poverty in America. There are now 34 million people in poverty, 15 percent of our Nation. Twenty-three million are White, 11 million Black, Hispanic, Asian and others, mostly women and children. By the end of this year, there will be 41 million people in poverty. We cannot stand idly by. We must fight for change now. (Applause)

Under this regime, we look at Social Security. The 1981 budget cuts included nine permanent Social Security benefit cuts totalling $20 billion over five years.

Small businesses have suffered on the Reagan tax cuts. Only 18 percent of total business tax cuts went to them, 82 percent to big business.

Health care under Mr. Reagan has been sharply cut. Education under Mr. Reagan has been cut 25 percent. Under Mr. Reagan there are now 9.7 million female head families. They represent 16 percent of all families. Half of all of them are poor. Seventy percent of all poor children live in a house headed by a woman, where there is no man.

Under Mr. Reagan, the Administration has cleaned up only six of 546 priority toxic waste dumps.

Farmers' real net income was only about half its level in 1979.

Many say that the race in November will be decided in the South. President Reagan is depending on the conservative South to return him to office. But the South, I tell you, is unnaturally conservative. The South is the poorest region in our Nation and therefore with the least to conserve. In his appeal to the South, Mr. Reagan is trying to substitute flags and prayer cloths for food and clothing and education, health care and housing. (Applause)

Mr. Reagan will ask us to pray, and I believe in prayer. I have come this way by the power of prayer. But then, we must watch false prophecy. He cuts energy assistance to the poor, cuts breakfast programs from children, cuts lunch programs from children, cuts job training from children, and then says to an empty table, "Let us pray." (Applause) Apparently he is not familiar with the structure of a prayer. You thank the Lord for the food that you are about to receive, not the food that just left. (Laughter and applause) I think that we should pray, but don't pray for the food that left. Pray for the man that took the food—to leave.

We need a change. We need a change in November. (Applause)

Under Mr. Reagan, the misery index has risen for the poor. The danger index has risen for everybody. Under this Administration, we have lost the lives of our boys in Central America and Honduras, in Grenada, in Lebanon, in a nuclear standoff in Europe. Under this Administration, one-third of our children believe they will die in a nuclear war. The danger index is increasing in this world.

All the talk about the defense against Russia; the Russian submarines are closer, and their missiles are more accurate. We live in a world tonight more miserable and a world more dangerous. While Reaganomics and Reaganism is talked about often, so often we miss the real meaning. Reaganism is a spirit, and Reaganomics represents the real economic facts of life.

In 1980, Mr. George Bush, a man with reasonable access to Mr. Reagan, did an analysis of Mr. Reagan's economic plan. Mr.George Bush concluded that Reagan's plan was "voodoo economics." He was right. (Applause)

Third Party candidate John Anderson said "a combination of military spending, tax cuts, and a balanced budget by 1984 would be accomplished with blue smoke and mirrors." They were both right.

Mr. Reagan talks about a dynamic recovery. There is some measure of recovery. Three and a half years later, unemployment has inched just below where it was when he took office in 1981. There are still 8.1 million people officially unemployed, 11 million working only part-time. Inflation has come down, but let's analyze for a moment who has paid the price for this superficial economic recovery.

Mr. Reagan curbed inflation by cutting consumer demand. He cut consumer demand with conscious and callous fiscal and monetary policies. He used the federal budget to deliberately induce unemployment and curb social spending. He then waged and supported tight monetary policies of the Federal Reserve Board to deliberately drive up interest rates, again to curb consumer demand created through borrowing. Unemployment reached 10.7 percent. We experienced skyrocketing interest rates. Our dollar inflated abroad. There were record bank failures, record farm foreclosures, record business bankruptcies, record budget deficits, record trade deficits.

Mr. Reagan brought inflation down by destabilizing our economy and disrupting family life. He promised, he promised in 1980 a balanced budget, but instead we now have a record $200 billion budget deficit. Under Mr. Reagan, the cumulative budget deficit for his four years is more than the sum total of deficits from George Washington through Jimmy Carter combined.

I tell you, we need a change. (Applause)

How is he paying for these short-term jobs? Reagan's economic recovery is being financed by deficit spending, $200 billion a year. Military spending, a major cause of this deficit, is projected over the next five years to be nearly $2 trillion, and will cost about $40,000 for every taxpaying family.

When the government borrows $200 billion annually to finance the deficit, this encourages the private sector to make its money off of interest rates as opposed to development and economic growth.

Even money abroad—we don't have enough money domestically to finance the debts, so we are now borrowing money abroad from foreign banks, governments, and financial institution: $40 billion in 1983, $70-$80 billion in 1984, 40 percent of our total, over $100 billion, 50 percent of our total in 1985. By 1989, it is projected that 50 percent of all individual income taxes will be going just to pay for interest on that debt.

The United States used to be the largest exporter of capital, but under Mr. Reagan, we will quite likely become the largest debtor Nation.

About two weeks ago, on July the 4th, we celebrated our Declaration of Independence, yet every day supply-side economics is making our Nation more economically dependent and less economically free. Five to six percent of our Gross National Product is now being eaten up with President Reagan's budget deficits. To depend on foreign military powers to protect our national security would be foolish, making us dependent and less secure, yet Reaganomics has us increasingly dependent on foreign economic sources.

This consumer-led but deficit-financed recovery is unbalanced and artificial. We have a challenge as Democrats to point a way out. Democracy guarantees opportunity, not success. Democracy guarantees the right to participate, not a license for either a majority or a minority to dominate. The victory for the Rainbow Coalition in the platform debates today was not whether we won or lost, but that we raised the right issues.

We could afford to lose the vote; issues are non-negotiable. We could not afford to avoid raising the right questions. Our self-respect and our moral integrity were at stake. Our heads are perhaps bloody, but not bowed. Our back is straight. We can go home and face our people. Our vision is clear. (Applause)

When we think on this journey from slaveship to championship, that we have gone from the planks of the boardwalk in Atlantic City in 1964 to fighting to help to write the planks in the Platform in San Francisco in 1984, there is a deep and abiding sense of joy in our souls in spite of the tears in our eyes. Though there are missing planks, there is a solid foundation upon which to build. Our Party can win, but we must provide hope which will inspire people to struggle and achieve, provide a plan that shows the way out of our dilemma and then lead the way.

In 1984, my heart is made to feel glad, because I know there is a way out—justice. The requirement for rebuilding America is justice. The linchpin of progressive politics in our Nation will not come from the North. They in fact will come from the South.

That is why I argue over and over again. We look from Virginia around to Texas. There is only one Black Congressperson out of 115. Nineteen years later, we are locked out of the Congress, the Senate and the Governor's Mansion.

What does this large Black vote mean? Why do I fight to win second primaries and fight gerrymandering and annexation and at-large elections? Why do we fight over that? Because I tell you you cannot hold someone in the ditch unless you linger there with them. (Applause) Unless you linger there. (Applause)

If you want a change in this Nation, you enforce that Voting Rights Act. We will get 12 to 20 Black, Hispanic, female and progressive congresspersons from the South. We can save the cotton, but we have got to fight the boll weevils. We have got to make a judgment. We have got to make a judgment.

It is not enough to hope ERA will pass. How can we pass ERA? If Blacks vote in great numbers, progressive Whites win. It is the only way progressive Whites win. If Blacks vote in great numbers, Hispanics win. When Blacks, Hispanics and progressive Whites vote, women win. When women win, children win. When women and children win, workers win. We must all come up together. We must come up together. (Spontaneous demonstration) Thank you.

I tell you, in all of our joy and excitement, we must not save the world and lose our souls. We should never short-circuit enforcing the Voting Rights Act at every level. When one of us rises, all of us will rise. Justice is the way out. Peace is the way out. We should not act as if nuclear weaponry is negotiable and debatable.

In this world in which we live, we dropped the bomb on Japan and felt guilty, but in 1984 other folks have also got bombs. This time, if we drop the bomb, six minutes later we, too, will be destroyed. It is not about dropping the bomb on somebody. It is about dropping the bomb on everybody. We must choose to develop minds over guided missiles, and think it out and not fight it out. It is time for a change. (Applause)

Our foreign policy must be characterized by mutual respect, not by gunboat diplomacy, big stick diplomacy and threats. Our Nation at its best feeds the hungry. Our Nation at its worst, at its worst, will mine the harbors of the Nicaragua; at its worst will try to overthrow their government, at its worst will cut aid to American education and increase the aid to El Salvador; at its worst, our Nation will have partnership with South Africa. That is a moral disgrace. It is a moral disgrace. It is a moral disgrace. (Applause)

We look at Africa. We cannot just focus on apartheid in Southern Africa. We must fight for trade with Africa, and not just aid to Africa. We cannot stand idly by and say we will not relate to Nicaragua unless they have elections there, and then embrace military regimes in Africa overthowing democratic governments in Nigeria and Liberia and Ghana. We must fight for democracy all around the world, and play the game by one set of rules.

Peace in this world. Our present formula for peace in the Middle East is inadequate. It will not work. There are 22 nations in the Middle East. Our Nation must be able to talk and act and influence all of them. We must build upon Camp David, and measure human rights by one yardstick. In that region we have too many interests and too few friends.

There is a way out, jobs. Put America back to work.

When I was a child growing up in Greenville, South Carolina, the Reverend Sample used to preach ever so often a sermon relating to Jesus and he said, "If I be lifted up, I will draw all men unto me."

I didn't quite understand what he meant as a child growing up, but I understand a little better now. If you raise up truth, it is magnetic. It has a way of drawing people.

With all this confusion in this Convention, the bright lights and parties and big fun, we must raise up the simple proposition: If we lift up a program to feed the hungry, they will come running; if we lift up a program to start a war no more, our youth will come running; if we lift up a program to put America back to work, and an alternative to welfare and despair, they will come running.

If we cut that military budget without cutting our defense, and use that money to rebuild bridges and put steel workers back to work, and use that money and provide jobs for our cities, and use that money to build schools and pay teachers and educate our children, and build hospitals, and train doctors and train nurses, the whole Nation will come running to us. (Applause)

As I leave you now and we vote in this Convention and get ready to go back across this Nation in a couple of days, in this campaign, I tried to be faithful to my promise. I lived in old barrios, ghettos and reservations and housing projects.

I have a message for our youth. I challenge them to put hope in their brains and not dope in their veins. (Applause) I told them that like Jesus, I, too, was born in the slum, and just because you are born in the slum does not mean the slum is born in you, and you can rise above it if your mind is made up. (Applause) I told them in every slum there are two sides. When I see a broken window, that is the slummy side. Train some youths to become a glazier; that is the sunny side. When I see a missing brick, that is the slummy side. Let that child in the union and become a brickmason and build; that is the sunny side. When I see a missing door, that is the slummy side. Train some youth to become a carpenter; that is the sunny side. And when I see the vulgar words and hieroglyphics of destitution on the walls, that's the slummy side. Train some youth to become a painter, an artist; that is the sunny side.

We leave this place looking for the sunny side because there is a brighter side somewhere. I am more convinced than ever that we can win. We will vault up the rough side of the mountain. We can win. I just want young America to do me one favor—just one favor.

Exercise the right to dream. You must face reality—that which is; but then dream of the reality that ought to be—that must be. Live beyond the pain of reality with the dream of a bright tomorrow. Use hope and imagination as weapons of survival and progress. Use love to motivate you and obligate you to serve the human family.

Young America, dream. Choose the human race over the nuclear race. Bury the weapons and don't burn the people. Dream—dream of a new value system. Teachers who teach for life and not just for a living; teach because they can't help it. Dream of lawyers more concerned about justice than a judgeship. Dream of doctors more concerned about public health than personal wealth. (Applause) Dream of preachers and priests who will prophesy and not just profiteer. Preach and dream! Our time has come. Our time has come.

Suffering breeds character, character breeds faith, and faith will not disappoint. Our time has come. Our faith, hopes and dreams will prevail. Our time has come. Weeping has endured for night, but now joy cometh in the morning.

Our time has come. No grave can hold our body down. Our time has come. No lie can live forever. Our time has come. We must leave the racial battleground and find the economic common ground and moral higher ground. America, our time has come.

We come from disgrace to Amazing Grace. Our time has come. Give me your tired, give me your poor, your huddled masses who yearn to breathe free, and come November there will be a change because our time has come.

Thank you and God bless you.

Notes

Introduction

1. For a collection of scholarly essays on the Jackson campaign, see Lucius J. Barker and Ronald Walters, *Jesse Jackson's 1984 Presidential Campaign: Its Meaning and Significance* (forthcoming).

Chapter 1

1. Convention diary, July 15,1984. Throughout my entire stay at the San Francisco Democratic National Convention, I kept a small notepad and recorded daily entries of on-the-spot observations and impressions of various convention activities and experiences. If particular circumstances precluded on-the-spot note taking, I made such entries at the first available opportunity following the activity or event. References to such materials are cited as convention diary and date.

2. For a symposium on this debate, see Lucius Barker, "Should A Black Run For President in 1984?" *PS* 16 (Summer 1983): 489-507. My views on this topic are discussed on 500-507.

3. For more detailed data and discussions on poverty and black unemployment see my chapter, "Jesse Jackson's Candidacy in Political-Social Perspective: A Contextual Analysis," in Barker and Walters, *Jesse Jackson's 1984 Presidential Campaign: Its Meaning and Significance*.

4. See, for example, William J. Wilson, *The Declining Significance of Race* (Chicago: University of Chicago Press, 1978).

5. Center for the Study of Social Policy, "A Dream Deferred: The Economic Status of Black Americans, A Working Paper" (Washington, D.C., 1983), p. 1.

6. Ibid.

7. See detailed discussion of these developments in Drew Days, "Turning Back the Clock: The Reagan Administration and Civil Rights," *Harvard Civil Rights/Civil Liberties Law Review* 19 (1984): 309.

8. For an overview of this struggle over the Civil Rights Commission, see "Civil Rights Commission Reconstituted," *Congress Quarterly Almanac* 39 (1983): 292-95.

9. For summary of the news conference at which the president equivocated on whether or not Martin Luther King was a Communist or Communist sympathizer, see *New York Times*, October 20, 1983. Also see Anthony Lewis, "The Real Reagan," Ibid., October 24, 1983.

10. *Brown v. Board of Education of Topeka*, 347 U.S. 483 (1954).

11. Barker, "Should a Black Run for President in 1984?"

12. David Broder referred to Marguerite Barnett's article in his column in the *Washington Post*, August 24, 1983.

13. Except as otherwise indicated, quotes and materials in this section are taken from Barker, "Should a Black Run for President in 1984?"

Chapter 2

1. Jesse Jackson, "The Quest for a Just Society," speech announcing his candidacy for the Democratic presidential nomination, Washington Convention Center, Washington, D.C., November 3, 1983.

2. *New York Times*, November 2, 1983.

3. *New York Times*, November 12, 1983.

4. Aldon Morris, *The Origins of the Civil Rights Movement* (New York: The Free Press, 1984).

5. Edelman, p. 20. See note 8, chap. 3, *infra.*

6. Ronald Smothers, "The Impact of Jesse Jackson," *New York Times Magazine*, March 4, 1984, pp. 40ff.

7. For more detailed and systematic discussion of the political-social context out of which the Jackson campaign developed, see Barker and Walters, *Jesse Jackson's 1984 Presidential Campaign*, ch. 1 and 2.

8. Matthew Holden, Jr., *The Politics of the Black Nation* (New York: Chandler Publishing Co., 1973), pp. 17-26.

9. Comments of Eddie Williams, president, Joint Center for Political Studies, Washington, D.C., November 10, 1983.

Chapter 3

1. Alvin Pouissant, *New York Times*, November 14, 1983.

2. See Marguerite Ross Barnett, "The Strategic Debate over a Black Presidential Candidacy," *PS* 16 (Summer 1983): 489-91.

3. Coretta Scott King, *St. Louis Post Dispatch*, November 10, 1983.

4. Richard Arrington, *New York Times*, January 6, 1984.

5. Charles Rangel and Hazel Dukes quoted in ibid, November 30, 1983.

6. Julian Bond, quoted by Thomas Ottenad, *St. Louis Post Dispatch*, February 26, 1984.

7. For an analysis of these criticisms, see Lucius J. Barker, "Jesse Jackson: A Viable Candidate," *Student Life* (Washington University student newspaper), April 13, 1984, p. 6.

8. For a penetrating analysis of the role and importance of symbols in American political life see Murray Edelman, *The Symbolic Uses of Politics* (Urbana: University of Illinois Press, 1967).

9. See Lucius J. Barker and Jesse McCorry, *Black Americans and the Political System*, 2nd ed. (Cambridge: Winthrop Publishers, 1980), esp. pp. 179-83.

10. See, for example, Barbara Reynolds, *Jesse Jackson: America's David* (formerly *Jesse Jackson: The Man, The Myth and The Movement*) (Washington, D.C.: JFJ Associates, 1985), and Thomas Landeas and Richard Quinn, *Jesse Jackson and the Politics of Race* (Ottawa, Ill: Jameson Books, 1985).

11. See Pat Press, "Jesse Jackson and the Family Feud," *Washington Post*, November 18, 1983.

12. Tom Cavanagh, *Inside Black America* (Washington, D.C.: Joint Center for Political Studies, 1985), pp. 3ff. Survey results from the 1986 JCPS-Gallup poll, however, show increasing agreement between blacks and whites on primary problems facing the country but sharp disagreement on how to deal with those problems, principally on the role that government should play in dealing with such problems.

13. Norman H. Nie, Sidney Verba, and John R. Petrocik, *The Changing American Voter* (Cambridge: Harvard University Press, 1979), pp. 247-56, quotes on p. 255.

14. *New York Times*, November 19, 1984.

15. Ibid., January 1, 1984.

16. Ibid., January 5, 1984.

17. *Washington Post*, January 5, 1984.

18. *New York Times*, January 5, 1984.

19. *Washington Post*, January 5, 1984.

20. Edward Kennedy, quoted by Howell Raines, "Jackson Coup and '84 Race," *New York Times*, January 4, 1984.

21. *New York Times*, January 4, 1984.

22. *Washington Post*, January 5, 1984.

Chapter 4

1. *Regents of the University of California v. Bakke,* 438 U.S. 265 (1978).

2. James Baldwin, "Negroes Are Anti-Semitic Because They're Anti-White," *New York Times Magazine,* April 1967.

3. Except as otherwise indicated, information in this section is taken from Ronald Smothers, "Jackson and Jews," *New York Times,* November 7, 1983.

4. For a discussion of the Andy Young Affair in the context of its larger implications for black politics, see Lucius J. Barker and Jesse McCorry, *Black Americans and the Political System* (Cambridge, Mass.: Winthrop Publishers, 1980), pp. 334-42.

5. Rick Atkinson, "Peace with American Jews Eludes Jackson," *Washington Post,* February 13, 1984.

6. Ibid.

7. Howell Raines, "Jackson's Candor Is Praised but Remark Critized," *New York Times,* February 28, 1984.

8. Ibid.

9. Ibid., April 12, 1984.

10. Ibid.

11. Ibid., April 10, 1984.

12. Ibid.

13. Ibid.

14. Ibid., April 13, 1984.

15. Ibid.

16. Ibid.

17. Ibid.

18. Ibid., June 29, 1984.

19. For text of Jackson's statement see Ibid.

20. Ibid.

21. Ibid.

22. Ibid., June 30, 1984.

23. Ibid., June 29, 1984.

24. Ibid., June 30, 1984.

25. *Congressional Record,* 98th Cong., 2nd sess., vol. 130, p. S-8671 (1984).

26. Cf. Timothy Crouse's account of the dynamic interplay of influences that affect how and what news reporters write or cast their stories: *The Boys on the Bus* (New York: Ballantine Books, 1973).

27. See William Schneider's interesting review and commentary of relevant data from the *Los Angeles Times* poll in "How Farrakhan Divides the Delegates," *National Journal Convention Daily,* July 17, 1984, p. 25.

28. *Congressional Record,* 98th Cong., 2nd Sess., vol. 130, p. 8677 (1984).

Chapter 5

1. *St. Louis Post-Dispatch*, January 5, 1984.

2. *New York Times*, January 12, 1984.

3. *Christian Science Monitor*, April 19, 1984.

4. For a discussion of the importance of oratorical competence in black culture, see Holden, *The Politics of the Black Nation*, pp. 21-22.

5. These excerpts from various Jackson speeches and comments can be found in the following: *Washington Post*, May 21, 1984; May 22, 1984; *Congressional Quarterly Weekly Report*, January 7, 1984, 10; *National Journal*, March 24, 1984, 575; *National Journal Convention Special*, July 21, 1984, 25; and *Chicago Tribune*, July 15, 1984.

6. *New York Times*, January 16, 1984.

7. Ibid.

8. Ibid.

9. See Howell Raines, "Debate Among Demos Draws Sharpest Exchanges of Campaign," Ibid.

10. For a transcript of the debate, see *New York Times*, February 13, 1984.

11. Ibid.

12. Ibid.

13. Ibid.

14. "TV Turns Campaign into 'Fritz, Gary, and Jesse Show,' " *Christian Science Monitor*, March 30, 1984, p. 36.

15. *New York Times*, March 29, 1984.

16. *Wall Street Journal*, June 1, 1984.

17. *New York Times*, March 31, 1984.

18. For discussion and commentary on how the runoff primary and similar structures impact on blacks and minorites, see E. Colette Wallace, "Runoff Primaries: Is There a Discriminatory Result?" *The Journal of Law and Politics* 2, no. 2 (Fall 1985): 369, and my unpublished paper on "The Runoff Primary in Political-Legal Context: Some Findings and Observations" (Washington University, August 21, 1986).

19. For more discussion on how the rules disadvantaged Jackson, see chapter 8 of this volume. For an overall informative review and analysis of the matter of reform in both major parties from the 1960s through early 1980s, see William Crotty, *Party Reform* (New York: Longman, 1983).

20. Thomas E. Cavanagh and Lorn S. Foster, *Jesse Jackson's Campaign: The Primaries and Caucuses*, (Washington, D.C.: Joint Center for Political Studies, 1984), pp. 11-12.

21. Ibid., p. 12.

22. Ibid.

23. C. Anthony Broh, *A Horse of a Different Color: Television's Treatment of Jesse Jackson's 1984 Presidential Campaign* (Washington, D.C.: Joint Center for Political Studies, 1987).

Chapter 6

1. Except as otherwise noted, this chapter is based on information and impressions I gained as an active participant-observer in delegate selection process in the Missouri River Township and Second Congressional District caucuses and in the state Democratic convention.

2. See, for example, Richard Fenno, *Home Style: House Members in Their Districts* (Boston: Little, Brown, 1978).

3. Barker and McCorry, *Black Americans and the Political System.* Professor Mack Jones of Howard is serving as co-author with me for the third edition, presently under revision for publication by Prentice-Hall, Inc.

4. My detailed account of the 1960 Kennedy-Humphrey contest in the Wisconsin primary is set forth in my unpublished manuscript, "The Wisconsin President Primary of 1960."

5. See my article, "A Split Delegation and a Neutral Governor," in *Inside Politics: The National Conventions. 1960*, ed. Paul Tillett (Dobbs Ferry, N.Y.: Oceana Publications, Inc., 1962), pp. 222-39.

6. Congressman Young was defeated in his re-election bid in the 1986 election.

7. *St. Louis Post Dispatch*, May 23, 1984.

8. See Edward F. Waite, "The Debt of Constitutional Law to Jehovah Witnesses," *Minnesota Law Review*, 28 (March 1944): 209.

Chapter 7

1. Except as otherwise indicated, information and impressions in this chapter are based on notes in my diary and additional insights gained from active participant-observation as a delegate at the 1984 Democratic National Convention.

2. For an informative commentary on the *Los Angeles Times* delegate survey, see William Schneider, "The Dividing Line between Delegates Is Age," *National Journal* 29 (July 21, 1984): 12.

3. I profited greatly from the informative guides provided by the Joint Center for Political Studies and the *Congressional Quarterly*, both of which helped me as a delegate to gain a better feeling and understanding of the flavor and facts about the Democratic convention. See Joint Center for Political Studies, Election '84, Report #3, *Blacks and the 1984 Democratic National Convention: A Guide* (July, 1984); and Congressional Quarterly's

Guide to the 1984 Democratic National Convention (San Francisco, July 16–19, 1984).

4. See *Washington Post*, April 25, 1984.

5. *New York Times*, July 19, 1984.

6. *Official Proceedings of the 1984 Democratic National Convention* (July 16-19, 1984), pp. 400-402.

Chapter 8

1. See Marguerite Barnett and James A. Hefner, *Public Policy for the Black Community* (Port Washington, N.Y.: Alfred Publishing Co., 1976), ch. 1 and pp. 257-70.

2. *Blacks and the 1984 Democratic National Convention*, p. 1; Thomas Cavanagh, *Inside Black America* (Washington, D.C.: Joint Center for Political Studies, 1985), p. 68.

3. See Jackson's convention speech, Appendix, p. 211.

4. See, for example, data showing marked increases in black voter registration and turnout in Thomas Cavanagh and Lorn Foster, *Jesse Jackson's Campaign: The Primaries and the Caucuses*, Election '84, Report #2 (Washington, D.C.: Joint Center for Political Studies, June, 1984), pp. 16-17.

5. *New York Times*, August 18, 1984.

6. For more discussion of this matter see Lucius Barker and Mack Jones, *Black Americans and the Political System*, 3rd ed. (Englewood Cliffs, N.J.: Prentice Hall, forthcoming), ch. 1.

7. For discussions of these and other functions of national party conventions see V. O. Key, *Politics, Parties and Pressure Groups*, 5th ed. (New York: Thomas Crowell Co., 1964), p. 431.

8. See E. E. Schattschneider, *The Semisovereign People* (Hinsdale, Ill.: The Dryden Press, 1975), p. 47; and David Truman, *The Governmental Process* (New York: A. A. Knopf, 1958).

9. Barker, "The Runoff Primary in Political-Legal Context."

10. See Margaret Shapiro, "Jackson Asks Manatt for 'Stolen' Delegates," *Washington Post*, April 24, 1984.

11. *New York Times*, August 18, 1984.

12. A succinct discussion of Jackson's campaign organization and finance may be found in the concise and excellent analysis of that overall campaign by Cavanagh and Foster, *Jesse Jackson's Campaign*, pp. 12-14. For reference to Jackson as a "black presidential candidate" in the preceding paragraph, see Ibid., p. 12.

13. *New York Times Magazine*, March 4, 1984, pp. 40, 53.

14. It is instructive to note that, when polled on their personal willingness to vote for a "qualified" black candidate, a strong majority of blacks and

whites (above 80 percent) showed a strong willingness to do so. By contrast, an Illinois NBC exit poll suggests that when asked whether "voters of this country are ready to elect a black president", an overwhelming majority of whites (79%) and a slight majority of blacks (54%) believed that the country was not ready. See Howard Schuman, Charlotte Steeh and Lawrence Bobo, *Racial Attitudes in America: Trends and Interpretations* (Cambridge, Massachusetts: Harvard University Press, 1985), pp. 73-82; Cavanagh, *Inside Black America*, pp. 63-66; and Linda Williams and Lorenzo Morris, "Jackson and the Rainbow in the Primary and General Elections," in Barker and Walters, *Jesse Jackson's 1984 Presidential Campaign*, pp. 13-14.

15. Ibid.

16. Preston, "The 1984 Presidential Primary Campaign," pp. 4-8

17. Quoted in Sydney H. Schanberg, "Other Voices," *New York Times*, May 5, 1984.

18. Cavanagh and Foster, *Jesse Jackson's Campaign*, p. 11.

19. C. Anthony Broh, "A Horse of a Different Color" (Jackson Campaign and the Media) Joint Center for Political Studies (April 25, 1985), p. 2 (mimeographed).

20. Williams and Morris, "Jackson and the Rainbow in the Primary and General Elections," p. 7.

21. For a concise graphic description of the intimidation and obstacles encountered by blacks in their attempts at voting, see Harrell R. Rodgers, Jr., and Charles Bullock III, *Law and Social Change: Civil Rights Laws and Their Consequences*, (New York: McGraw-Hill, 1972), pp. 18-23.

22. See the *Washington Post*, July 6, 1985; October 17, 1985; and the *New York Times*, July 2, 1987. For additional commentary see Ray Jenkins, "Scottsboro Deja Vu: II," *Baltimore Evening Sun*, November 16, 1985; and Alabama Black Belt Defense Committee, "Vote Fraud Trials Threaten Democracy," Printed Statement, 4 pp., undated.

23. Cavanagh and Foster, *Jesse Jackson's Campaign*, pp. 16-17.

24. Ibid., pp. 12-14, and Williams and Morris, "Jackson and the Rainbow in the Primary and General Elections."

25. See Milton Morris, *The Politics of Black America* (New York: Harper and Row, 1975), pp. 204-6; and Hanes Walton, Jr., *Black Political Parties* (New York: The Free Press, 1972), esp. pp. 56-59.

26. See "Reagan Leaving Conservative Mark on Courts," *Congressional Quarterly Weekly Report* (November 1, 1986), pp. 2727-29.

27. See Dan Balz, "Heads, Hearts Battle in Alabama Today," *Washington Post*, December 10, 1983.

28. For news report and excerpts from the Democratic Policy Commission's Statement of Principles see the *New York Times*, September 21, 1986. For reactions to statement see Ibid., September 24, 1986. See also "Officials

Seek Moderation in Party's Image," *Congressional Quarterly* (March 9, 1985) 43:457.

29. For a succinct discussion of the impact of the black electorate on the 1986 elections, see Linda Faye Williams, "Black Politics in 1986" (speech to the Board of Governors of the Joint Center for Political Studies, Washington, D.C., November 8, 1986).

30. Tyrone Brooks, quoted in David Broder, "A Two-Party System for Blacks, Too?" *St. Louis Post Dispatch*, September 30, 1986.

Note on the Author

Lucius J. Barker is the Edna F. Gellhorn Professor of Public Affairs and professor of political science at Washington University in St. Louis, Missouri. A co-editor of *Jesse Jackson's 1984 Campaign: Its Meaning and Significance*, Barker is the co-author of *Black Americans and the Political System, Civil Liberties and the Constitution*, and *Freedom, Courts, Politics: Studies in Civil Liberties*.